PANAMA MONEY IN BARBADOS

PANAMA MONEY IN BARBADOS 1900–1920

BONHAM C. RICHARDSON

THE UNIVERSITY OF TENNESSEE PRESS
KNOXVILLE

Copyright © 1985 by The University of Tennessee Press / Knoxville.
All Rights Reserved.

Frontispiece: Barbadians arriving in Panama aboard *S.S. Ancon,*
September 2, 1909. *Courtesy Still Picture Branch, National Archives,
Washington, D.C.*

Library of Congress Cataloging in Publication Data

Richardson, Bonham C., 1939–
Panama money in Barbados, 1900–1920
Bibliography: p.
Includes index.
1. Alien labor, Barbadian—Panama—Panama Canal—
History—20th century. 2. Barbados—Social conditions.
3. Barbados—Economic conditions. I. Title.
HD8178.5.B37R53   1985   330.97298'1   85-6127

ISBN 0-87049-477-5 (cl. alk. paper): 1st printing, 1985
ISBN 1-57233-306-5 (pbk. alk.paper): 1st printing, 2004

For Eliza

Old Barbadian Man: "Sitting here or there it come to me how things make a change. Time wus when money flow like the flood through these here hands, money as we never ever know it before. We use to sing in those times gone by 'twus money on the apple trees in Panama. 'Tis Panama my memory take me back to every now an' again where with these said hands I help to build the canal, the biggest an' best canal in the wide wide world."

George Lamming, *In the Castle of My Skin*

Contents

Preface, xi

1. Introduction, *1*

2. Barbados at the Turn of the Century, *13*

3. The Black Barbadians in 1900:
   "Ned Is in the Land," *53*

4. "Hit de Manager in de Head, and
   Come Along wid We!," *105*

5. Panama Men and Panama Money, *140*

6. The Social and Economic Changes:
   "Money Is a Blessed Thing," *170*

7. Epilogue: The 1937 Riots and Beyond, *233*

Notes, *249*

Bibliography, *269*

Index, *279*

Illustrations

Photographs (*following page xiv*)

Bridgetown waterfront
Transporting canes, Barbados
"Third-class" child labor gang, Barbados
Bridgetown Carenage
Bridgetown market
Moving a "syrup spider," Bridgetown
Fruit vendors, Swan Street, Bridgetown
Roebuck Street, Bridgetown
McGregor Street, Bridgetown
Barbadian chattel house
Barbadians leaving for Panama
Barbadians arriving in Panama
Shifting railroad track, Canal Zone
Dynamite crew, Canal Zone
Paving street, Panama City
Cooking meals in the Canal Zone
Camp Bierd, Canal Zone

Figures

1. Barbados and its parishes *14*
2. Contract workers to Panama, 1906–1907 *127*
3. St. Michael parish, Barbados, in 1920 *128*
4. Contract workers from St. Michael parish to Panama, 1906–1907 *129*

Tables

1. Population of Barbados, 1891, *20*
2. Barbados Savings Bank Depositors in 1904, *71*
3. Barbados Infant Mortality per 1,000 Live Births, *78*
4. A Portion of the 1906–1907 Contract Laborers to Panama by Barbadian Parish, *126*
5. Barbadian Returnees from the Canal Zone and Their Declared Money, *144*
6. Postal Remittances Sent from the Panama Canal Zone to Barbados, 1906–1920, *157*
7. Barbados Government Savings Bank Accounts, 1901–1920, *165*
8. Depositors in Barbados Savings Bank, 1915–1917, *167*
9. Population of Barbados, 1911, *171*
10. Population of Barbados, 1921, *172*
11. Barbadian Sugar Tonnage, 1901–1920, *182*
12. Persons Owning Fewer than Five Acres of Land in Barbados, 1912, *190*
13. Barbadian Friendly Societies, 1901–1920, *206*

Preface

The profound influences exerted by the United States on the peoples of Latin America and the Caribbean have not been limited to those stemming directly from military, political, and economic relationships between the United States and particular nations. American influences have also affected the peoples of these regions in innumerable indirect ways. Indeed, the more subtle ways have been perhaps the most far-reaching, affecting individuals and families, altering the fabrics of local societies, and changing the ways people regard themselves and each other. An example of such indirect yet massive change was that resulting from the impact of the construction of the Panama Canal on the peoples of the small islands of the Caribbean. Early in the twentieth century, men and women from throughout the West Indies traveled to work in the Canal Zone, sending and taking "Panama money" back home to those who stayed behind. Nearly every Caribbean island was affected by the Panama Canal construction, some more than others. On the British West Indian island of Bardados, probably more than any place else outside Panama, influences from the Canal Zone created momentous demographic, economic, and social transformations.

This book is a historical geography of Barbados during the era of Panama money. It might also be considered a study of social change. Furthermore, it presents a case study of how human migration can produce such change. The first part of the book describes the semifeudal conditions that existed on Barbados at the turn of the century, emphasizing the plight of the island's black laborers and the ways they coped with oppression and poverty. The middle chapters depict the remarkable emigration of tens of thousands of black Barbadians to Panama and the accompanying return of people and money. The final chapters assess the social changes, at both the individual level and island-wide, that took place on Barbados during the era of Panama money.

This study is based on one year of archival research and interviewing in Barbados during 1981–82, followed by one and one-half years of intermittent research and writing. Earlier, in June 1980, I spent two weeks in Barbados, supported in part by a small projects grant from the Association of American Geographers, in order to seek material for a formal research proposal. The research year in Barbados, and subsequent library work at the National Archives in Washington, D.C., was funded by the Geography and Regional Science Division of the National Science Foundation. A summer stipend awarded by the Humanities Division of Virginia Polytechnic Institute and State University allowed me to devote the summer of 1983 to full-time writing. I am most grateful to everyone who made these various research funds possible and to the many colleagues, both near and far, who commented and criticized so helpfully on several research proposal drafts.

My wife, daughter, and I resided in Barbados from August 1981 through July 1982. During this period I had the good fortune to be a Visiting Research Fellow at the Department of History at the University of the West Indies at Cave Hill. Participation in Woodville Marshall's Saturday morning history seminars at UWI was a stimulating experience; the West Indian historians there paid me the compliment of being every bit as critical and demanding of me and my ideas as they were of each other. Many persons at UWI, Cave Hill, were extremely helpful and willing to discuss with me their own areas of expertise as they related to my research interests, especially Kathleen Drayton, Ronnie Hughes, Keith Hunte, Dawn Marshall, Woodville Marshall, and Velma Newton. But knowledge about Barbados's history is not a strictly academic pursuit on the island, and there is a lively and fruitful exchange there between professional historians and several nonacademics whose knowledge is profound. Among the latter, I am most grateful for help, interest, and encouragement to Warren Alleyne, Gordon Bell, Peter Campbell, Frank Gibbons, Robert Morris, and Edward Stoute. The eminent H.A. Vaughan, lawyer, statesman, and historian—who recalled personally many events and trends during and after the era of Panama money in Barbados—graciously offered advice and information during my several visits to his house in Christchurch parish.

Preface   xiii

I devoted the first half of my research year in Barbados to archival work in libraries and newspaper offices. Usually my wife accompanied and assisted me. The great bulk of our work was accomplished at the Barbados Department of Archives, at Black Rock, St. Michael. I would like to thank Christine Matthews, the director of the archives, Bruce Bates, Michael Chandler, and all of the staff members for a great deal of help.

At the Barbados Department of Archives we reviewed a wealth of published and unpublished material pertaining to the Panama money era in Barbados, including reports published annually as well as those dealing with particular problems or events. Issues of the colony's *Official Gazette* contained annual reports by medical officers, sanitary inspectors, police officers, harbor masters, registrars of friendly societies, bank officials, and others. The planters' perspectives and controversies were available in the published debates from the Barbadian House of Assembly and Legislative Council. The newspapers from 1900 to 1920 were particularly helpful. Perhaps the most important documents we consulted at the archives were handwritten "Emigrants' Registers." The registers listed nearly 6,000 (of the total 20,000) Barbadian contract workers, and their villages of residence, who had emigrated to the Panama Canal. With the kind assistance of Robert Williams of UWI, we then developed from these data a computer printout showing each Barbadian village community and its contract workers.

During the second half of the research year, we interviewed older persons in the key village areas from which the Panama Canal emigrants had traveled. Usually, the first stop in each village we visited was the school or church. After explaining our research to school headmasters or clergy, we were directed to older persons in the community who were thought to know about the Panama Canal era. This "method" of locating interviewees entailed repetitive explanation on our part; it meant that daily we were the objects of villagers' curiosity; and it led to many blind alleys. It also yielded dozens of invaluable interviews with older Barbadians who had lived in Panama as children or who recalled Barbados during the Panama money days. Few of George Lamming's "old men" who worked on the canal are still alive, but we did locate one ninety-six-year-old who had his original service contract with the Isthmian Canal Commission from 1907. We returned to speak with him on several different occasions as we did other key informants.

The debt I owe to the older Barbadians with whom we spoke can never be repaid. In nearly every case they were friendly and eager to speak about their own experiences and what they remembered from earlier days. Of course, it soon became obvious—as it has in my interviewing people on other Caribbean islands—that attempts to guide the interviews were much less effective than simply allowing interviewees to discuss their experiences in an unstructured fashion. In all but a very few cases I have chosen to render the interviewees anonymous when I have quoted them. This choice results in a somewhat repetitive manner of introducing relevant quotations as from, say, "an eighty-year old man of St. Joseph parish." But this device seeks to avoid possible embarrassments for those persons who were kind enough to describe their feelings and experiences with me but who may not be anxious to see their names associated with a particular assertion or quotation.

During the writing of this book I have sought the help of friends and colleagues. Robert Dirks read early drafts of each chapter and provided his usual valuable combination of criticism and encouragement. All or parts of the manuscript have been read and commented on by Susan Brooker-Gross, Michael Conniff, Edward Cox, Larry Grossman, Franklin Knight, and Linda Richardson. I am grateful for their many suggestions. Karen Waldrop created and drafted the maps. Jane Vyula, Vanessa Scott, and Glenna King deciphered my longhand writing and typed chapter drafts and revisions therefrom at an extraordinary rate of speed. Charles Good and Bob Morrill helped in no small way by creating in the geography department at Virginia Tech an atmosphere in which mutual support and high academic standards reinforce one another.

While my wife and I daily researched and interviewed in Barbados, our seven-year-old daughter attended the "top infants" form at St. Gabriel's school at Collymore Rock in Bridgetown. Through her friendships, school experiences, infrequent illnesses, and enthusiasm, I learned much more about Barbados and the Barbadians than I ever could have without her. This book is dedicated to her.

Bridgetown waterfront in the early twentieth century. *Courtesy Edward Stoute.*

Transporting harvested canes in rural Barbados in the early twentieth century. *Courtesy Edward Stoute.*

"Third-class" child labor gang, ca. 1900. *Courtesy Colin Parkinson.*

Bridgetown Carenage and Carlisle Bay, ca. 1918. *Courtesy Colin Parkinson.*

Bridgetown market in the early twentieth century. *Courtesy Colin Parkinson.*

Moving a "syrup spider" in Bridgetown, ca 1905. *Courtesy Val Millington.*

Fruit vendors on Swan Street, Bridgetown, ca 1900. *Courtesy Edward Stoute.*

Roebuck Street, Bridgetown, ca. 1900. *Courtesy Edward Stoute.*

McGregor Street, Bridgetown, ca. 1900. *Courtesy Edward Stoute.*

Modern chattel house with iron roof and concrete groundsel. *Photograph by the author.*

Barbadians leaving for Panama, ca. 1907. *Courtesy Colin Parkinson.*

Shifting railroad track by hand, Canal Zone, January 1912. *Courtesy Still Picture Branch, National Archives, Washington, D.C.*

Dynamite crew, Canal Zone, February 1912. *Courtesy Still Picture Branch, National Archives, Washington, D.C.*

Paving Arosamena Street, Panama City, ca. 1907. *Courtesy Still Picture Branch, National Archives, Washington, D.C.*

Cooking meals in the Canal Zone. *Courtesy Still Picture Branch, National Archives, Washington, D.C.*

Camp Bierd, Canal Zone. *Courtesy Still Picture Branch, National Archives, Washington, D.C.*

CHAPTER 1

Introduction

The construction of the Panama Canal Between 1904 and 1914 provided a showcase for the burgeoning industrial and technological might of the United States. In 1900, Americans already had accomplished dramatic environmental transformations within the circum-Caribbean region; as the twentieth century opened, American engineers, surveyors, and planters—imbued with a sense of destiny and a righteous, unalloyed view of progress—were converting rainforest and scrubland of Central America and the Greater Antilles into enormous banana and sugar cane plantations. But the American undertaking of the Panama Canal, where the French recently had failed, held unprecedented promise. Indeed, historical superlatives soon became synonymous with the American effort in Panama. Not only would the building of the Panama Canal itself become one of the premier engineering feats in all of history, but scores of advances in fields as disparate as finance and medicine would be achieved in support of the construction.[1]

Superlatives were also necessary to describe the army of workers assembled to dig the canal. In 1915, the year following the project's completion, American engineers boasted that "the construction of the Panama Canal called together the largest number of men that were ever employed at one time on any modern or medieval peaceful enterprise."[2] Individual laborers came from all over the world. The great majority of the workforce, however, were black West Indians from British Caribbean colonies.

From the Americans' point of view, the overall engineering triumph in Panama—symbolized by the grandeur and sweep of the locks and waterways of the isthmus—far outweighed the indispensable, though relatively unnoticed, role played by the labor force. Furthermore, such a comparison probably rarely, if ever, crossed the minds of American supervisors. The photographic records from the Panama Canal, for example, indicate that in the view of the Americans the black laborers were of far less importance than were the physical dimensions of the canal.[3] Picture after picture portrayed the immensity and scale of the project; black workers, when photographed, usually appeared distant and antlike. Comparatively few blacks were pictured close up, as individual people. Similarly, American foremen commented only infrequently about the West Indian laborers they supervised. The odd-sounding British West Indian accents amused American bosses, as did the assertions by individual black workers that they were British subjects, as indeed most were. But the workers' particular islands of origin meant little, if anything, to American supervisors. "We need more niggers," was a common request by the Isthmian Canal Commission's chief engineer, John Stevens, to his labor recruiters in the islands at the height of the blasting and earth moving. The wording of Stevens's oft- repeated request was eloquent testimony to the racist anonymity accorded individual black workers by American supervisors during the construction of the Panama Canal.[4]

Despite racism and oppression on the job, black men from throughout the Commonwealth Caribbean—not to mention those from Danish, Dutch, and French islands—eagerly sought work on the isthmus. At ten cents per hour, construction wages in Panama were, at the very least, double what individuals could earn on the seasonal sugar cane estates of their home islands. The black workers themselves, of course, made finer distinctions about their own insular identities and those of fellow laborers than did their American supervisors. Black men from Jamaica, Barbados, drought-prone Antigua, the volcanic Windwards, and all the other British islands worked alongside one another. The money they sent and took back to their families on the islands softened the local effects of a savage economic depression that had afflicted the British Caribbean since the 1880s. The impact of the creation of the Panama Canal in the early twentieth century was therefore not limited to scientific, engineering, and geopolitical spheres. Throughout the small islands of the British Caribbean, migrating men—and a smaller number of women—

sent and brought "Panama money" back home, an achievement of momentous local importance still discussed on those same islands today, late in the twentieth century.

Barbados was the British Caribbean colony most affected by the construction of the Panama Canal. Early in 1905, the Americans established their main labor recruiting station in Bridgetown. Of the total 45,000 contract workers recruited for the isthmus from all sources during the next decade, black Barbadians numbered 20,000, far more than from any other place. Possibly as many as 25,000 other Barbadian men and women went informally, paying their own passage to the isthmus during the Panama Canal construction. So altogether a possible 45,000—from a Barbadian population of less than 200,000—emigrated to the Canal Zone. Thousands of the Barbadian emigrants died in Panama from accident and disease, thousands stayed in Central America or moved on, and thousands returned home to families and friends. Overall, the exodus to Panama and the return of workers and money had profound effects on every facet of Barbadian life. In the late twentieth century, almost every black Barbadian recalls a great-grandfather or an old uncle who worked in Panama, although direct recollections are becoming hard to find, and stories passed on from parents to children to grandchildren are beginning to take on the vague, exaggerated, and embellished character of myth and legend.

But the impact of the Panama Canal on Barbados went far beyond the circulation of people and money, and the importance of the canal construction era on Barbadians today is much more than a collection of stories. The loss of many people and the gain of unprecedented amounts of cash by the black working class on Barbados set significant social and economic forces in motion. The workers' exodus undermined an antiquated sugar cane industry and inspired its modernization. Barbadian planter-worker relationships then changed. The infusion of money dissolved traditional food-sharing relationships among black Barbadians. Mutual-aid societies were transformed. A decline in planter paternalism was accompanied by heightened class consciousness and incipient political activity on the parts of black Barbadians. In a broad sense, the Barbadian exodus to Panama was a creative, grass-roots catalyst of social change, not simply a pathetic drift of labor to capital.

The chapters of this book follow chronologically the changing conditions of the black Barbadian working class during the first two decades of the twentieth century. In chapter 2 I describe the setting—including the institutionalized racism, planter oppression, and general black landlessness—in 1900. Chapter 3 is an assessment of that setting from the point of view of black Barbadians of the time. In chapter 4 I discuss the exodus to the Canal Zone of thousands of young, black, mostly male Barbadians, and in chapter 5 I attempt to capture the exuberance of "Panama men" returning home and to track the astonishing sums of money remitted to Barbados from the Canal Zone. In chapter 6 I focus on some of the many interrelated social and economic changes of Barbados that followed the Panama experience. Chapter 7, the book's epilogue, contains the suggestion that the socioeconomic underpinnings of the Bridgetown riots of 1937—an event of momentous political and economic significance for Barbados—were related, at least indirectly, to the changes that occurred during the era of Panama money on the island.

This book provides only indirect accounts of the Barbadian workforce in the Canal Zone itself. The workers' lives on the isthmus were, obviously, extremely important to the Barbadians who lived them, wrote home about them, and returned to describe their sojourns to family and friends. Moreover, experiences in Panama often activated Barbadians to follow certain directions once they returned home. But in this study I concentrate on Barbados, emphasizing the actual Panama experiences only insofar as they directly affected the British island. Readers interested in the story of the West Indian workforce in the Canal Zone itself will be pleased to learn, if they are not already familiar with it, that a growing scholarly literature exists dealing explicitly with the black labor force on the Panama Canal.[5]

Although in this study I focus on the socioeconomic impacts of the Panama Canal on Barbados during the first two decades of the twentieth century, I fully intend to treat the Barbadians' Panama Canal experiences within the broader framework of Barbadian geography and history, a plantation background that has been evolving since the mid-seventeenth century. For example, in the first decade of the twentieth century, although the Central American isthmus was by far the most important migration destination for Barbadian blacks, it was only one of a surprisingly wide array of outside destinations for Barbadian migrants. Prior to Panama, nearby British Caribbean colonies—as amplified in chapters 3 and 4—had for decades been visited annually by hundreds, if not thousands, of Barbadian labor migrants. Then a few years later, as the American authorities in Panama began to send West Indian workers home upon the canal's completion, the United States itself—as discussed in chapters 6 and 7—emerged in the century's second decade as the principal external migration destination for Barbadian blacks.

The era of Panama money on Barbados is more fully understood, furthermore, by realizing that many events on Barbados between 1900 and 1920 were linked much more closely to the island's traditional economic and colonial heritage than they were to events in Panama. In 1900, Barbados already had been a British sugar cane plantation colony for two and one-half centuries. Tied directly to the historical trajectory of Western capitalism, the island's residents—planters and workers alike—had for decades experienced the rhythms of capitalism's advances and retreats, high prices and low, and booms and busts. The first twenty years of the twentieth century were no different. The economic depression affecting Barbados in the years immediately after the turn of the century was offset partly by spectacularly high West Indian sugar prices in the century's second decade, which were influenced, in part, by World War I. In short, the Panama Canal experience for black Barbadians was imbedded in the cumulative and complex history of Caribbean colonialism, a history which was undergoing its own internal changes in the early twentieth century.

The severity of externally influenced economic downturns, however, never had affected individual West Indians equally. Rather, the level of suffering always had depended on a person's position within the region's socioeconomic hierarchy. During slavery, for example, when prices for exported agricultural staples were less than the costs of imports, white planters experienced short-term financial losses. Black slaves, on the other hand, sometimes suffered malnutrition and even early death because planters were unwilling or unable to pay the high prices of imported foodstuffs. After full British slave emancipation in 1838, newly freed blacks, whose freedom rarely included access to any but the tiniest and most marginal plots of land, possessed a new means of dealing with externally influenced economic perturbations. This means was their own mobility or migration, and thousands of former slaves in the British Caribbean began to migrate from their home islands, usually to nearby destinations, before the middle of the nineteenth century. They sought higher wages to bring back home or better living conditions elsewhere. In any case, by 1900, British Caribbean migration was a traditional means of black livelihood rooted in the region's plantation history. Accordingly, scholars of the Caribbean have begun to document labor migration as a livelihood strategy of long standing in the islands.[6]

Local geographic conditions influenced more nineteenth-century migration from some British Caribbean islands than from others and perhaps more from Barbados than from any. Barbados is fertile and flat, or nearly so, when compared with most of the other islands of the Lesser Antilles. At emancipation, planters monopolized nearly all of Barbados's land, leaving most black Barbadian freedmen only tiny, rented, estate-controlled, subsistence gardens whose output often had to be supplemented with imported foodstuffs. "There are no Crown Lands on Barbados," was the unvarying reply from local administrators in the annual colonial reports of the nineteenth century, meaning that sugar estates covered nearly the entire island, leaving no unoccupied, public lands. More important for black Barbadians, it meant the lack of a local subsistence refuge like the swamplands of Trinidad and British Guiana or the highlands of Jamaica and the Windwards, where working people could fish, gather firewood and mangoes, and get away from planters. The absence of a local subsistence refuge, in turn, meant the lack of an indigenous buffer against external economic fluctuations or climatic hazards such as drought or hurricane. In response to this precarious combination of local and external conditions, many black Barbadians of the nineteenth century emigrated seasonally, permanently, and by the thousands, mainly to Trinidad, British Guiana, and some to other, non-British destinations.[7]

Introduction

Most British colonial administrators had only a vague awareness about black West Indian migration patterns of the nineteenth century. The issue of migration had arisen during the hearings of the 1897 British Royal Commission in the region. A few observers testified before the commission that moving "surplus" black populations from one place to another might be advisable, although migration was not mentioned in the commission's concluding recommendations. A few years later, the Americans, who knew nothing of black West Indian migratory habits, initially had favored the Jamaicans over other West Indians for the construction work on the Panama Canal. And the Isthmian Canal Commission officials probably had little, if any, inkling that, in eventually locating their main recruiting station in Barbados, they were tapping a reservoir of black laborers whose fathers and grandfathers had been migrating and returning for decades. Neither did the Americans understand that this mobile livelihood behavior had created an awareness among the Barbadian populace of the rewards, as well as the hazards, of labor migration.

The eventual decision by the Americans to establish their main Panama Canal labor collecting point in Barbados, a decision discussed in chapter 4, thereby dovetailed neatly with the presence of a laboring population conditioned by earlier migration experiences. The Americans were seeking a source of mobile, cheap, dependable labor. The black Barbadian laborers, from their own point of view, had located a reliable, decade-long, nearby source of relatively high wages. In other words, the Panama Canal experience for black Barbadians could be interpreted as an extension of the past, another destination in a wide-ranging migration that they had been involved in since slave emancipation.

The Panama Canal eventually would prove to be a wage source of unprecedented magnitude for black Barbadians, and unprecedented numbers of them would travel to work on the isthmus. Moreover, the demographic, social, and economic changes brought about from the Panama Canal experience would create pivotal changes in Barbadian social history, so much so that the old-fashioned means of labor coercion and social domination by the white Barbadian plantocracy would no longer be tolerated by black Barbadian laborers. So by indulging in migration—a mode of livelihood that was, by 1900, a traditional means of coping with local landlessness and oppression as well as external uncertainties—black Barbadians created something new. In Barbados, migration therefore was not, nor has it been since, simply a "safety valve" to relieve population pressures or a one-dimensional response to a given problem. For generations of Barbadians, migration has been fundamental and a way of life.[8]

A number of scholars of human migration would doubtless take issue with the assertion that the black Barbadian exodus to Panama was in part a creative act of individual or group volition. This is because a "structural" school of human migration, currently fashionable in many quarters, stresses that labor migrations are simply some of the more visible components in the broader historical process of the development of the world capitalist system.[9] Migration structuralists have criticized, quite appropriately in my view, the earlier microeconomic model of migration in which individual migrants or actors move through space, uninhibited by coercion, immigration officials, or similar impediments, "to achieve an equilibrium of the spatial distribution of the factors of production through the geographic mobility of labor."[10] Migration structuralists, furthermore, criticize the earlier models for lacking a historical dimension, although there remain surprisingly few thoroughly researched historical studies of labor migrations, by migration structuralists or anyone else.[11] I am most sympathetic with much of the structuralist argument, but I feel it falls short of providing an accurate interpretation of many facets of human migration. Most important, in the case of the black Barbadian exodus to Panama in the early twentieth century, I feel that a structural, macrolevel approach probably would downplay unnecessarily the ingenuity of the individual migrants themselves. But I make no pretense to attempt to assess thoroughly the voluminous scholarly literature that purports to address itself to migration "theory," a literature that now grows annually at a staggering rate.[12]

Caribbeanist scholars, emphasizing the behavior of the people they have lived and worked with and also aware of the external constraints impinging on insular West Indians, have begun to build an impressive fund of migration studies. The working

Introduction

peoples of the islands and rimlands of the circum-Caribbean region, inhabiting small, sometimes worn-out isalnds, often have had little choice but to move about in order to make ends meet. To most West Indians, migration "is simply one of many ways of pursuing one's life objectives, of getting by in a world over which one has no control."[13]

The perspective I take in this book combines the microlevel approach that Caribbeanist scholars have employed so effectively in village studies and migration studies with a broader macrolevel view assessing historical conditions and economic changes not only in Barbados but also in other parts of the Caribbean and beyond. Above all, this study stresses that black Barbadians, pushed and pulled by internal and external forces and given remarkably little latitude for maneuver, responded with doggedness and a keen survival instinct in setting out for the Panama Canal and, in so doing, were responsible eventually for important social and economic changes on their own home island. In this way, black Barbadians have much in common with working peoples everywhere. And historians and social scientists have learned to appreciate that, for centuries, working classes, tribesmen, and peasants throughout the world often have been the "agents in the historical process" rather than "its victims and silent witnesses."[14]

Although the migration to Panama was of extreme importance to Barbados in the early twentieth century, this study does not deal exclusively with migration. Its focus is on Barbados and the Barbadians from, roughly, 1900 to 1920. And while the Panama Canal emigration, discussed in depth in chapters 4 and 5, was the most important external event affecting all Barbadians at the time, some of them never went to Panama or anywhere else. Those staying behind, however, felt the impact of the changes created by those who did emigrate to Central America and elsewhere, just as those Barbadians staying home late in the twentieth century cannot avoid the influences of the many who have traveled abroad.

Throughout this study I assert that white planters oppressed black workers in Barbados during the early part of the twentieth century. This assertion is not to suggest that there was a state or islandwide political apparatus modeled along totalitarian lines, as in the Soviet Union or South Africa today, which narrowly circumscribed the daily lives of a segment of the local population. Rather, the planters used their political domination of the local economy in order to bolster the export of sugar. And in so doing, they often exerted remarkable control over individual members of the black Barbadian working class. The local planters, however, never possessed ultimate political control over the lands and peoples of the island, because that control was held in London where officials at the Colonial Office at times acted to curb excesses by members of the Barbadian plantocracy. These points are discussed further in the following chapters, especially at the end of chapter 4, where a discussion of black Barbadian expectations at the time involving the "right" to emigrate is presented.

Although the emphasis of this study is on the achievements of Barbadian blacks and, as a corollary, how they overcame oppression by whites, Barbados has never been totally divided into only a white minority and a large black working class. Poor whites and a large "colored" group on Barbados have represented intermediate and ambiguous social and economic categories whose interests and identities have sometimes coalesced, often differed, and occasionally overlapped with those of the black majority. These complexities as they existed in 1900 are discussed further at the end of chapter 2.

A related and final introductory comment is in order about race relations in Barbados in the early twentieth century. According to many Barbadians, of any color, racial discrimination is still, at the end of the twentieth century, more pronounced there than in any of the neighboring West Indian islands. This assertion may or may not be true. But at the beginning of the twentieth century a withering racism among members of the white plantocracy of Barbados provided an ideological rationalization for the economic subjugation and deprivation of Barbadian blacks. Furthermore, this racism seems to have ascended to the level of a psychological imperative for some Barbadian whites of 1900. For those few planters who still felt pangs of conscience about the plight of the black laborers, they sometimes were (incorrectly) reminded that, after all, some European laborers were even worse off. An article in the Barbados planter

Introduction 11

newspaper, adapted from a piece in a British journal at the time, made the ludicrous yet reassuring point that black West Indians, whose needs were simple, few, and easily achieved, lived actually quite comfortable lives:

> There are hundreds and thousands of our own [British] countrymen living in the darkness of the slums of our great cities more in need of sympathy and generosity than these West Indian negroes... If a negro's house is destroyed by fire or tempest, how long do you think it will take him to build another? Nature will give him food almost for the asking... and disease does not decimate him as it does the poor at home.[15]

Assertions such as these, stressing the supposed carefree, innocent, even childlike makeup of black people, were relatively common in published material and public pronouncements in Barbados early in the century. It takes little imagination to suppose what rumors and misinformation on the subject circulated unofficially among white Barbadians.

These points about racial discrimination are raised not to serve as a vehicle for the expression of polemical indignation but rather to point out the background and climate of the conventional racism prevailing at the turn of the century against which Barbadian blacks were forced to struggle both at home and in the Canal Zone.[16] Neither should these points, nor the discussions of the political economy of Barbados when they occur in the ensuing chapters, be interpreted to condemn every planter, every parish doctor, or every government official of Barbados during the period in question, a few of whom were sensitive, kind, caring, and even committed to the betterment of the black workers and members of their families.

The institutional racism at the turn of the century was only one dimension of an interrelated complex of obstacles facing black Barbadians. Landlessness, disease, and economic depression were other dimensions. These obstacles, moreover, were not simply short-term problems but were similar to those that had been facing black Barbadians for generations. Perhaps the years of suffering had conditioned them to avoid becoming demoralized and to keep alive at least the hope for better times against impossible odds. Early in the twentieth century, their goal was achieved in part by the men and women of Barbados who traveled away to Panama. Because of the efforts of these migrants, the history of the construction of the Panama Canal is linked as closely to Barbados as it is to the United States. And the story of hardship, migration, return, and achievement of black Barbadians in the first two decades of the twentieth century is a testimony to a most remarkable people.

CHAPTER 2

Barbados at the Turn of the Century

The geographer's assertion that the past often is reflected in the landscape would have come as little surprise to most Barbadians in 1900. The cumulative weight of two and one-half centuries of plantation colonialism had created the roads, settlements, and crop combinations, and had even determined, through the Atlantic sugar and slave trade, the nature of the people residing there. Other fundamental characteristics of the island at the turn of the century, although not necessarily visible landscape phenomena, also reflected Barbados's plantation history. Among them were the local political economy, the entangled financial web that helped explain an anachronistic resistance to change, and even the tragic health conditions of many black estate workers.

Land and People

As any Barbadian will tell you, Barbados is different from all of the other islands in the Caribbean. Barbados (figure 1) is the most easterly of the islands, and—except for wind-carried volcanic ash that has occasionally drifted to Barbados—it is geologically unrelated to the igneous Windwards, which are one hundred miles to the west. Accordingly, the island's topography is less dramatic than that of its neighbors. The highest point, Mt. Hillaby (a mere 1,115 feet) is part of the eroded and hilly Scotland district in the northeastern part of the island. But on the rest of Barbados, sedimentary marine deposits capped with coral underlie a gently rolling landscape, making the island ideal for agriculture and easily accessible from most everywhere else. Barbados is therefore without the mountainous core that has served as village

13

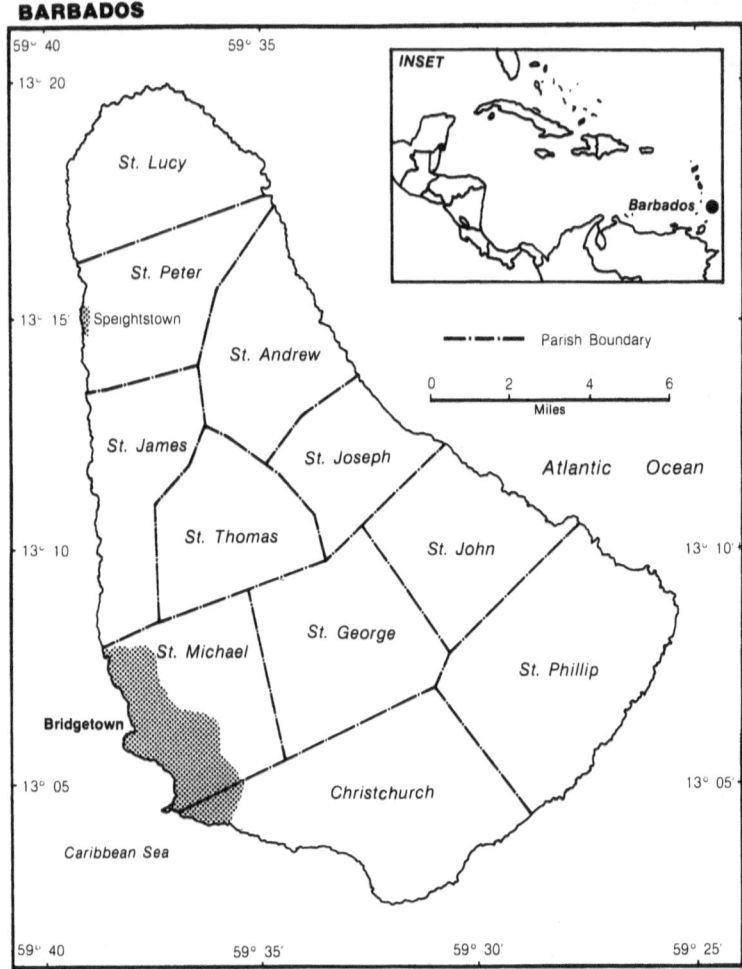

Figure 1. Barbados and its parishes.

region, subsistence zone, or maroon (runaway slave) sanctuary at various times elsewhere in the Commonwealth Caribbean. The low-lying, coral-based soils of Barbados have, in contrast, been nearly monopolized by a sugar cane plantocracy for three and one-half centuries.

The planting and harvest of the sugar cane on Barbados have

always followed seasonal climatic rhythms. The average annual sixty inches of rainfall is distributed unevenly between the rainy season (generally June to November or December) and the dry season (January to May). The island's temperatures are only rarely higher than 90 degrees or lower than 60 degrees Fahrenheit, and cloudy days are relatively few.[1] The benign character of the Barbadian climate historically has been sought by North Americans and Europeans for therapeutic reasons. In the late nineteenth century one enthusiastic visitor proclaimed the Barbadian climate "as sparkling and invigorating as champagne," an exuberance matched only by the tourist brochures that describe Barbados today, one century later.[2]

Barbadians themselves, however, have learned to be wary of their climate. The hurricane season, August to October, always poses potential danger. As the twentieth century opened, Barbados had not yet fully recovered from the effects of the hurricane of September 10, 1898; the storm had roared through the island's southern parishes killing 112 people (and innumerable livestock), destroying the wooden cottages of more than 11,000 black laboring-class families, and leaving surviving inhabitants in a "dazed and water-soaked" state.[3] Barbadians with short memories were again reminded of the hazards of late summer three years later; an incredible twenty-five inches of rain poured down during a twenty-four-hour period beginning on the morning of July 5, 1901. The storm flooded low-lying areas, filled drainage channels, and drowned a plantation manager and his five-year-old son in St. Peter parish when it washed away their horsecart.[4] At the other extreme, drought was a recurrent, more insidious menace. Drought desiccated provision grounds and drove black Barbadians to brackish water holes. Prolonged dryness was common, especially in St. Lucy and St. Philip parishes at the low-lying northern and southeastern ends of the island, where rain-bearing winds passed over parched settlements and estates. In 1895, severe drought, combined with economic depression, had led to widespread hunger in rural areas, causing desperate black Barbadians to invade neighboring plantations and provision grounds seeking edible fruit and root crops. As in past decades, drought would recur in the first years of the twentieth century.[5]

Problems of prolonged aridity were compounded by the lack

of forests on the island. The government's Forestry Committee met in 1899 and noted what everyone already knew—that their island, more than any other in the West Indies, was nearly devoid of natural forest vegetation. The level topography and excellent agricultural potential of Barbados combined with the "energy of its inhabitants" had caused the island long ago to be given over to the nearly exclusive cultivation of sugar cane.[6] The committee further noted that forested areas might protect streams, inhibit runoff and erosion, and create recreational benefits. The Forestry Committee happily concluded business by recommending that (1) waste lands be forested, (2) prominent ridges be bought by the government and forested, and (3) existing wooded areas be preserved—platitudes that immediately became dead letters.[7]

The unique character of Barbadian geography had been observed firsthand by the British Royal Commission of 1897, which had been appointed to investigate Caribbean economic and social conditions. During hearings in the Council Chamber at the Public Buildings in Bridgetown on February 18, 1897, the Reverend C.T. Oehler, a Moravian minister familiar with both Jamaica and Barbados, testified before the commission. Oehler explained that, unlike Barbados, in some areas of Jamaica land was available almost for the asking and that rural Jamaicans were in the habit of exploiting their mountainous, government-owned Crown lands for mangoes, citrus, firewood, and other provisions. Two other ministers, the Reverends Sealy and Payne, further commented that the working classes of the Windwards were similarly better off in terms of access to interior Crown lands and therefore better off in terms of subsistence than were their Barbadian counterparts.

Black Barbadians, the overwhelming majority of whom inhabited rural plantation "tenantries," faced markedly different circumstances. Their tiny subsistence gardens normally were rented from the estates, and access to these garden plots was contingent upon their working (usually exclusively) on the same estates. On Barbados, firewood was imported and purchased, not gathered, as were some foodstuffs that were, in contrast, locally cultivated in Jamaica and the Windwards. Black Barbadians, lacking a local highland area that the planters did not dominate, were therefore without a physical refuge outside direct planter control. The relative lack of homegrown foodstuffs, a shortcoming invariably worsened during periods of drought, helped to explain why infant mortality rates on Barbados were always so tragically high. In the conclusions of their report, the members of the Royal Commission of 1897 remarked that Barbados was the Caribbean colony most dependent on sugar and its products (97 percent of exports). Further, the commission summarized the geographical and demographic character of Barbados as have so many observers before and since: "The condition of Barbados is markedly different from that of any other Colony in the West Indies. It is very thickly populated. . . . There are no Crown lands, no forests, no uncultivated areas, and the population has probably reached the maximum which the island can even under favourable circumstances support."[8]

The general Barbadian settlement pattern of 1900 had, of course, been inherited from the past. The sugar cane introduced during the first half of the seventeenth century had swept all before it. Richard Dunn suggests that by late in the same century the island already was cleared and "was as fully cultivated as it is today, a sea of cane accented here and there by a clump of trees, a sugar works, or a Negro village."[9] Then, one and one-half centuries later, in the 1830s, when black slaves were emancipated, they were unable to assert themselves as truly free and independent from former masters because the planters continued to hold the land.[10] At emancipation the landless Barbadian freedmen were "turned loose like a pack of wild goats on a barren mountain, and they had to return to the house whence they came to work for a mere crust of bread."[11] The land, the means of producing either subsistence or wealth on Barbados and available in only finite quantity on a mostly level island of 166 square miles, was jealously preserved by the planter class at emancipation. And the protection of land and power as domains of the local plantocracy seems to have been the main source of inspiration for the planter-dominated legislature of Barbados during the rest of the nineteenth century.

The buildings and grounds supporting the usually antiquated methods of producing raw sugar on Barbados in 1900 typified the postemancipation landscape of the island. In 1911, two-thirds of Barbados's 329 plantation mills still relied on windpower, the remainder on steam.[12] Unlike in Trinidad and British Guiana, where enormous steam-driven factories commanded extensive areas of sugar cane, the prototypical estate of Barbados at the turn of the century was only two hundred to three hundred acres in extent. Unlike in Trinidad, where neat, macadam roads led to towering factory stacks, rutted trails in many parts of Barbados approached ramshackle windmills and tiny wooden boiling houses that were "mere sheds."[13] Unlike in other West Indian territories, where "outside capitalists" now controlled local events, the typical resident owner or proprietor on Barbados had eschewed the adoption of central cane milling and the dislocation it certainly would create. But the estate owner-planter of Barbados could still take pride in being master of his own affairs and in producing the hogsheads of semirefined muscovado sugar from the island's fertile soils as his forefathers had done for so many decades.

Although the planter's house was often inauspicious, it was opulent compared with the wooden houses of the nearby tenantry settlement occupied by the estate's black labor force. Estate tenantries were often sited on "rabland," stony or sloping areas unsuited for cane cultivation. The main road leading through an estate was usually graveled, the coralline stones crushed to a chalky powder by the metal wheelrims of the owner's horsecart or those of the donkey "trucks" carrying sugar and molasses to Bridgetown. Foot trails, on the other hand, led to the estate tenantry and were nearly impassable during the rains of late summer.

The Political Economy

Planter control over the land in 1900 guaranteed planter control over the government. A Barbadian man could vote for House of Assembly members only if he controlled land that yielded at least £5 per year, or earned a salary of £50 per year, or had a university education—qualifications that only 1,986 electors could meet in 1911. Those electors meeting the landholding qualifications were eligible to help elect each year the vestrymen for every parish. The vestry system was another throwback to the seventeenth century. Apparently begun in 1630 when the Barbadian parishes themselves were formed, the parish vestries had provided for the maintenance of ministers of the Church of England and the initial construction of churches in each Barbadian parish at a time when intraisland communications were poor and "parishioners" were called upon to manage their own local affairs.[14]

The vestry system had, however, persisted into the early twentieth century, continuity sustained by a succession of legislative acts over the years. Each vestry in 1900 was empowered to levy taxes on the land (from which the overwhelming amount of parish revenue was derived), buildings, animals, vehicles, and Anglican church pews of its particular parish. From this revenue, vestries were then obligated to repair and maintain parish church buildings, remunerate church officials, and provide road repair (the latter obligation usually accomplished with financial help from Barbadian general revenues). Parish vestries, moreover, were required to provide for the education and "maintenance" of the poor. Each parish vestry was responsible for an almshouse where the most impoverished of the black laborers and their families could receive food and medical care and for paying annual stipends to parish sanitary inspectors. In theory, parish vestries of Barbados in 1900 represented an admirable case of local political autonomy: parish funds collected and disbursed for the benefit of all who resided within parish boundaries. In practice, the vestry system—implemented by the same planters who controlled the land—was a formidable weapon in the planters' arsenal directed toward the domination of a large and dependent black labor force. Barbadian vestry minutes from the early twentieth century invariably suggested that parish vestrymen at the time felt little responsiblity to help provide proper sanitation and related services in their particular districts; rather, their principal collective goal seemed to have been to seek ways to keep parish expenditures (derived from taxes on their land) as low as possible.

A Barbadian's parish of residence in 1900 was therefore of more importance than simply being included in one census district or another. A rural black Barbadian "belonged" to a particular parish just as he "belonged" to a particular estate. And vestrymen made very sure that parish funds were not being used to support outsiders from beyond the district's boundary line, who were thereby the financial responsibility of others.

The population of Barbados had been officially enumerated in 1891 (table 1) and would not be counted again until 1911. Although the great majority of the island's 182,306 inhabitants in 1891 were rural (plantation) dwellers, greater Bridgetown—including urbanized St. Michael parish and the western end of Christchurch parish—accounted for roughly one-third of all Barbadians. Bridgetown, moreover, was the commerical and communications center for the island as it always has been. The gravel highways of Barbados, during the dry season some of the finest in the West Indies, progressively improved as they approached Bridgetown. The island's railway, which had run east to the St. Philip coast since 1881 and extended north to terminate at Belleplaine in St. Andrew parish in 1883, had its main station on Fairchild Street near the Carenage, or waterfront. Horse-drawn

Table 1. Population of Barbados, 1891

	White	Mixed	Black	Total
Bridgetown	3,336	9,227	8,433	20,996
St. Michael	3,646	9,609	21,932	35,187
Christchurch	1,483	3,081	16,928	21,492
St. Philip	1,301	4,025	13,337	18,663
St. George	694	3,087	12,273	16,054
St. John	1,170	1,850	7,936	10,956
St. Peter	825	2,663	7,312	10,800
St. James	486	2,351	7,667	10,504
St. Thomas	394	1,831	7,873	10,098
St. Lucy	509	2,332	6,921	9,762
St. Joseph	995	2,153	5,900	9,048
St. Andrew	774	1,767	6,205	8,746
Totals	15,613	43,976	122,717	182,306

Source: Data from *Report on Census of Barbados (1881–1891)*, 17.

trams carried passengers from the heart of Bridgetown to outlying areas at Hastings, Eagle Hall, Fontabelle, Roebuck Street, and Constitution.

Barbadians from St. Peter and St. Lucy parishes often traveled to "town" and back via the small, thirty-ton Speightstown schooners, a trip costing three pence (six cents) each way.[15] But intraisland traffic at Carlisle Bay and the Carenage was minuscule compared with the momentous function that the port played in linking Barbados's sugar cane economy with the outside world. Had a visitor stood at the inner harbor's wharfside in 1900, unmolested by horsecab drivers or untrammeled by donkeys laden with imported firewood, he or she would have witnessed a commodity flow that explained what the island's business was all about. Black Barbadian lightermen rowed small boats laden with bags of muscovado sugar or locally made wooden puncheons of molasses toward the freighters lying in wait at Carlisle Bay and destined for Europe, the United States, Canada, and Newfoundland.[16] On some days, a sailing schooner heading for British Guiana could be seen taking on potatoes and yams that had been produced on a Barbadian estate.

The returning lighters carried the many externally produced trade items on which all Barbadians, black and white, had depended for centuries: unground corn, barley, and wheat from North America; barrels of flour mainly from the United States; barrels of cornmeal from the United States and Canada; rice from India and British Guiana; coal from the United Kingdom; firewood from British Guiana and the Windwards; building materials—mainly pine and spruce lumber from Canada; animals and meat from near and far; nearly every kind of manufactured item from machinery and telephones to buttons and thread; liquors and tobacco; and a myriad of other trade commodities.[17] These items were off-loaded at the pierhead and taken to the warehouses of the island's commission agents before being consigned to stores and shops.

The Barbadian government in 1900, typical of governments throughout the Commonwealth Caribbean, imposed duties on these imports—mainly on spirits, food, and building materials—as its main source of colonial revenue.[18] The black working class's overall purchasing power was thereby related directly to the government's financial well-being, and changing wage levels on Barbados therefore had a "very marked" effect on government revenues.[19] The seat of the Barbadian government was Bridgetown, Barbados's political as well as commercial focal point. In Bridgetown—whether at the fashionable Savannah Club, the legislative chambers, business offices, or luncheons at the governor's residence—the important planters, businessmen, and politicians (designations that were by no means mutually exclusive) of Barbados regularly met and exchanged formal and informal views concerning the direction of the island's economy.

The most powerful body of Barbados's central government in 1900 was the recently formed Executive Committee. Headed by the island's governor, who represented the British Crown, the Executive Committee controlled government financial decisions as well as public works and institutions. The governor selected the Executive Committee's other four members from among the membership of the Legislative Council and the House of Assembly. The Legislative Council, or upper house, consisted of nine "selected" members, and the House of Assembly had twenty-four members elected by qualified voters—two from each of the eleven parishes and two from Bridgetown. The island's chief justice was the principal judicial officer of a court system that administered and interpreted the laws passed by the Legislative Council and House of Assembly.

The degree of autonomy of the Barbadian legislature (and therefore of the plantocracy) from direct metropolitan rule had been a source of contention ever since the navigation acts and protected English sugar market had tied Barbados irrevocably to its "mother country" in the mid-seventeenth century.[20] Thereafter, as British abolitionist sentiment grew, Barbadian legislation—especially those laws dealing harshly with slaves—came under increasing scrutiny in Britain. Barbadian planters had resisted, accommodated, and compromised at various times in responding to metropolitan demands and sanctions, but Barbadians never lost sight of their "special" semi-independent status from the Crown.

Their position was shaken in the emancipation era, when Barbadian assemblymen were forced by abolitionists through the Colonial Office to curtail what they regarded their "traditional constitutional rights."[21] Later, in the 1870s, Barbados survived the federation crisis with the Windwards and avoided possible Crown Colony status. Barbadian autonomy had, however, been further curtailed by the formation of the Executive Committee in 1881.[22] The committee's most significant responsibility was its exclusive authority in initiating all money bills, authority formerly invested in any member of the legislature.[23]

But concession was by no means capitulation by the Barbadian landed interests, who monopolized a local government that existed for and by the planters. The qualifications for membership in the House of Assembly at the turn of the century was ownership of freehold land worth £1,500 or an annual income of £200, requirements that restricted assembly seats not simply to any elector but to the more prosperous or well-to-do.[24] And the cherished self-rule and autonomy that Barbadian assemblymen demanded from Britain as a God-given right was by no means translated into obligations that individual Barbadian planters/legislators felt toward their parish "constituencies." Rather, assembly members usually considered their positions privately owned fiefdoms and confined their legislative duties and viewpoints to bettering their own positions and those of a small group of associates. As late as 1919, Governor C.R.M. O'Brien's secretary would lament that in Barbados "which claims to have Representative Government no member of the House of Assembly can be found to champion the cause of a large section of the population."[25] In 1921 the black Barbadian journalist Clennell Wickham summarized attitudes of members of the Barbadian House of Assembly in the first years of the twentieth century as follows: "There is no sense of duty to the individuals of the island as a whole. There is no sense of responsibility for broad and reasonable treatment. There is merely a sense of class."[26]

Wickham had brought into the open a most important and fundamental point. Though patterned after British common law, Barbadian law in 1900 was in no sense an objective code of rules whose ethical validity transcended the interests and attitudes of the several classes on the island. Rather, it represented a codified set of constraints by which a tiny white elite dominated a numerically dominant, technically free, largely landless, black laboring class. And the practice of blatant socioeconomic discrimination under the guise of participatory democracy was possible only if assembly members were willing to entertain pretense and hypocrisy as commonplace in the legislative chambers. For the white ruling class in general, the essential inequalities upon which the Barbadian sugar economy was based could be justified for external consumption along condescending, racist lines: a Barbadian black had few wants that could not be satisfied with a biscuit, a cotton shirt, or a tot of rum; he produced good work only when properly supervised; he preferred a vegetable diet; he cared little for his offspring. Another means of coping mentally with caste and class in Barbados in 1900 was simply to ignore one's surroundings. According to one American visitor at the time, Barbados could be "heavenly" for whites only if they were prepared to "ignore the frightful misery" of the black workers and were successful "in shutting their eyes to everything which is unpleasant or threatening."[27]

The persistence of the sugar plantocracy's domination depended heavily on the continuity and enforcement of laws that immobilized members of the black working class. Though modified since emancipation, Barbadian statutes generally referred to as "located laborer" acts endured with remarkable severity into the twentieth century.[28] The "Master and Servant Act" of 1891 no longer stipulated that agricultural workers be imprisoned for "breach of contract" as had the preceding master-servant law. The 1891 law, however, called for a written contract between estate owner and worker, indicating the general nature of the workday, the wage rate, and the *maximum* number of hours to be worked.[29] Significantly, no *minimum* work hours were guaranteed in the contract. Such an arrangement was entirely in the planters' favor. They could reward servile individuals with enough wage labor to keep their families alive and, conversely, they could send unruly workers home. On most Barbadian estates planters held contracts with many laborers so that an individual worker obtained "at most, three or four days work per week."[30]

The "Landlord and Tenant Act" of 1897 had evolved from an earlier master-servant statute. The landlord-tenant law, theoretically distributing mutual obligations and risks between estate owner and worker, allowed planters to seize property—

ing animals or food supplies—of tenants for rent payments. Planters used this law to intimidate workers who sought wage labor elsewhere. It was not uncommon for houses of troublesome tenants to be torn down and left conspicuously at the roadside. In theory, both the master-servant and landlord-tenant laws designated police constables or police magistrates of the parish to "arbitrate" any questions between parties. In practice, police (who were often plantation employees or planters themselves) acted as estate owners' legal accomplices in limiting severely the individual mobility and thereby the wage-seeking opportunities for black Barbadian laborers.

It is not surprising that black estate laborers, hemmed-in geographically and coerced legally, occasionally exhibited an "unwillingness to work" for arbitrary and capricious planters. Also, black unemployment—caused by planters' withholding work—could throw individuals and families onto the parochial relief roles, thereby causing indirect planter expense. So the planters resorted, as they had in the past, to further legal remedies to solve the problems that their oppressive laws had caused in the first place. The legal fine-tuning provided to counter black "laziness" and to save poor-relief expenses was the latest variation of the Vagrancy Act, a law passed in 1897. Descended from the vagrancy acts that British Caribbean planters had used since emancipation (many of the acts subsequently modified or disallowed in London), the 1897 act in Barbados called for punishment of persons who should "willfully refuse or neglect" to work and thereby cause himself or family members to become "burthensome upon any parochial or other public funds."[31]

The legal strictures allowing planter domination of Barbados in 1900 were simply the external forms of an unwritten but well-understood social system. White planters or plantation managers decided who would and would not work, or whose goats and sheep could graze the plantation yard. Black women and children gathering cane stalks for cooking fires might be sent home by a plantation manager who, in a better mood, would turn a blind eye to such harmless activity. A Barbados newspaper excerpt, which in 1910 served to remind potential "thieves" and "troublemakers" of penalities for wrongdoing, serves to remind us three-quarters of a century later of the severity of the island's legal system at the time and its punishments for incredibly trivial "offenses":

> Before Mr. Smith yesterday, a lad 18 years of age, named Evans Bridgeman of Canewood, St. Michael, was prosecuted by the manager of Canewood Plantation with stealing four breadfruits growing on lands of the plantation. . . . Defendant said he stole the breadfruits because he was hungry. He was sentenced to 14 days' imprisonment with hard labour.[32]

Poor Relief and Medical Mismanagement

The first comprehensive islandwide Poor Relief Act had been passed by the Barbadian legislature in 1880 and amended four times before the turn of the century. The act emphasized central administrative control over the poor relief that had been carried out by the parish vestries since immediately after emancipation. Unlike in Britain, Barbadian poor laws involved no workhouse tradition. Nor was there need in a socioeconomic system based mainly on color for poor laws, as in Britain, usefully "to stigmatize the self-confessed failures of society."[33] Indeed, Barbadian planters had resisted after emancipation the provision of any poor relief for freedmen who, by virtue of their freedom, were obligated to care for themselves and their families. But the Colonial Office had prevailed, and during the decade following emancipation Robert Schomburgk reported vestry care of the "deserving poor" throughout the island and was moved to describe a "commodious and large almshouse" in Bridgetown.[34] During the remainder of the nineteenth century, Barbadian vestries had provided grudging poor relief at the almshouse of each parish, supplemented by private benevolent and charitable groups. Hurricanes and similar disasters normally overtaxed existing local charitable agencies and usually attracted one-time imperial grants and also mimimal relief from nearby islands.

Because estate wages were so pitifully low, many black laboring families of Barbados in 1900 had firsthand experience with parish almshouses. As long as a worker was in good health he could eke out a hand- to-mouth existence; but illness, drought, or any similar accidental departure from the routine often meant one's candidacy for pauper relief. In 1908 a general rule of thumb expected 10 percent of the Barbadian population to be "relieved" annually, either at government agencies (hospital, lunatic asylum) or at the hands of parish vestries.[35] Serious accidents or illnesses usually justified "inside" relief at parish hospital wards and care by parish doctors. "Outside" relief was a more common means of aid to the poor; food, milk, rum, money, and free burials were provided for the aged, infirm, and poor of each parish. Relief doles varied qualitatively from parish to parish and from one year to the next. The changing validation systems and criteria for poor-relief candidacy usually were determined by parish vestrymen who were themselves the members of parish health boards and who therefore appointed parish medical officers and set local tax rates to pay for poor-relief obligations.

Overall assembly control of poor relief that, at the same time, remained the immediate responsibility of individual parish vestries of Barbados created a bewildering, redundant, and thoroughly inefficient means of providing aid to the poor. It never was entirely clear—at least to potential recipients of poor relief—what agency had responsibility for any particular case. Of course, a concerted mystification of poor-relief rules and responsibilities had a financial dimension in the form of short-term planters' tax savings. Boards, commissions, officers, and inspectors all were invested with varying, ill-defined, and overlapping authority. A poor-law inspector appointed by the governor, as was the Barbados General Board of Health, visited outlying parishes and collected reports from parish medical officers, who were paid from vestry funds. Each parish had health and sanitary inspectors (and subinspectors) plus vestry-appointed commissioners of health. The commissioners of health of St. Michael parish acted also as highway commissioners. Frequently they met as one body, adjourned, and then reconvened as another.

The confusion and bureaucratic inefficiency inherent in overlapping, parallel, and competing authorities served well to confuse and inhibit potential recipients of relief benefits. Institutionalized befuddlement also hindered government actions against "genuine" islandwide medical emergencies. When smallpox was introduced to Barbados in February 1902, the management and control of the epidemic came under the parish sanitary commissioners, though "some confusion" existed as to which authorities were responsible for such action. In August, after hostility and bureaucratic indifference had inhibited effective responses to counter the spread of the disease, Governor Frederick M. Hodgson mandated that the Barbadian Board of Health take direct control. In early September, Hodgson distributed circulars to the various parish vestries with specific instructions: subdivide parishes into vaccination districts and do not minimize the gravity of the situation. The smallpox epidemic eventually was declared ended on April 20, 1903, having brought about 119 deaths from a total of 1,466 cases and an expenditure from local resources of £26,500, almost certainly much more money than would have been necessary had the outbreak been handled more efficiently at the start.[36]

In combating the outbreak of smallpox, the Barbadian legislature had in May 1902 passed a bill calling for public vaccination, paupers to be vaccinated without charge and others to pay a fee. Few persons to be vaccinated complied with the act. Then in August, under pressure from Governor Hodgson, and in light of a worsening situation, a vaccination amendment provided that all persons vaccinated be paid a six-pence "bonus" from public funds. The epidemic was thereby controlled (150,000 Barbadians were vaccinated by March 31, 1903), but only after aggressive public health measures had been adopted by the highest government officials. "Lizzie and Joe," two perceptive street-corner conversationalists who appeared in Barbados's *Weekly Recorder* newspaper cartoons, at the time considered the government's action taken to curb smallpox as odd and inconsistent. The same government, after all, was willing to see food prices increase to impoverish further an already oppressed working class:

> Yuh vaccinashun bettuh? Wah yuh do wid you four cents?
> Deh might did leh de ting run and save de whole expense;
> Instid uh dah deh raise de price pun wah we got fuh eat
> Deh wan tuh see starvashun kill we niggahs pun de street.[37]

The answer to Lizzie and Joe's puzzlement could not be found within the confines of the island itself, but it was obvious in light of the potential disruption of Barbadian external trade brought about by quarantine. Barbadian public health bills in the early twentieth century were acted upon by the assembly with a good deal more interest in keeping the port open than in maintaining or improving public health, an attitude sometimes unwittingly blurted out on the floor of the legislative chambers themselves.[38] Quarantine was dreaded and beyond local control. The local legislature had no control, for example, over the governor of French Guiana, who in March 1902 declared that no one from Barbados could land in Cayenne without a vaccination certificate. Nor could they control the Royal Mail Company, whose steamers refused "communication with the shore" by the end of March because of the Barbadian small pox epidemic, whereupon the company transferred its West Indian headquarters from Barbados to Trinidad.

The decision by the Royal Mail Company and similar smallpox-inspired decisions by other shipping lines were disastrous. Barbados had for years enjoyed its position as the first Caribbean port of call for mail steamers from Britain and as the last West Indian destination for "homebound" ships.[39] Although the company's West Indian headquarters were to return to Barbados after the epidemic was over in 1903, the short-term economic effects were suffered by all Barbadians, most of all those who could least afford it. Economic isolation meant a nearly empty bay, an idle wharf, and no wages for the boatmen, waterfront workers, porters, taxi drivers, coal carriers, and all others.

Although Barbadian authorities had to act against smallpox in order to save their economy, some spokesmen were nevertheless convinced of an international conspiracy that was more semantic than medical. How could one distinguish between "Indian pox" and "water bumps" and smallpox itself? And why did the capricious steamer executives not penalize, rather than reward, the insidious Trinidadian authorities whose island, it was "confidently whispered," had the same disease as poor Barbados but simply called it a different name?[40] A noisy minority of influential Barbadian planters and businessmen depicted Governor Hodgson and his chief medical officer, Dr. John Hutson, as dupes and accomplices of those who would allow arbitrarily imposed quarantine to shut Barbados down. Hodgson and Hutson were "vaccinists" and "faddists," and, of course, Hutson and his "medicine-men" cronies stood to profit handsomely from mass inoculation. The governor, in their stated view, had taken himself and his executive powers much too seriously. Had not Governor Mouttet of Martinique exercised similar "overgovernment" in persuading the now-incinerated residents of St. Pierre to stay at home rather than flee Mount Pelée's ominous rumblings?[41]

The ludicrous insistence by many among the Barbadian plantocracy that those who recognized and acted against smallpox were automatically enemies was not an isolated instance in the first decade of the twentieth century. On November 5, 1907, the HMS *Indefatigable* arrived from Grenada with a seaman aboard apparently suffering from yellow fever. The ensuing epidemic finally ended in April 1909, but meanwhile Barbados was again avoided by the Royal Mail Company and also the Royal Dutch Line. From December 1908, thirty-six Barbadians died of yellow fever with twenty-two cases alone at Pie Corner, St. Lucy. Sir Rupert Boyce, dean of the Liverpool School of Tropical Medicine, came to Barbados and confirmed the existence of yellow fever. Displaying boundless energy and enthusiasm, he orchestrated a laudable and effective grass-roots mosquito control program that successfully ended the epidemic.[42] Boyce's efforts, however, were not appreciated by several leading public figures and a segment of the press who preferred to refer to yellow fever as "gastric influenza."

After the economically disastrous smallpox epidemic of 1902–3, Barbadian government officials decided to take action in an attempt to exert some control over externally imposed quarantine sanctions. A local committee, organized in 1903, recommended cooperation, rather than competition, among neighboring West Indian colonies. The result was the West Indian Sanitary Convention of 1904, which met in Barbados and included representatives from throughout the Commonwealth Caribbean except Jamaica. They agreed to notify one another about the existence of the major, internationally agreed-upon quarantine diseases—yellow fever, smallpox, and cholera—and they further agreed not to declare quarantine against one another as readily as in the past and to leave much of the responsibility for identification and prevention in the hands of local health officials. That the intercolonial convention in 1904 was much more a common strategy to avoid quarantine than it was an alliance to combat local disease seems evident from the following clause ratified by the conferees: "No measures shall be taken against any ship *merely* because it has come from or called at any place where typhus fever, enteric fever, cerebro-spinal fever, scarlet fever, diphtheria, measles, whooping cough, chicken-pox or dengue exists" (emphasis added).[43]

Grateful planters agreed that the provisions of the 1904 convention had eased quarantine restrictions against Barbados during the yellow fever outbreak of 1907–9. Perhaps Barbadian political control could extend beyond the island, after all. Recurrent diseases and quarantine dangers notwithstanding, there was still no doubt where the power lay in Barbados, and the planters would exert that power even if it meant making astonishingly cynical and self-serving decisions to preserve it. During House of Assembly debates in 1907, H.G. Yearwood of St. Joseph parish spoke out against a government-sponsored amendment to the Public Health Act that would make typhoid a "notifiable" disease, thereby marking it for special government attention. If the bill were passed, reasoned Yearwood, the Barbadian Board of Health actually would be legally committed to creating "regulations as to how a man with typhoid fever was to be treated." Yearwood's planter colleagues took the point. They could not imagine that a board of doctors, and not they, would actually be in a position to make decisions about overall health standards on their island. On February 26, 1907, the Barbados House of Assembly rejected the typhoid amendment to the Public Health Act by a vote of ten to six.[44]

Economic Depression and Plantation Inertia

The world system and core-periphery models of socioeconomic history associated with the relatively recent writings of such scholars as Andre Gunder Frank, Immanuel Wallerstein, and Eric Wolf probably have created less of a sense of revelation for Caribbeanists than for others. The history, settlement, and "development" of the Caribbean have been so closely associated with metropolitan decisions and strategies that scholars of the region have largely eschewed viewing particular islands or coastal zones as microcosms or geographical isolates and have been long aware of external causes creating local effects.

The "bounty sugar depression" of 1884 to 1903 in the Commonwealth Caribbean is a case in point. In the late nineteenth century, Western European nations filled British open markets with cheap, government-subsidized beet sugar; German and French governments paid bonuses or "bounties" to their own sugar processors based on refining standards. Because of the greatly diminished demand for West Indian sugar, the London price for it fell dramatically in the 1880s. On Barbados in 1882 the average price for one hundred pounds of sugar was $3.80. The price fell to $2.20 by 1892, plummeting further to $1.06 by 1902.[45]

Economic ruin and hardship followed throughout the British West Indies. By all accounts, Barbados, the British Caribbean colony most dependent on sugar and its derivatives as export products, suffered the most. For a number of reasons—Barbados's inherent fertility, the avoidance of overhead expense that would have accompanied any modernization, and, above all, low labor costs because of the large local labor force—Barbadian planters had not been compelled earlier to modernize sugar production on their island. In Trinidad and British Guiana, in contrast, the overhead of modern central factories now was spread over large areas, leading to unit production costs a good deal cheaper than in Barbados. When the bounty depression hit, Barbadian planters, bearing the double burden of antiquated production methods and an ever-widening network of debts and creditors, responded as they had before to lowered sugar prices; they dropped workers' wages even lower.

George Carrington, a resident Englishman whose mother owned the second largest sugar estate on Barbados, had visited the family property in 1895 and pronounced the black laborers on the Carrington plantation "admirable" in the stoic way they accepted lower wages. Even during the depths of the bounty depression, asserted Carrington, estate workers exhibited a sense of "clanship," having lived on the plantation all their lives. He recalled with admiration the subservient, almost grateful, way his workers had responded to his reasoned and logical explanation of things: "we know, master. . . . we must have our wages cut down, and we must take the hard times with you."[46]

Carrington's testimony before the Royal Commission, given in London and typical of an absentee planter's viewpoint, was refuted many times over when the commissioners visited Barbados. Carrington probably was accurate in suggesting that rural workers comprehended the planters' explanations of lower prices, but the laborers also understood that a monetary pie, although smaller, still would be divided up by white planters and officials when sugar payments came from abroad. The newspaper cartoon characters Lizzie and Joe almost certainly captured rank-and-file laborers' attitudes toward economic depression much more accurately than did Carrington:

> De backras [whites] isn got no shame, deh nebbah does ack fare,
> De King sen lots uh munny fuh all we get we share,
> But not one cent deh gie we, deh keep all fuh dehself—
> We en get not a glass uh rum fuh drink de po King helf.[47]

Interpretations of black perceptions of economic theory notwithstanding, the bounty depression led to poverty, deprivation, and hardship on Barbados. These local results of macroeconomic perturbations, all filtered through a plantation system, are considered at length in the following chapter.

European beet sugar had made subtle inroads into British markets, thereby competing with Barbadian cane sugar, as early as the 1840s. Barbadian planters had been shaken much more, however, by the act of the British Parliament in 1846 that removed preferences on colonial sugar imported to Britain. British West Indian planters nevertheless had profited most years of the following four decades, despite the prevailing British era of free trade. But irrevocable social changes in Britain and technical improvements in world agriculture in the late nineteenth century pointed to a collision course between British interests, narrowly defined, and the interests of her Caribbean sugar colonies.

The Great Depression of 1873–96 in Europe was marked by slowed industrial output in Britain and "universal catastrophe" for European agriculture.[48] Cheap agricultural surpluses sent to Western Europe from the Pampas, the Ukraine, and the heartlands of the United States and Canada undermined traditional, and now more expensive, European farming methods. But cheaper food imports into Britain's open market led to better working-class living standards, especially among city dwellers. Eric Hobsbawm suggests that the last three decades of the nineteenth century in Britain were marked by important changes in workers' diets with meat, fruit, and jam—items formerly considered luxuries—consumed at an accelerating rate by the country's urban poor. Cheap, bounty-induced beet sugar from Europe represented an important part of this boon to working-class diets. Therefore, when British West Indian planters pleaded for countervailing British duties against European bounty sugar to protect the Caribbean sugar industry, they faced intense competition in the "mother" country. British politicians and industrialists, the latter depending on a growing world market for manufactured goods, could mask their indifference toward West Indian colonial interests with pious abstractions about the moral superiority of laissez-faire economics. The vested interests of the British jam and confectionery trades, prospering from unprecedented low sugar prices and increasing worker demand, were not without slogans of their own: a "free breakfast table" for working-class Britons certainly could not be sacrificed for a protected home market.[49]

The Barbadian planters were indignant. The London price for muscovado sugar had fallen by one-third during 1884 alone. Financial pressures were intensifying while foreign politicians negotiated about sugar bounties in a leisurely fashion. The British seemingly had turned their backs on the loyal Barbadians who were thus left to depend on "false markets and false sales and false prices." Barbadian sugar was the "finest" in the world, but even it could not compete against handicaps imposed from afar. Bounty sugar and "the present conditions of things" thus pervaded conversations, correspondence, and the thoughts of the forlorn Barbadian sugar planters at the turn of the century. Local politicians and individual estate owners desperately sought political leverage; Sir Neville Lubbock, chairman of the West Indian Committee, had presented the sugar colonies' case before the Colonial Conference in 1887. Barbadians even considered producing a "monster petition" signed by "every man, woman, and child" in the Caribbean; it would ask the British Parliament "for what ought never to be denied to any British subject, namely, just and equal treatment."[50]

A less-hysterical solution to the dilemma of the bounty depression was to seek markets elsewhere. Though a British colony,

Barbados was not compelled to send her sugar to the home market if she could find more demand and a better price somewhere else. Several alternatives were considered. Governor Hodgson, for example, explored the possibility of exporting rum and sugar to West Africa, corresponding with firms in the Gold Coast while he was on leave in England in 1903. Though Barbadians made trial shipments to West Africa in April 1904, the results were disappointing.[51]

The North American market, especially in Canada and neighboring Newfoundland, was more promising. Transportation costs from Europe to Canada were high, and the fiscally autonomous Canadian government in 1898 began to admit British West Indian sugar for refining and molasses while at the same time placing a surtax on imported German beet sugar. The Canadian market thus offered some short-term relief for the beleaguered Barbadian planters. The island's exports to British North America rose accordingly, from £86,000 in 1897 to £291,000 in 1906, the latter figure nearly doubling that year's exports to the United Kingdom.[52] A shift to the Canadian market, however, meant meeting new demands and standards. The Canadians, for example, complained about the acidity of Barbadian molasses, attributing it to the poor quality of the containers. In September 1903, the island's leading sugar producers and exporters met at Commercial Hall in Bridgetown and agreed on uniform barrel staves and uniform production standards for wooden molasses puncheons in order to satisfy the Canadian market. In addition, the Barbadian muscovado sugar that was sold in Canadian groceries, although not fully refined, was nevertheless subject to higher Canadian duties, an unfair decision according to the Barbados Agricultural Society.[53]

Although Canadian markets, and those in the United States to some extent, offered relief, the undermining of Caribbean cane sugar by European bounties on the London market was a source of continuous distress to Barbadian planters. Most fortunately for the Barbadian plantocracy, their case in Britain was championed—and eventually won—by Joseph Chamberlain. Chamberlain, the former mayor of Birmingham, England, and later depicted as the "savior" of the West Indies, became the British secretary of state for the colonies in 1895. He considered the bounty system to be unfair and the root cause of Caribbean economic problems. He created the West Indian Royal Commission of 1897, led financial relief efforts for the West Indies, and influenced Europeans to abolish the sugar beet bounties at the Brussels Convention of 1902.

Chamberlain saw Britain's formerly prosperous, and now distressed, Caribbean colonies as the "Empire's darkest slum." He countered arguments against open-market advocates by pointing out the £3 million worth of British manufactured goods purchased annually in the West Indies and proclaimed that economic protection for the Caribbean sugar cane colonies was a "necessary expense of asserted Empire." To compensate for possibly higher sugar prices in the United Kingdom itself, prices potentially burdensome for Britain's working classes, Chamberlain offered a corresponding reduction of the home duty on tea.[54]

The findings of the Royal Commission of 1897, the first such investigation of the region in fifty years (and indicative of its downward slide in the colonial hierarchy), were revealing but not unanimous. In general, the commission members agreed that bounty sugar was to blame for many of the Caribbean's economic problems, but they fell short of unanimously endorsing countervailing tariffs. They recommended the establishment of the West Indian "labouring population on small plots of land as peasant proprietors," new crops and new markets, and better agricultural production methods. Most significant for Barbados, the commissioners recommended a loan from the imperial exchequer for the establishment of central milling facilities on the island.

The actual results of the commission's findings heartened Barbadian planters even further. In 1902, Parliament approved a £250,000 "free grant" for Caribbean colonies, £80,000 of which was to be set aside for the resuscitation of Barbados's relict sugar cane industry. Also, Barbados was to become the site of the new Agricultural Department of the West Indies, led by Dr. Daniel Morris, assistant director of Kew Gardens and an original member of the 1897 commission. Joseph Chamberlain also had been instrumental in securing—as a result of the 1898 hurricane—a £40,000 grant for the repair of laborers' dwellings in Barbados and an additional £50,000 loan for the repair of sugar plantation buildings of the colony.[55]

The black Barbadian working class was relieved only indirectly by the imperial grant. Though the commission had heard poignant testimony everywhere about the plight of Commonwealth Caribbean labor and had recommended a greater degree of workers' access to the land, Chamberlain refused to restrict colonial governments' "liberties" as a condition of receiving imperial funds. The Barbadians, in particular, had "an ancient constitution, more than two hundred years old [that] had worked well."[56] Barbados, moreover, with its cultivable terrain and abundant labor had "special advantages" for the continued production of sugar cane. The planters thus received the grant, maintained their legislative control over the island, and still had the luxury of indulging in self-righteous complaining about the capricious constraints externally imposed on their economic destiny.

Chamberlain's diplomatic triumph over sugar bounties at Brussels in March 1902 (aided by antibounty tariffs imposed by British India) was received in Barbados with relief but without unqualified gratitude. "Promises," proclaimed a Barbados planter newspaper, "are too often compounded of pie crust. And it does not appear that the Brussels convention . . . offers us more than the mere hope of being able to sell a few tons more."[57] Dr. Morris, now of the Agricultural Department, was hopeful but wary. He suggested that, as a result of the Brussels convention, Barbadian planters foresaw an improvement of "about 100 per cent," although bounty-depressed prices had been so low that such an improvement actually might mean very little.[58]

By any measure, the antiquated Barbadian sugar cane industry of 1902 would need all of the £80,000 in grant money for improvement and modernization. Rickety windmills, their stone walls bearing the stress of heavy equipment attached inside, often "choked" on canes during the grinding season when light breezes turned sails slowly. On the other hand, in the island's central and northern parishes the possibility of squalls meant windmills had to be worked with caution lest high winds cause too much speed and wreck the buildings' rotting interior timbers.⁵⁹ Moreover, the old-fashioned boiling, clarifying, and evaporation of sugar juice in open pans involved many steps and much handling.⁶⁰ Although perfected to an art through the years on Barbados, this "open tayche" method produced low-grade muscovado sugar for outside markets, not the more desirable vacuum-pan "dark crystals" that metropolitan refiners could process more easily and cheaply.

Even though imperial funds had been allocated, plantation transformation was a good deal more complex than simply purchasing new milling equipment and retraining personnel. Barbados's sugar industry and plantocracy had been in place for two and one-half centuries; agricultural backwardness easily could be rationalized by planters as "time-honored" virtue. More important, Barbadian financial complexities had long involved British creditors whose interests also would be affected in any major agricultural reorientation. Further, during the bounty depression of the previous twenty years, local merchants and creditors had become heavily involved in financing Barbadian sugar estates and their operations.

The buying and selling of estate land in Barbados in 1900 was, moreover, far from straightforward and was fraught with local legal entanglements. If a planter defaulted on interest payments to creditors, for example, a foreclosure bill was filed in the Barbados Court of Chancery. The estate then was managed by a receiver for a year, appraisals solicited, and the property "set up for sale." The estate could not be sold at a price below the appraised value which almost always was far too high and an inaccurate reflection of sugar's depressed prices at the turn of the century. Creditors, who stood to lose as much or more as did estate owners with lower prices, supported the artificially high plantation prices, which thus created a stagnant, slow-moving land market.⁶¹ Some estates had been in and out of the Court of Chancery for years without being sold. During the 1897 Royal Commission hearings in Bridgetown, Walter Marston, a Bridgetown watchmaker, condemned the chancery system as "rotten to the core" and the artificial appraisement system a legal ploy to maintain estates in large blocks, thereby inhibiting the development of a landed peasantry on the island.⁶²

The bounty depression had forced an increasing number of

foreclosure suits in chancery by the turn of the century. As West Indian sugar prices plunged, the Agricultural Aids Act of 1887 in Barbados had allowed owners to borrow locally in order to pay working expenses, using the growing crop as security. By 1896, 138 estates, representing more than 30,000 acres—more than one-third the plantation acreage in Barbados—were being operated under provisions of the act. Increasing local indebtedness meant that any agricultural transformation would involve the interests and investments of layers of local managers, attorneys, merchants, and "ordinary investors" such as the Barbados Mutual Life Assurance Society, which held an increasing number of estate mortgages by 1900.[63]

Further complicating the Barbadian land issue, a legacy of British credit systems had persisted from more prosperous times. W.K. Chandler, Barbados's master-in-chancery since 1882, reported in 1897 that "the greatest portion of the land in the island was in the hands of firms or consignees in England" who had "assisted men of straw to bid and purchase plantations" in order to have the crops shipped to them. This arrangement saw British consignees pay only down payments, and the mortgages then passed from one local planter generation to the next, all creating a complex and enduring system of indebtedness. Officially, only one-third of Barbados's sugar cane estates were owned by residents of Britain. Wallwyn P.B. Shepheard, an English lawyer who owned two Barbadian estates but who never had been "out there," lamented the difficulties involved in land transfers in Barbados, suggesting that any legal improvement in conveyancing property there would be of immense value.[64]

So when the £80,000 grant was transferred from the imperial exchequer to the government of Barbados in 1903 for the resuscitation of the island's sugar industry, the money's investment was a subject about which few members of the local elite lacked an opinion. Its deployment in the sugar industry would, of course, affect directly the vested interests of individual Barbadian planters, attorneys, estate managers, merchants, creditors, politicians, and shipping agents, not to mention British consignees, absentee landowners, and their business associates. Vociferous debate followed in the Barbados Legislative Council and House of Assembly, principally over the issue of central milling. Central factories now were active or planned elsewhere in the Caribbean—in the Greater Antilles, the French islands, and in those British possessions where sugar cane cultivation still merited serious capital outlays. And the Royal Commission had advocated specifically a system of central factories for Barbados.

But who would lose and who would gain if Barbadian central factories preempted muscovado mills and if consolidated estates and improved transportation facilities on Barbados provided the efficiency to compete with, say, Cuba and Puerto Rico? If a central factory were, for example, established in St. Lucy parish, would all neighboring estate owners be obliged to ship their canes there in order to ensure continuous factory operation and thus its efficiency during the grinding season? What about original creditors' claims on individual estates under such an arrangement? Many similar issues were raised. Local complications aside, the greatest fear among Barbadian planters was of "outside capitalists," not locals, preempting the commanding heights of the sugar cane industry. Stanley Robinson, a planter of St. George parish, acknowledged that central factories, controlled cooperatively, were necessary. Indeed, they should be constructed "but not by capitalists . . . [or] we will have these companies or capitalists reaping the whole benefit of the sugar industry, and other men will simply degenerate into cane farmers."[65] One way to resolve the problem of how to use the £80,000 was simply to divide it among planters, an idea that never was popular because, again, of the fear that absentee owners and outside creditors would take most of it.

The questions surrounding the disposition of the £80,000 grant eventually were resolved by the establishment of the Barbados Sugar Industry Agricultural Bank, which husbanded the funds and used them for loans to individual Barbadian planters. In 1902 the legislature passed the first of a series of annual Plantations-in-Aid Acts which called for the grant funds, as well as borrowed money from abroad, to be advanced to individual estates to keep the industry alive. By 1904, of the 411 Barbadian estates on the island, 108 had borrowed under provisions of the act.[66]

In 1911 a bill mandating the establishment of central milling "along cooperative lines" was passed by the Barbadian legislature. The act was more symbolic than substantive, yet, as discussed in chapter 6, a noticeable shift toward central milling did occur on Barbados in the century's second decade. But these inevitable changes in cane milling would have to overcome formidable and entrenched obstacles. The burden of long-standing credit, marketing entanglements, and an infrastructure developed to sustain a decrepit muscovado sugar industry had produced a life of its own. Local capital was tied up, and even the uses of "free" outside capital seemed to be limited to propping up what already was in place. Partially buffered from external realities by imperial funds and their own traditions, the Barbadian planters in the first decade of the twentieth century avoided rapid innovation just as they dreaded interference by "outside capitalists." Changes of scale, planters feared, would upset a delicately balanced system. In a finite world of 166 square miles, nothing was left to share around, and rearranging the status quo might have lamentable implications.

Because the great majority of Barbadian land was held by planters, central milling—even if it were adopted—would give only a limited boost to small-scale cane farmers, certainly a more limited one than it had provided to indentured Indians in Trinidad, where more land was available. In any case, the plight of the black Barbadian working class was only an ephemeral subject, rarely raised during legislative debates over possible agricultural reorientation. The most common point in regard to workers was the problem of labor dislocation or redundancy if small muscovado mills were abandoned or reorganized. This issue was brought up on occasion within the context of the highly questionable, yet popular assertion that the black Barbadians "needed" the sugar industry and that social responsibility, of course, compelled local planters to maintain the industry unchanged for the benefit of workers and their families.

The more candid planters realized who needed whom more. Black workers cleared pastures, repaired roads, maintained mills, built fences, and acted as house servants, not to mention their principal activities of planting, harvesting, and processing the sugar cane. But for most planters, the varied quality of black roles seemed less important than the quantity of workers at hand. "In our supply of labour lies our strength" asserted the *Barbados Agricultural Reporter* in 1905.[67] A good deal of inefficiency and "time-honored" techniques could be preserved, at no great loss to the planters, with an inexhaustible labor supply residing in the estate tenantries.

Among the many advantages of a large labor force to the planters was that its energies could be directed toward agricultural intensification, which would compensate, at least in part, for a lack of modernization. A central theme of the West Indian Agricultural Conference in Barbados in January 1900, presided over by Dr. Morris, was the redoubling of plantation efforts to save money—through good agricultural husbandry—in an era of low prices and competition. Most Barbadian sugar planters already fertilized their canes mainly with farmyard manure, a combination of animal droppings and cane trash applied by hand to the cane holes. Planters also were learning that the judicious application of inorganic fertilizers would improve sugar cane output, but modern fertilizers had to be imported, and cheap sugar often made them prohibitively expensive.

During the agricultural conference, the Barbadian John R. Bovell—known for his experiments with cane seedlings throughout the Caribbean—addressed conferees about the importance of proper crop rotation and the "catch crops" cultivated after the summer cane harvest and then reaped when sugar cane was planted at the first of the year.[68] Bovell's tentative analysis, hampered by the notorious lack of reliable agricultural data for any Barbadian crops, suggested that additional attention to fodder and "green manuring" using leguminous plants would improve sugar cane yields substantially. Perhaps even more important, if planters throughout the island cultivated fields carefully, Barbados could realize as much as £175,000 in savings by replacing expensive American food imports with corn, beans, and peas planted and harvested in the fallow periods within the Barbadian sugar cane cycle.

For any intensification strategy to become successful, however, the labor lorce would have to be properly motivated. Despite the landlord-tenant and master-servant laws that tied workers to estates, worker dissatisfaction was obvious to anyone who cared to listen. Disquieting attitudes among young plantation workers suggested that they preferred clerical work, or anything other than agricultural labor for that matter. The Barbados General

Agricultural Society regularly sponsored small-scale livestock exhibitions throughout the island in conjunction with ploughing and forking contests at various estates. Winning cane-hole diggers and forkers could realize up to five shillings for a Saturday afternoon's work. These contests and programs were designed to create excitement and a love for "honest toil" among agricultural laborers and, not incidentally, to prepare areas of particular estates for the ensuing season.

An overriding concern, therefore, was to "educate" black West Indians to appreciate and respect agricultural labor. The heads of colonial education departments and also local school superintendents had been among those attending the agricultural conference in 1900. They had heard Dr. Morris explain that the archbishop of the West Indies himself had noted that capable "peasant" boys were seeking office work but really "should be trained in an atmosphere favourable to agriculture . . . that they should learn that tilling the soil and caring for crops is . . . worthy of being studied by intelligent minds."[69]

In Barbados's case, the archbishop's fears that agricultural laborers would leave the land really could not be realized to any great extent simply because of the lack of local alternative opportunities. Indeed, in 1899 the Barbadian inspector of schools, J.E. Reece, reported that most children of agricultural laborers went on to become agricultural workers themselves. Primary school education was available throughout Barbados under Anglican auspices for a penny per week per student. And although school attendance was not compulsory, the 1878 Education Act, reinforced by the recommendations of the Bree Commission Report of 1896, had called for school attendance, not employment, for any Barbadian child under the age of twelve.[70]

But in 1900, contrary to the abstractions of local education rules and recommendations, many poor children of Barbados did estate work rather than attending school. Necessities of survival, produced by landlessness and low wages, traditionally had driven black children into child labor gangs ("third-class gangs") on the plantations in the nineteenth century and well into the twentieth. Throughout the island the children of the poorer black families toiled on sugar cane estates along with their fathers, mothers, and siblings. In practice, then, it was Barbadian plantations that provided the children with on-the-job training and "education."

Advocates of "education" for Barbadian agricultural workers knew very well, of course, that they really meant "training," because education without provisos could become a powerful tool to upset the equilibrium of the existing social order. Eventually, real education could provide undesirable results, to say the very least. Therefore it would be necessary to educate the black agricultural masses just enough, certainly not too much, so that they would provide reliable labor. Proper "handling" of the educational process could modify unrealistic expectations that black children of Barbados might learn from books or pamphlets. The planter newspaper in October 1905 was explicit in this regard:

> It is admitted that the Negro, if properly handled, is an excellent labourer. The question then is one of proper handling. Handle the negro properly, and there would be no lack of workers. Such handling would involve, amongst other things, the giving of a sound practical education. Some book learning is of course essential, but the mistake of conveying the child the idea that such education as he acquires at school is calculated to make him eligible for the highest honours in life must be avoided.[71]

Barbadian Society In 1900

The words *color* and *class* often are used together in efforts to analyze the varying social and economic relationships among Caribbean peoples.[72] The two words combined serve to summarize usefully general social characteristics of the region. At the same time, this word combination is potentially troublesome, since it obliterates complexity and also suggests the existence of a scientifically vertifiable theory linking the two. Beyond pointing out the "color continuum . . . paralleling the economic and social structures of the societies" throughout the Caribbean,[73] these two abstract variables always must be modified and redefined in the analysis of any particular West Indian locale. Subtlety, nuance, and uniqueness of place are therefore subject to potential sacrifice to a dogmatic, uncritical lumping together of Caribbean "color" and "class."

By the turn of the twentieth century, for example, Barbadian society had been evolving for 250 years and, although rigidly hierarchical, it was exceptionally complex. For Gordon Bell, who wrote under the pen name of George Bernard and was a most perceptive observer of Barbadian society in the early twentieth century, any attempt to describe the island's "coloured communities" alone was likened to "attempting blindfolded to find one's way through the catacombs of ancient Rome."[74]

Neither perceptive skills nor splitting sociological hairs was necessary, however, to understand which group occupied the apex of the Barbadian social order in 1900. The white planter elite formed a colonial prototype of the aristocritic "landed interest" of pre-industrial Britain where political and social domination was interrelated with the monopolization of land.[75] The center of the Barbadian white elite's social life was the Savannah Club near the boundary of Christchurch and St. Michael parishes, just down the coastal road from Bridgetown. At the club's parade grounds on "a polo day," the scene depicted perfectly the "English ideal of gayety." Pretty girls, iced drinks, croquet, afternoon tea, black waiters in starched whites, and all the rest recalled "some of Kipling's stories of the 'hill life' at Simla."[76]

It is from the official sources mirroring the plantocracy's perspective, of course, that we derive the great majority of our published information about Barbados in the early twentieth century. Furthermore, these reports reveal the arrogance, indifference, and superficiality with which many, probably most, of the white elite observed the lower classes of the island as people when they noticed them at all. Miss Dora Alleyne, home from boarding school in Scotland and the daughter of a St. James planter, composed a school essay in 1903 about her stays in Barbados. The innocent yet animated style of a portion of Miss Alleyne's essay renders an appallingly clear picture of white elite perceptions of black Barbadians at the turn of the century:

> As soon as the steamer anchors in Carlisle Bay . . . a crowd of noisy negro boys . . . come out in little canoes; they dive in a marvelous way for cents. . . . We drive through the streets of Bridgetown, which are crowded with carts loaded with barrels of sugar drawn by teams of mules or oxen. If we stop for a moment we are beset by negro-women with large trays of fruit, bananas, oranges, pineapples, guavas and limes on their heads. . . . The tennis courts are kept

in very good condition, as they are in constant use. . . . It is a very heating pastime, although we have little black boys to pick up the balls. . . . The negroes who work on the estates live in little wooden huts along the roadsides, which consist of two rooms only. . . . They eat wonderfully little, and will work from 7 in the morning till 12, without eating anything, and then they will just eat a little rice or a biscuit, and work on till 5 in the evening, and they either have another frugal meal, or sometimes go without.[77]

Looking the other way, black working-class perceptions of white planter families were almost certainly a good deal more accurate. On many Barbadian plantations, black domestics and "nurses" were intimately familiar with white family life and practically brought up planters' children, a throwback to slavery. Black servants thereby often came to know whites as individual people by sharing with them the daily travails of family life, a perspective of blacks rarely if ever gained by Barbadian whites.[78] This intimacy involved personal bonds—between black women and white women and especially between black women and white children—that in a small way bridged the social chasm separating the white elite and black workers.

But familiarity did not necessarily guarantee either kindness on the part of white plantation mistresses or respect from their black servants. A ninety-two-year-old informant from Orange Hill Village, St. James, recalled her days as a maid at a nearby sugar cane plantation in about 1910: The planter's wife, she remembered, acted like "a pig," ignoring the hired help, hardly even speaking to them. During croptime she occasionally gave household servants small packages of sugar; at other times she doled out breadfruit that had been gathered from trees in the plantation yard. These meager gifts (for which she expected profuse thanks) could not compensate, however, for her rudeness and lack of civility.

The personal familiarity among individual members of the various social classes was evident on the larger Barbadian sugar cane estates. The relatively high percentage of resident proprietors in 1900 meant that many Barbadian plantations still had a paternal characteristic, quite different from the corporate impersonality found elsewhere in the British Caribbean by this time. The same Barbadian planter who was unspeakably harsh in his attitudes toward social and legal matters in the abstract could also exhibit goodwill and kindness, in a noticeably lordly and distant way, toward "his" faithful workers. For the black worker, the estate had been his birthplace and contained the small garden plot from which he derived subsistence for his family. These patterns have been noted throughout the Caribbean at different times and other places where the pre-modern, family-owned plantation historically has represented a curious amalgamation of "a capitalistic enterprise cloaked in a version of manorial tradition and isolation."[79]

Job differentiation among the black plantation workers was most noticeable at harvest time in the windmill yard of a small estate. This differentiation is captured in the following quotation which also carries with it the "happy plantation" image put forward by the plantocracy:

> the processing of sugar was by no means the whole story. There were cartwrights, wheelrights, coopers, carpenters, blacksmiths, welders and metal workers, sailmakers, leather workers, together with . . . tradespeople of all kinds plying their trades. In and around the millyard there was a hive of rhythmic activity, often musical and pleasant to the ear, especially if the wind was favourable and there was plenty of cane juice to quench thirsty throats. Youngsters played in the drying megass spread on the roads and bare patches of yard, mingling their play with happy laughter.[80]

But although important differences existed between and within the ranks of black artisans and field laborers, black Barbadians rarely held positions of real authority and responsibility on sugar cane estates. Most large plantations had white bosses or "managers" in charge of all laboring activities. For absentee owners, resident managers were virtually the estate proprietors, running field operations and coordinating daily financial decisions with the plantations' agents who usually were Bridgetown attorneys.[81] Larger estates also had white "overseers" who supervised particular laboring gangs and maintained handwritten journals of agricultural data and workers' hours. Then there were white estate bookkeepers and even assistant bookkeepers. The larger estates, of course, had the more complex managerial and clerical hierarchies. Small-scale estate owners often managed their own plantations with the help of an overseer and a single bookkeeper.

The conventional image of the brutish and hard-hearted Barbadian plantation manager at the turn of the century is a more accurate statement about relations among social classes at the time than it is a verifiable stereotype valid for all white managers (and overseers) for all plantations. White estate officials usually were drawn from white middle and lower classes on Barbados that collectively exhibited "bitter race hatred" against the black and mixed-blood majority on the island.[82] Indeed, elderly black Barbadians recall white estate managers who capriciously discounted an entire day's work in the record books for tardiness or who seemed to enjoy dismantling and removing an estate worker's house from the tenantry grounds because of late rental payments. Nearly as often, however, former field workers remember particularly kind acts (possibly because they were relatively rare) of managers, such as their giving food at Christmas or calling a doctor in the case of sickness or childbirth in a black laborer's family.

Unlike in later years, Barbadian field managers in 1900 often worked on a single estate for a lifetime. Daily interactions between the same manager and workers over the years meant that continuous cruelty would, very simply, be counterproductive. In any case, it is not surprising that particular plantations earned reputations among black workers for being benevolent or otherwise because of the personality of an individual manager. Few black laborers, however, had the luxury of seeking optional, or even reasonable, work conditions based on managerial reputations; the located laborer laws tied plantation workers to particular places and, not incidentally, to particular managers and overseers.

A number of observers have suggested that the racist character of Barbadian society is underlain in part by the presence of a relatively high percentage of local whites at all social levels throughout the island's history.[83] Table 1 shows that 15,613—nearly 9 percent—of the island's population was considered white for the 1891 census. Neither the total number nor the percentage of white individuals is high in an absolute sense, but Barbados was far from the demographic polarities of, for example, the Windwards at the same period with its tiny number of whites and vast black majorities. Besides the different social and economic positions held by Barbadian whites on sugar cane plantations, local whites also acted as merchants, attorneys, police officers, clergy, minor government and commercial officials, and small-scale farmers. It was therefore probably inevitable that clear-cut distinctions would exist among white Barbadians and that pretense, snobbery, and other forms of social discrimination would not be exhibited exclusively on the basis of skin color.

The richest planters who owned the most land within a particular parish were the lords of the countryside; they dressed well and kept "a good cellar and well-stocked larder, good horses, flash buggies."[84] They often occupied seats in the House of Assembly or the Legislative Council and could count on being reelected to these positions of power because of their domination over "pocket boroughs" of a tiny number of voters, who were the smaller planters in the vicinity.[85] The latter were intimidated by the importance of a neighboring large-scale planter and avoided even his suspicion by casting votes in his favor. Big planters influenced vestry decisions and controlled the most modern cane-milling facilities in a neighborhood, facilities to which a favored small planter might be given access in the event of the breakdown of his own antiquated grinding equipment.

The lines between the white planter elite and the white middle classes (small-scale planters, Bridgetown merchants, attorneys) were not so rigid that merchants' daughters could not ascend into the planter elite through astute marriages. But children of the white upper and middle classes often left Barbados permanently. The limited professional possibilities on the island meant that higher education or the pursuit of law, medicine, or suitable marriage partners might be more successful in England or Canada. Educated sons of tropical Barbadian planters were ideal candidates for Britain's colonial posts or foreign embassies, and a number of them, like the lieutenant returning from the Boer War to Barbados in Eric Walrond's *Tropic Death,* found their way into the officer ranks of the British armed forces.

At the turn of the century there also were pockets of "poor whites" in Barbados, the "Redlegs" or "Poor Backras" or "Red-

Leg Johnnies" who inhabited small, stony plots of land in the island's windward parishes. These poor whites, traced historically to a shipload of indentured servants who arrived in Carlisle Bay in 1627, had been thereafter supplemented by the periodic arrival of other white, small-scale farmers.[86] In 1900 the poor whites studiously avoided social contact with nearby blacks although economic necessity often dictated that individuals of the two groups work together in a planter's fields. At their worst, the Barbados "Redlegs" represented pitiful sights with mottled skin and other unattractive physical features possibly enhanced by a lmited gene pool made smaller by a closed social circle. Some poor whites, however, were able to improve themselves economically; their skin color allowed them "to enjoy a sort of monopoly" over the position of assistant bookkeeper on many Barbadian estates.[87] Also, like white children of the upper and middle classes, Barbadian poor whites at century's turn were emigrating in increasing numbers, many to Canada.

One group of whites in Barbados—members of the clergy—stood, formally at least, outside the plantation hierarchy. But the established Anglican church on Barbados merged with, rather than paralleled, the plantocracy in many ways. The well-developed and long-standing parish vestry system meant that local planters and clergy collaborated continuously on social and economic issues within each parish. Representing the state religion, the Anglican church was committed to performing official baptism and burial services, and in order for an individual to conduct any kind of official business it was necessary to have an official certificate of baptism. The parish minister, moreover, headed the public schools in his district and hired (and terminated) public school teachers. In 1891, of a total of 182,867 Barbadians listed, more than 147,000 were counted as Church of England adherents in census records.[88] For many black Barbadians at the time, however, the attraction of Anglicanism possibly was similar to the "attraction" of work at a nearby plantation. Anglican clergy, especially in rural parishes, were powerful individuals. A favorable letter from an Anglican minister, for example, was a sound recommendation for a better job. Ministers thereby often controlled what limited upward mobility might exist for members of the laboring class.[89]

Other religious denominations, notably Methodists and Moravians, who together accounted for close to 19,000 Barbadians in 1891, had made inroads, but the Anglican church and the state formed a formidable coalition. Unlike elsewhere in the Caribbean, where planters and Christian ministers often had disputed the well-being of slaves and their descendants, the lasting alliance between the plantocracy and the church—unbroken for nearly three centuries—offered little in the way of an indigenous religious buffer with which Barbadian blacks might have dealt more effectively with planters' demands.

Occupying the middle ground within the "color and class" continuum in Barbados at the turn of the century was the island's numerous (table 1) "mixed" or "colored" group. To suggest that this group, or groups, constituted a "middle class" would be a helpful identification in terms of economic well-being or job description, but it might also suggest an interclass fluidity that really did not exist, especially at the point where the smallest taint of black ancestry excluded a person from the category of "white."

The ambivalent status of brown Barbadians did not fit well into the hierarchical social system on large estates; when they did work on sizable sugar cane plantations, "mixed" Barbadians usually held positions of minor supervisory or clerical authority. Some "colored" Barbadians were small-scale planters themselves and thereby entitled to vote. More often, mixed-blood Barbadians' economic roles in rural parishes were those of shopkeepers, small landholders, head teachers, artisans, clerks. By the early twentieth century the talented Barbadians of mixed ancestry were recognized, at least in some quarters, as "a growing force . . . in the colony's industrial and commercial life."[90]

Brown Barbadians' equivocal standing—between the whites who shunned them and the blacks whom they themselves avoided socially—drew them in disproportionate numbers to the Bridgetown area. Greater economic and residential differentiation within the city offered a variety of social and economic opportunities outside a plantation context. Well over 40 percent (table 1) of "mixed" Barbadians resided in Bridgetown and St. Michael parish when the 1891 census was taken. This disproportionately high percentage was not new historically; freedmen of color also had gravitated to Bridgetown, probably for the same general reasons, well before emancipation.[91]

In Bridgetown itself, the mixed-blood group occupied a variety of clerical jobs, never approaching the pinnacles of government or commercial power, but never descending to the ignoble level of wheeling syrup "spiders" (mechanical pushcarts) along the waterfront or hawking fruit from door to door, positions held exclusively by blacks. Within the city itself, moreover, status and attainment for colored Barbadian jobs exhibited a spatial dimension, with positions of higher prestige in the most exclusive stores and shops near the Carenage.[92] An example of the type of higher-level situation accorded a Barbadian of mixed blood was as manager of A. Barrow and Company, booksellers on High Street; in 1909 this position was held by Mr. J.G. Dear, a light-skinned brown man who was described for external consumption as "a gentleman of culture and refinement."[93]

Locale and occupation type were only two criteria in differentiating status and success among colored Barbadians at the turn of the century. Clothing, mannerisms, religious affiliations, social relationships, reading preferences, and many other variables all were combined with skin color—the overriding distinction—in locating a brown Barbadian at his or her social level. The distinction within and among the ranks of the colored Barbadians, moreover, provided formidable complexity, classes within classes, and a social context within which a good deal of a person's behavior might be better understood and commented upon. The variety within the brown Barbadian middle class, and the behavior attributed to individuals attempting to improve their positions within this broad category, has, furthermore, provided typologically oriented gossip and conversational grist for discussions by Barbadian wags for a good many decades.

CHAPTER 3

The Black Barbadians in 1900: "Ned Is in the Land"

Two-thirds of all Barbadians were classified as "black" in the 1891 census (table 1), and the vast majority of Barbadian blacks resided in the tenantries of the rural estates. The typical adult head of household on a plantation tenantry was a male who lived with his family in his own wooden chattel house on a rented house plot, tilled a rented subsistence garden of one-quarter to one-half acre, owned his own tools, furniture, and some small yard animals, and earned cash wages from laboring on the plantation from which the house and garden plots were rented. The legal basis of occupying rented estate ground was a written contract signed or marked by the planter or his agent and the black head of household. Enforcement of the interrelated rental and laboring agreements was authorized by the islandwide "located laborer" acts discussed in chapter 2. Variations in subsistence crops, plot sizes, working conditions, and, to a limited extent, wages existed from parish to parish and from one Barbadian sugar cane estate to another.

The collective term for the black Barbadian working class used in colonial and government publications at the turn of the century was usually "the peasantry," a term with which some social scientists of the late twentieth century would probably disagree. In the brief typological discussion here, I seek not to categorize with finality the typical rural wage earner of Barbados in 1900 as either "peasant" or "proletarian." Rather, I seek to point out the ambivalence of his situation and, more important, to illuminate the material bases for his and his family's ultimate subsistence and security.

On a commonsense level, the term *peasant* seems inappropriate for the black Barbadian estate worker. Direct planter control of the land and the predominance of wage labor suggest that *rural proletarian* is a better description.[1] Indeed, in a recent essay dealing with peasantry as a process throughout the Caribbean region, Sidney Mintz proposes "that it would be misleading to call such [Barbadian] cultivators a 'peasantry.' " On the same page, however, Mintz infers the shortcomings of either/or categories by noting the ambivalence of the Barbadian case in which "the inclusion of a garden plot and a cottage gave the Barbadian plantation workers a somewhat curious post-Emancipation stake in their own wage labour."[2]

When Teodor Shanin posited the "family farm" as the basic unit of production among peasant families, he probably did not have rented subsistence plots in mind.[3] But, although owned by the planter who collected rent for its use, the Barbadian land plot provided at least partial subsistence—in some cases, nearly everything a tenantry family needed to eat and in good years even a few extras for barter or sale. Some Barbadian workers tilled the same rented plot for a lifetime, visiting and caring for it after a day of estate work. The immediate ties to the land among Barbadian estate workers meant that rural-estate tentantries in Barbados certainly were more peasantlike than were rural proletarian settlements near modern, large-scale, Caribbean sugar cane factories elsewhere. And the Barbadian plantation laborers' access to land and usufruct rights over tiny plots of land suggest that, if access to land were the sole criterion, they might be considered "peasants" in the same sense that some rural Africans have been.[4]

A major drawback, however, in suggesting "peasantry" as a category for Barbadian estate workers is that, although climatic conditions provided some good years, drought and pestilence meant that long-term subsistence production could never really be assured on the tiny land plots surrounded by seas of estate sugar cane. The homegrown "caloric minima" outlined by Eric Wolf as a key consideration in defining peasants thus was not realized in many years by black Barbadians.[5] Therefore, fathers, mothers (occasionally carrying infants), and children became wage workers controlled by estate managers and overseers, not a family labor team whose principal activities were devoted toward the agrarian activities on a family farm. In other words, the tenantry inhabitants could not reproduce themselves without estate work, especially if poor subsistence yields—from drought, for example—wiped out what tiny food surpluses they had accumulated. An eighty-two-year-old man in Boscobel, St. Peter, made the point better when I asked him about the importance of acquiring small land plots in the early twentieth century as insurance against planter demands. Yes, he said, land was very important "but you still had to work for money. You couldn't get along without it."

Probably the most telling argument against categorizing Barbadian tenantry workers of 1900 as "peasants" was simply the omnipresent legal and economic domination of them by the plantocracy. The extraction of surpluses from peasants by others that is so often cited as a key characteristic of a peasantry was, in the Barbadian case, not because of indirect market linkages or the paying of rent to a distant, town-based landlord. Rather, domination of the rural Barbadian wage workers was daily, locally circumscribed, and went to the very heart of a laborer's existence. For example, when C.J. Lawrance, the Barbadian inspector of police, explained to the Royal Commission in 1897 that "our labourers are chiefly vegetarians," his remark apparently was intended to suggest dietary preference on the part of black workers.[6] What Lawrance really was saying, as he well knew, was that tiny subsistence plots, minuscule wages, and a lack of local livelihood alternatives meant that most black workers and their families could afford to eat nothing else.

Not all rural black Barbadians were tenants. Though data on such matters were notoriously unreliable, it was estimated in 1897 that roughly 8,500 small proprietors had acquired about 10,000 acres of land throughout the island as a cumulative index of the "establishment of peasantry" on the island since emancipation in 1838.[7] These numbers, regardless of accuracy, doubtless included petty proprietors of mixed blood, poor whites, and some small landholders in the Bridgetown area. In any case, small-scale black landowners in rural areas, whatever the number, had several advantages over tenantry renters: they had assured access to a means of subsistence; they could choose to work seasonally on estates as carpenters or even cane cutters but were not under daily estate supervision; and many were artisans or small shopkeepers. These distinctions, among many others, between black landholders and black tenantry renters in Barbados prompted an elected witness for the working class to assert before the 1897 Royal Commission that it was "the ambition of every Barbadian to own a piece of land."[8] This point, furthermore, helps us to understand better any attempt to categorize rural black Barbadians in 1900. Even under repressive social conditions on the estates, Barbadian blacks aspired to better themselves by accumulating enough cash for a small plot of their own land; landed and landless were therefore fluid, not static, categories. In a more general sense, we are reminded that rural peoples often possess a heterogeneity that may not be fully appreciated by outside observers.[9] This heterogeneity, moreover, may itself help explain individual ambitions and motivations. In the case of Barbados in 1900, the small-scale black landowners, though vastly outnumbered by plantation tenantry dwellers, represented an independence and an ideal toward which the landless could strive.

The Rural Parishes

Beyond asserting that the typical black rural household was composed of a nuclear family of father, mother, and children, we cannot discuss with any certainty the magnitude of variation from this norm for Barbados as a whole in 1900. Typical of other Afro-Caribbean societies, small houses sometimes had three generations residing therein, and in other cases children were raised by aunts, uncles, or older siblings. Black Barbadian households were, moreover, changeable in their composition. Migration, "visiting," and the well-known Afro-Caribbean tendency to keep kinship and friendship ties open and active elsewhere meant that the personnel residing in a given house at a particular time could differ from season to season or from year to year.[10] Not the least of the complications in obtaining valid family data was the reluctance of the black Barbadians of the period to reveal to their "superiors" any of the details of their domestic lives on the rare occasions when such information was sought.[11]

Most unions between black men and women in rural parishes

were not sanctified by legal marriage. These "illegal" unions, of course, went untabulated by record keepers, but the 55 to 60 percent "illegitimacy" rate among the 7,000-odd births on the island each year in the first decade of this century gives some notion of the magnitude of marriage versus nonmarriage among Barbadian blacks. (One must assume here that nearly all "illegitimate" births were to black and mixed-blood mothers.) Vestrymen continuously bemoaned the evils of "concubinage" and related immorality that led to unwanted offspring who eventually swelled the rolls of the parish almshouses. Black immorality, furthermore, invariably was cited as underlying ill health and high infant death rates among black Barbadians. And readers of the planter newspapers occasionally were treated to vivid details of black immorality and irresponsibility. Publicizing the sad case of an eighteen-year-old mother who threw her stillborn fetus into a well in Christchurch parish in 1902, for example, reinforced preconceived notions about the hopelessly primitive, near-savage character of the black laboring class.[12]

Official rationalization for the impoverishment in plantation tenantries also seized often on a parallel theme, the problem of the absent father. A man who sired a child and who then failed to provide proper support could be fined or imprisoned under the Bastardy Act. This act, again, was designed to relieve parish almshouses and to place financial responsibility on the shoulders of a child's biological father. But convictions under the Bastardy Act never were easily accomplished. Reputed fathers sometimes had left Barbados altogether. Moreover, in most Barbadian police districts a deposit of one shilling was necessary before a court summons could be issued against a reputed father, and the plaintiff mother, so desperate that she had taken her case to the authorities, was "always too poor to pay it."[13]

The fundamental inanimate object of reference for a black Barbadian, whether of "legitimate" birth or not, was the house he or she lived in. To most European visitors to Barbados, the small wooden houses of the plantation workers were pathetic gray hovels, and the clusters of dwellings on tenantry grounds were unattractive, if necessary, landscape phenomena. To the rural blacks themselves, however, the house was "far more than a fabrication of wood and thatch, the yard far more than a locale for the house."[14] The few sensitive observers noted the children and small animals in the yard and the care with which vegetables and flowers had been planted in the tiny house plot. The denial of land to the vast majority of black Barbadians could not influence them to abandon the pride and industry they devoted to their modest dwellings:

> The house itself speaks volumes of the struggle to keep the little homestead together. Standing on rough lumps of lime-stone placed in disorderly rows and in wonderful pillars, which somehow as if by good luck keep upright, the building is industriously patched with sundries. Patch is piled over patch, like the sail of a barge, but it is a home; its rough walls shelter a dozen honest folks or more.[15]

The nature of the dwellings themselves was directly related to the impermanence of land tenure on the sugar cane plantation tenantries. Of the 39,999 dwellings enumerated in the 1911 census, 34,623 were constructed of wood.[16] And although house type was unspecified, it seems certain that the wooden dwellings were nearly all the distinctive Barbadian "chattel houses."[17] These houses were (and still are) small, portable dwellings standing on heavy wooden stakes ("uprights") at the four corners. Further support for the structure came from the foundation, or groundsel, of stones that elevated the small houses a foot or two above ground level, thereby inhibiting the entry of floodwaters or centipedes. The floor or "bottom plate" of the chattel house was occasionally as small as ten by ten feet. Normally the gabled wooden roof had a cover of wooden shingles that was surprisingly impervious to heavy rains. An individual desiring a chattel house purchased lumber and nails in Bridgetown and then arranged for transportation of the materials and for carpenters, usually neighbors, to construct the dwelling. The cost of a chattel house was minimal by most standards, but it represented a substantial cash outlay for most tenantry dwellers. In preparing his estimates of damage inflicted by the hurricane of 1898, Acting Governor Ralph Williams estimated £2 1s as the reconstruction cost for a typical worker's house.[18]

Small both in size and in number of component parts, the most distinctive feature of the wooden chattel house was its portability. Estate tenants, subject to eviction from their rented ground plots, could take apart, move, and reassemble their chattel houses on a nearby estate with the help of a few friends and a donkey cart in a matter of hours; more lengthy moves or moves over slightly hilly areas took considerably longer. Visitors to Barbados at the turn of the century were amazed to meet "a house on the highway" on a cart "like a puzzle taken to pieces . . . as if they were pieces of scenery from a theatre." The procession along the road sometimes was headed by the owner with "the front door on his head" accompanied by children and neighbors carrying windows and doorsteps.[19] This bizarre chattel-house parade usually was interpreted as a curious local custom. It actually was a manifestation of the constriction of the working class and, probably more accurately, a demonstration of the lengths to which the people were prepared to go in order to preserve their own individuality and dignity in a plantation society that had denied them all but the most meager possessions.

When black workers occasionally acquired their own land plots (even tiny "house spots"), through either cash accumulation or inheritance, their landed status was soon evident from observing their houses. The wooden chattel dwellings could now be elaborated and supported by concrete groundsels rather than stacks of stones. Wall foundations were therefore visible symbols of upward mobility via the possession of land. Permanent stucco or wall houses, or stone additions to the chattel house core, could be built on one's own land, not only for the present but also for future generations. On rare occasions, a working-class family who had inhabited a rented house plot for several generations would regard it as their own and build permanent stone dwellings on ground controlled legally by the estate. A few wall houses in Colleton and Clifton Hall in St. John parish in 1910 were occupied by black workers on plantation grounds, a legal incongruity better understood by the fact that the wage workers' ancestors had occupied the same plots: "These people had lived there not only themselves, but their fathers and forefathers had done so, and they built really good houses."[20]

But the overwhelming majority of black Barbadian tenantry dwellers lacked acreage of their own or the generations-old continuity with a particular plot of land which would give them the confidence or, more important, the legal basis for erecting more permanent houses. In compensation, the tiny wooden chattel home itself—with a banana or papaya plant growing nearby, a goat tethered in the yard, and children playing about—took on enormous importance for the black working class. The Barbadian preference for individual dwellings, moreover, distinguished them from other West Indians when they traveled abroad for periodic work sojourns. In the late nineteenth century, Mr. Agostini, owner of the St. Augustine plantation in Trinidad, went so far as to have individual workers' houses erected on his estate. The reason was to encourage migrant Barbadian laborers, whose preference for houses over plantation barracks was well known, to settle there.[21]

The few modest possessions inside a given house in a rural parish of Barbados provided compelling evidence of poverty. Despite the oft-heard pronouncements that improvident blacks habitually "spreed out" their wages on gaudy clothing and baubles, a typical black family's possessions were few and well used. Beds (when families had them) doubled as chairs, but more often, family members slept on straw mattresses or hammocks. Mothers cooked outside on three-legged iron pots, and the family ate meals on well-worn enamelware. Children's toys were homemade. Though they were poor, Barbadian market women, in their starched white dresses and headscarves, provided handsome, picturesque sights for visitors to the island. Men wore cotton shirts and headkerchiefs in the fields. Shoes were rarities and owned by only the most prosperous. For the poorest black families, clothes for children were nonexistent, and lack of school attendance occasionally was attributed to the children in question literally having nothing to wear. For the black working class in general, accumulated material possessions were pitifully small. On February 22, 1911, for example, a fire destroyed a thatched hut and a "quantity of clothing" belonging to Abraham Shepherd, a plantation laborer at Work Hall, St. Philip. Shepherd's total loss—including the house—was valued at slightly more than £2.[22]

Black Barbadians further distinguished themselves from other West Indians, mainly from Trinidadians and Guianese, by their propensity for keeping small livestock.[23] In rural Barbadian parishes a high population of small animals—especially pigs and yardfowl—was sustained from potato peelings, food scraps, and, in no small way, milling by-products from plantation windmills. Tenantry dwellers had no dogs because there was so little for them to eat. Cattle were rare and considered a luxury; there was, very simply, little land available on which to graze the animals. Old Barbadians recall that tenantry dwellers sometimes secretly grazed cattle on plantation lands at night. When black workers were able to acquire their own lands, a proliferation of grazing animals on the landscape—asses, cows, pigs, goats, and sheep— was sure to follow.[24]

The black Barbadian predilection for keeping small animals represented, among other things, a means of small-scale investment in an environment controlled by others. Chickens, sheep, and goats also were valuable sources of protein in black laborers' diets. Rocky hillsides, gullies, or patches of grass along roads and pathways were the only uncontested grazing areas for the animals of black tenantry residents attempting to subsist in the interstices of a plantation economy. But, as in the other small islands of the Caribbean region, black Barbadian workers—by maintaining and husbanding small animals and by selling them back and forth—realized incremental profits if rains provided adequate forage or if food scraps were available as animal feed.[25] A seventy-four-year-old retired school headmistress in St. James parish remembered that parents taught their children lessons in thrift and hard work by entrusting small animals to their care: "A boy would receive a sheep from his parents; later it would represent enough money to purchase a suit of clothes for Christmas if he cared for it properly." And Lizzie and Joe suggested that rural black Barbadians were often ill-advised to trust their spare bits of pocket change to investments other than animals for the family:

> But uh oughttah did know bettah, dis berry time las yare
> Uh had a few cents by muh,—sum munny uh coud spare,
> Uh wuz gwine put um in sum stocks, but like a fool uh went
> An len Miss Kitty dawtah tuh pay up she lan rent.[26]

Making do with very little, a function of the few local livelihood alternatives and the relative lack of access to the land, also was reflected in the intensity with which black Barbadians tilled their tiny subsistence plots, whether rented or owned outright.

Moreover, similar to other traits, this one was most noticeable when compared with farming practices of other West Indians. The Reverend Dr. Morton, a member of the Agricultural Society in Trinidad, was much taken with the conservation practices of a black smallholder from Barbados who had emigrated to Trinidad and whose house and land were nearby. Morton considered the man's husbandry laudable and a model for other West Indians; not only did he plow leaves, grass, and straw back into his land, but he even borrowed animal droppings from neighbors, using the material to enrich his soil. "He was a Barbadian," concluded Morton, "and knew the value of manure."[27] Innumerable elderly Barbadians reinforce this point when they remember their fathers, and their mothers, who also worked the gardens, hoeing and weeding the last square foot of a subsistence plot and throwing the clods of soil stuck to a hoe or fork back into the garden after work in the evening.

Crop diversity also was a feature of small subsistence plots on Barbados where black tenantry dwellers cultivated "the cereals, Indian and Guinea corn, and peas and beans . . . [crops] not grown separately, because, in most cases, the plot is not large enough."[28] Diversity, of course, was not simply a function of plot size but was typical of family-level subsistence agriculture everywhere; a variety of products cultivated in a given area limited the severity of insect pest or disease attack that might devastate completely a monocultural crop. Moreover, garden variety provided kitchen variety when the only consumers were members of the immediate family.

Subsistence crop heterogeneity also was reflected islandwide. In the drier southern parishes of Christchurch and St. Philip where sugar cane was not ratooned, corn was the subsistence staple. Okra predominated in the arid Marley Vale district of eastern St. Philip. Arrowroot grew in the northern parishes. Yams were more plentiful in the wetter central parishes. Timing or seasonality was an important dimension of Barbadian subsistence agriculture in 1900. Cassava, bananas, and pumpkins ripened and were harvested year-round; yams and eddoes, in contrast, were planted in May and ripened in December. White potatoes were grown on nearly all rented provision plots and by the plantations too. With good weather, potatoes were "plentiful and cheap," one hundred pounds of them selling for 1s 8d.[29] Barbadian planters routinely exported potatoes to British Guiana via vegetable sellers who took sackloads of Barbadian potatoes to Georgetown on sailing schooners.

Small-scale Barbadian cultivators, though mainly concerned with subsistence agriculture, also sold some of their produce for cash. Freeholders and even renters often grew small patches of sugar cane themselves. The money derived from their cane harvests (from a land area as small as half an acre) usually was devoted to a major expense, such as house purchase or shingles for a new roof, rather than meeting day-to-day living needs. Food crops for sale were carried to Bridgetown by female hucksters. With only small profits to be made on provision crops, especially when a particular item was in season and therefore a glut on the market, rural Barbadian marketing women extended their efforts extraordinarily to earn even the tiniest bits of cash. Groups of market women walked together to Bridgetown from the farthest points of Barbados, all laden with baskets of fruits and vegetables from the countryside. Once in town, they often sold their goods from door to door, seeking out customers rather than remaining at the designated market area. Police constables fined and harassed market women who were described on occasion as "nuisances" or "vagrants." There were no official comments of how convenient it must have been for the white residents of Bridgetown to have cheap and fresh produce from the country carried to their doors each day.

Just as seasonality affected the activities of market women, it also influenced the diets of black Barbadians in rural parishes. "When yams were in season" according to elderly Barbadians "it was yams, yams, yams, but in other times of the year often there was not enough to eat." Meals in the countryside tenantries were indeed usually the "vegetarian" fare described by the police inspector Lawrance in 1897. The bulk of the food was produced on the small plots of land, whether rented or owned outright. At the same time, imported grains (mainly corn and barley and a smaller amount of wheat) from North America were vital, cash-purchased dietary supplements, important especially in the case of drought. Flying fish were "ten for a penny" in season in villages at the water's edge. Imported salt fish was consumed, although not in great quantities, by black Barbadians, and ham was a Christmas luxury. The increase in both quality and quantity of food intake at Christmastime among black Barbadians in 1900 probably had its origins during slavery. British West Indian planters had always imported considerable quantities of food for slaves at Christmas, in part to modify and redirect their potential for rebellion.[30]

Seasonal food surpluses for the island as a whole did not always reach the poorest tenantry dwellings, where food scarcity and malnutrition were common. When sugar cane was being harvested in the first half of the year, regular wages meant that estate workers could buy food supplements if they had to. But, as Lizzie and Joe pointed out, hunger was common among the poorest people ("peetle") of Barbados, the most heartbreaking cases among the children whose parents could not afford to purchase anything for them to eat:

> When we big peetle hungry we kin draw weself in tight
> An we kin stan de hungry till wen we gets uh bite,
> But little children diffrunt, um nuf fuh drive yuh wile
> Wen yuh en got not uh biskit fuh gie yuh starvin chile.[31]

A widespread, although probably unquantifiable, means of compensating for food deficits in rural Barbados in the first decade of the twentieth century was reciprocal food sharing. Old Barbadians, when interviewed about local food production and diet, unanimously and spontaneously emphasize that food, especially vegetables, was shared back and forth: "When I have food I give some to you; when you have, you give to me. That's the way we used to live in the country." The quantity, in weight or caloric value, probably always will remain unknown, but it appears that subsistence reciprocity among rural black Barbadians was ubiquitous and possibly an extremely important means of coping with food scarcities. When small animals were butchered and eaten, portions of meat were shared similarly with kinsmen and friends, a practice that is well-known among non-Western folk not yet completely bound up into a monetized market economy.[32]

But even sharing food surpluses back and forth among friends and families could not provide necessities that were unavailable on the island. The "open economy" and "food deficit" status of Barbados, characteristics of the island for centuries, were much more than economic abstractions for black rural dwellers at the turn of the century if external lines of supply were interrupted. During the smallpox epidemic of 1902–3, for example, the traffic of sailing schooners from the Windwards was curtailed. These vessels normally brought charcoal and cordwood for use by the black Barbadian working class. Soon "many of the few remaining trees" in rural Barbadian parishes were "being cut down and converted into firewood."[33] But emergency livelihood strategies could go just so far; no one could compensate for subsistence crops that did not exist on the island or for crops that had withered because of prolonged aridity.

Hunger among rural tenantry dwellers frequently was marked by a "potato raid," a strictly Barbadian term that is more specific than the prosaic "praedial larceny" used throughout the rest of the British Caribbean to indicate rural crop pilferage. Potato raids, not surprisingly, were much in evidence during the years of the bounty sugar depression when Barbadian workers' wages were cut. On July 1, 1898, about three hundred men and women, armed with cutlasses and clubs, assembled near Bowmanston Plantation in St. John parish. They surged into the estate's potato field, looted the crop, and beat the watchman who attempted to intervene. This incident came to a close only after Inspector Lawrance personally led a detachment of police to Bowmanston from Bridgetown. Nineteen potato raiders were convicted and sentenced.[34]

The Bowmanston raid was among the more sensational events in an era during which the thievery of food in the Barbadian countryside was exceptionally common. Colonial officials routinely condemned the acts as "criminal" or "lawless." Legislators and police officers, moreover, devised a classification that distinguished between a "raid" and what was simply spontaneous food scavenging. A potato raid was "where three or more persons are concerned in making a raid on a field of provisions."[35] The actual cause, of course, had little to do with criminal tendencies; food pilferage was, very simply, a last resort among desperately hungry people. Members of the Barbados General Agricultural Society acknowledged in December 1904, the well-understood fact that the theft of food from Barbadian estates was common throughout the rural parishes although "very few prosecutions were instituted."[36] The raids themselves usually were focused toward the estate grounds that had been planted in potatoes (possibly intended for export to British Guiana and Trinidad). In light of local conditions, the lack of prosecutions for provision stealing by Barbadian estate owners and managers early in this century was not indicative of either indifference or inconsistency. The planters doubtless understood that forceful defense of plantation potatoes might lead to general insurrection in the countryside, and common sense suggested that the close proximity of near-starving people and plantation potato fields could lead to only one thing. As in other times and other places "the coincidence of severe hunger with available stocks of food in the possession of landowners or the state is a call to action."[37]

Widespread hunger in the countryside was not, however, necessarily accompanied by rural, antiestate solidarity. People afflicted with hunger pangs themselves and responsible for their near-starving children were less ideologically motivated than they were inspired by more fundamental, short-term subsistence needs. Planters' descriptions of Barbadian potato raids, such as the Bowmanston affair, all seemed to suggest a cunning and prior planning when actually the raids were probably more spontaneous. Hungry tenantry dwellers seeing their bolder neighbors advancing into an estate's potato fields would naturally join them. Furthermore, rural food scavenging, although directed mainly toward plantations, was by no means uncommon among the small rural tenantry plots cultivated by the estate workers themselves. Nocturnal food stealing among fellow workers further suggests that the activity lacked an ideological, class-based cause and was simply a reaction to hunger.

Among the environmental nooks and crannies of a sugar cane island—in gullies, gutters, along pathways, and around chattel houses—rural black Barbadians gathered a wide range of plants and herbs from which they concocted a variety of medicines or bush teas.[38] Most of these plants grew wild, although some were cultivated by women in their house gardens. Black folk medicine usually involved remedies and potion formulas handed down from parents and grandparents. Special medical advice was occasionally sought from local black "bush doctors," men who gathered plants either for a particular illness or for house-to-house sale by female acquaintances. Bush teas were applied to parts of the body for, say, a burn or a sprain. They also were taken internally. Bush teas were common antidotes for malnourished children in rural Barbadian tenantries in the early twentieth century. Since many of the home remedies were altered on the spot by the individual practitioner, it is not unlikely that doses of bush teas taken indiscriminately were responsible for worsened health or even death.

The ecological devastation that had accompanied the seventeenth-century conversion of Barbados into a sugar cane island eliminated much of the natural plant raw material with which black Barbadians subsequently might have experimented for medical purposes.[39] At the same time, the slave supply was continuously replenished from West Africa from the seventeenth to the early nineteenth centuries. Among many other things, this replenishment meant that imported African folk medicine practitioners would have constantly experimented with familiar plants encountered in Barbados, reinforcing the continuity of an African tradition that doubtless has persisted in part into the twentieth century. In some cases, the African continuity involved the same plant. Lemongrass (*Cymbopogon* sp.), for example, was introduced to Barbados from West Africa between 1750 and 1830. Both West Africans and Afro-Caribbean peoples use lemongrass commonly as a medicine to reduce fevers.[40]

The gathering and processing of wild plants for medicinal and other uses was one activity among the black working class not regimented and controlled by the Barbadian plantocracy. Whereas black subsistence acreage was curtailed and fuel gathering monitored, "no one bothered you from collecting the wild plants in the gullies" according to elderly Barbadian informants. And if the collection, experimentation with, and dissemination of medicinal plants and herbs were the exclusive domain of the black workers, it follows that bush teas may have been important daily elements of a black cultural identity that provided at least symbolic resistance to white oppression.[41] Locally collected plants and herbs doubtless provided important functional remedies for black Barbadian household problems as diverse as the need for a laxative (Porter bush, *Synedrella nodiflora*) or a purgative (belly ache-bush, *Jatropha gossipiifolia*). Bush teas also were used by persons who professed a deep Christian identity in public but who drank "bush tea pun de sly" to ward off spirits and spells.[42]

Just as the Barbadian plantocracy controlled the overwhelming majority of the land and thereby access to most agriculture, grazing rights, and house locations in 1900, the planters and their associates also controlled the local supply of money. Low wages, combined with tiny ground plots, were calculated to keep the black labor force in a perpetually dependent condition. The concerted strategy to limit money in the countryside—and thereby limit a possible means of working-class independence—was stated as a conclusion of the 1878 Commission on Poor Relief. In response to an issue raised about possible plantation wage increases to alleviate poverty, the commission was unequivocal: "More money per day would, in by far the majority of the cases, probably mean more idleness per week."[43]

Twenty years later, the 1897 Royal Commission was given the following data on daily wages for Barbadian sugar estate laborers: mechanics, 2s; men field laborers, 10d to 1s; women, 7½d; and children under sixteen, 5d.[44] Probably these figures were too high; from 1901 to 1910–11, the colonial *Blue Books* quoted 8d per day for "agricultural labourers" and in 1912 quoted an increase to 1s per day.

A Barbadian sugar estate manager usually traveled to Bridgetown each Friday to collect money from the bank for wage payment the next day. On Saturday at noon, laborers assembled and queued in alphabetical order and received their wages from the plantation bookkeeper when their names were called. In addition to his own pay, a father usually collected the pay earned by his wife and children if they worked on the estate: "I came along in third-class time, but I never saw the money" recalled one old man in St. Peter parish, referring to his days in an estate's child-labor gang. After being paid, the father gave the coins to the mother who had dressed up to go shopping. She could afford to purchase more for her family with the larger amounts of money paid out during the December–June cane harvest than she could during the other half of the year, when two or three days' estate work per week was all a black tenantry dweller could expect. Barbadian banks, moreover, adjusted their supply of copper and silver British coins seasonally so as to serve more adequately the cyclical changes in plantation wage payments and the associated islandwide amplitude in commercial activities.[45]

Money—as payment for land, in conjunction with land or by itself—represented a means by which rural black Barbadians could buy at least partial escape from plantation oppression in 1900.[46] This obvious point must be interpreted, however, in light of the critically low wage levels in Barbados, wages which, for all practical purposes, represented the only local source of money for rural tenantry dwellers. For a worker to toil endlessly on an estate in pursuit of money in Horatio Alger fashion—a livelihood strategy blithely prescribed for estate workers by colonial officials—was usually to condemn oneself to lifelong poverty. For one thing, the lack of full-time work and the seasonal plantation regimen could not guarantee money wages even if one were willing to work endless hours. For another, plantation laborers never received pay raises but simply worked for the set wage scale that applied to all workers. Short-term subsistence emergencies, moreover, often ate into what little cash a black woman or man had set aside for long-term upward mobility. Starving children could not be fed with food purchased with nonexistent wages, so a balance was necessary—indeed mandatory—for most rural black families between the accumulation of money through wage labor and the family-level production of foodstuffs on rented estate plots. This dual commitment to earning small amounts of cash and cultivating small subsistence plots—a combination which might mean survival—locked most rural black Barbadians irrevocably into the island's plantation workforce.

The dual efforts toward subsistence cultivation and wage labor suggest that the two endeavors were, at least on occasion, parallel and could not always be reduced to cash equivalencies. The reciprocal exchange of food among friends and families existed alongside a money exchange system in the Barbadian plantation tenantries. Although Barbados clearly was within a European-centered commercial orbit, the majority of the island's labor force still regarded money, in part, as a "special purpose" medium of exchange, a medium that was not used to measure all transactions.[47] If for no other reason, the scanty wages paid to estate laborers meant that money simply was unavailable to reckon equivalencies at all times among all tenantry dwellers. Furthermore, a money economy had not always imposed its own values on black Barbadian country dwellers, because in some cases black Barbadians had imposed their own values on it: in the mid-nineteenth century, rural market women, for example, valued heavier copper coins more highly than their recognized worth, thereby affixing "what value they please[d] upon the current coins."[48]

Despite their frightfully hemmed-in and economically depressed position in 1900, black Barbadians somehow saved small amounts of money. It has been said, probably not altogether inaccurately, that "for every penny saved by other people, the Barbadian will save a shilling,"[49] and the particularly stringent economic circumstances traditionally imposed on black Barbadians may help to explain that trait. The extent to which black tenantry dwellers put coins aside in jars and cupboards can never be determined, but in 1904, for the first time, an effort was made to classify Barbados Savings Bank depositors by occupation (table 2). Assuming that Seamstresses, Artisans, Domestics, Agricultural and other laborers, and Hawkers were members of the black working class and that the listings "No occupation" and "Unenumerated" might also have included many, we can appreciate the surprising extent to which black Barbadians patronized the island's single savings bank at the turn of the century.

The only bank was located in Bridgetown. Recent attempts to establish rural bank branches had been unsuccessful because of a lack of patronage by the laboring class. One interpretation of this behavior was that rural depositors preferred the anonymity associated with the bank in town; neighbors and family members could not ask to borrow savings that had been hidden away in the Bridgetown bank.[50] Almost certainly more important was that local savings bank laws called for police magistrates to manage rural savings banks.[51] It hardly needs emphasis that black estate workers were loathe to hand over what little savings they earned in a plantation system to the same rural police officers who enforced it.

Table 2. Barbados Savings Bank Depositors in 1904

Occupation	No. of Depositors
Professional men	509
Public Officers	447
Planters	790
Merchants	214
Shopkeepers	446
Clerks	1,139
Teachers	257
Soldiers	45
Police constables, etc.	249
Seamen	234
Seamstresses	674
Artisans	2,265
Domestics	2,009
Agricultural and other laborers	1,434
Hawkers	454
Friendly societies, etc.	316
No occupation	1,762
Unenumerated	968
Total	14,212

Source: Data from P.P. 1905/LI/43, "Barbados, Report for 1903–1904," 16.

The propensity for black Barbadians to save tiny amounts of cash in impossible circumstances had not gone unnoticed. Some local planters, moreover, made little effort to conceal that they disliked the savings trait because it represented at least the possibility of black Barbadians earning a way out of the plantation regime. The idea of a local savings bank had been considered and rejected as early as the apprenticeship period. In 1848 the first savings bank bill "was passed by the Barbados House of Assembly after several acrimonious debates and adjournments."[52] Though the bank had existed ever since, there were those in Barbados who continued to condemn its presence at the turn of the century. The reason? "[I]t would do harm to the people for them to save money, for it would make them independent and idle."[53]

The accumulation and savings of small amounts of money by black Barbadian tenantry dwellers in 1900 was a possibility, however faint, of gaining some degree of control over their own destinies. The accumulation of land or money, or one of the two gained from the other, provided an edge over the landless tenantry workers whose activities were divided between subsistence tillage and plantation labor. Small-scale landowners and shopkeepers and artisans of Barbados were in financially advantageous positions. They had obtained those positions via hard work, luck (alliances with benevolent planters), inheritance, education (at a penny per week, frightfully expensive for the poorest people), skin color, or a combination of these factors. During the latter half of the nineteenth century, one important way members of the black working class had accumulated money outside the local plantation system had been by traveling away from Barbados to work.

Poverty, Disease, and Infant Mortality

A combination of land hunger and few local employment opportunities help to explain such characteristics of black working-class Barbadians at the turn of the century as agricultural intensification, thriftiness, an absorbing interest in small livestock, and even occasional food pilferage. But in 1900 the situation was much worse than usual. The bounty sugar depression although far beyond Barbadian control was nonetheless brutal in the hardship it dealt to the island's laborers. Conscientious colonial administrators and parish medical officers reported "chronic pauperism which like a chonic disease is . . . undermining the population of this island."[54] In the small wooden chattel houses of the estate tenantries, old men and women proclaimed in hushed tones that "the men are out," and "Ned is in the land," the traditional Barbadian sayings telling everyone that desperate times had arrived and no relief was in sight.

Unlike black workers in the nearby Windwards, where mountainous interiors provided subsistence buffers during economic depression, black Barbadians often did without. All through the Barbadian countryside the effects of poverty and malnutrition were obvious to anyone who cared to notice: children without clothing, a lethargic workforce, general ill health. Planters occasionally resorted to the tiresome refrains about "laziness" and "unwillingness to work" in order to explain the general malaise. But the obvious distress within the rural tenantries could not be rationalized that easily. A general view of the Barbadian countryside in early 1903 is typical of scores of similar statements about conditions on the island at the turn of the century:

> The prevalence of ulcers has been a marked feature of the half-year. The careless habits of the people no doubt contribute somewhat to the formation of ulcers from slight injuries and bruises, but it is to be noted that these wide-spread epidemics of ulcers occur at times of depression when the vitality of the people is lowered from the difficulty in obtaining an ample supply of nourishing food.[55]

Economic depression, moreover, amplified the effects of drought and the cyclical nature of wage-earning possibilities. In the last half of each depression year, an annual period when local wages had always been low, conditions were dismal in the Barbadian tenantries. And a lack of rain during any year of the bounty sugar depression, either islandwide or in a particular parish, undermined the subsistence portion of local livelihood which, of course, had taken on greater importance because wages had been reduced. In the latter part of 1908 in the coastal districts of St. Philip parish, for example, "much privation" and "an increased amount of illness" followed a drought that desiccated the provision gardens and killed small livestock in the neighborhood.[56]

Poverty and desperation in the years of the bounty depression inevitably brought many black tenantry dwellers to seek help from parish vestries. Poor-relief rules, the quantity and quality of records kept, and the attitudes of particular poor-relief officials varied from one parish to another. For all Barbadian blacks, however, parochial budget stringencies and bureaucratic indifference exacted a high price indeed for those unfortunate enough to seek official help. Usually relief applicants had no other recourse, and often they were young mothers seeking medical aid for children whose fathers were absent. Officials could, and did, deal heartlessly with these young black women with little fear of retribution. Occasionally such harshness came to public attention. A case in St. George parish in December 1904 called for a coroner's inquest against a poor-relief inspector, a case possibly indicative of many similar but unrecorded episodes. A woman approached the parish health inspector for hospital care for her sick infant. The inspector pronounced the woman "not destitute" and sent her to the supposed father for money. She returned to the inspector for help on Wednesday, December 21, and he issued a hospital ticket good for the following Monday, but the child died on December 22. During the inquest, the health inspector (against whom no action was taken) explained that the parish health board recently had instructed him to give fewer hospital tickets to single women "and impressed upon me the expense."[57]

The care with which poor-relief officials guarded against providing aid to those residing outside parish boundaries proved fatal to Edward Weekes, a tenantry dweller on Spencer's Plantation, which was located partly in Christchurch and partly in St. Philip. Weekes, suffering from stricture, was admitted to the Christchurch almshouse on June 20, 1901, but the inspector soon discovered that Weekes resided on the St. Philip portion of the estate. Weekes's son was summoned to remove his father to the St Philip almshouse via a jolting donkey cart. Edward Weekes died at the St. Philip almshouse the day after his admission there.[58]

The logistical and bureaucratic requirements of gaining almshouse admission in Barbados in 1900 were enough to keep all but the most determined applicants away. Sick people who arrived at an almshouse hospital without an admission slip were redirected to the health's inspector's office, which was often two or three miles from the almshouse, for an admission ticket (the issuance of which, of course, was not a foregone conclusion). Then they could return and be admitted to the almshouse if there was room. The traveling back and forth and haggling with skeptical white officials would have been monumentally frustrating for any healthy tenantry dweller. For sick or malnourished peoples running fevers, these arduous requirements must have been agonizing ordeals. Once admitted to the parish almshouse, a patient was by no means assured of adequate care or nutritious diet. Almshouse menus were notoriously skimpy, as vestrymen learned that by providing only sweet potatoes and other starches to eat, they could reduce daily costs for an inmate to three or four pence. Occasionally, as at the almshouse in St. Lucy parish in 1908, hospital cooks stole the food meant for the inmates.

Proper health care for members of the black working class, hampered at the parish level by local inspectors and islandwide by planter hostility and official constraints (discussed in chapter 2), also was occasionally thwarted by the suspicion harbored by the blacks themselves. During the dark hours of the 1902 smallpox epidemic, some of the victims actually were concealed from local health authorities and sanitary inspectors. Barbadian blacks were distrustful of the islandwide vaccination campaign, distrust ironically orchestrated by the planter newspaper which suggested an "anti-vaccination crusade," publishing frightening letters about the dangers of doctors going "about the country injecting vaccine lymph into the arms of people."[59] Not all of the black suspicion and dislike for vaccination can be attributed to naïveté or "primitive" attitudes toward medical science, however. In October 1902, in St. Thomas parish, blacks were reluctant to report for vaccination; they could apply for almshouse help if they caught the disease, but no one would support them if they became sick from the vaccination itself and had to miss several days' wage labor.[60]

Although the epidemics of quarantinable illnesses received more official attention than any other outbreaks of disease in Barbados in the first decade of this century, smallpox and yellow fever were simply two of many diseases that ravaged the black tenantries. If health records from the period were complete, reliable, and accurate, several other types of sickness probably could be proven to have been more deadly to the population as a whole. "It is a pity Typhoid is not a quarantinable disease" lamented the parochial medical officer of St. George parish in 1910, adding that "many other diseases . . . kill far more people every year than small-pox, yellow fever, plague and cholera."⁶¹ Influenza, measles, pellagra, whooping cough, dysentery (and a variety of other bowel disorders) varied in their severity from season to season and year to year, seeking out their victims in the crowded estate tenantries that were nearly devoid of sanitation facilities. Parish health officials probably noted only a small fraction of the cases of communicable diseases that preyed on malnourished tenantry dwellers and thereby sapped the vitality of both individuals and the Barbadian workforce in general.

The particular severity of typhoid among black tenantry dwellers could be explained in large part by the crowded, unsanitary conditions of the tenantry settlements. Fetid cesspits and open latrines overflowed during heavy rains and contaminated local ponds and springs that were sources of washing and drinking water. In rural areas served by piped water, clogged drains and stagnant pools around standpipes emitted noxious odors and were ideal reservoirs for the typhoid bacilli. In 1897, Dr. C.E. Gooding, the medical officer of St. Philip parish, visited a typhoid victim at Perry's Tenantry. The ghastly scene he described was by no means unusual among the parochial health reports filed in Barbados at the turn of the century:

> I found no less than seven little children bathing in the pond around which several women were also engaged in washing clothes; and the woman in the house where the fever boy lay, told me that for several days she had been washing the bedclothes, soiled with typhoid excrement in the same pond. It is needless to go further to seek the source of infection.⁶²

Similarly unsanitary conditions throughout the Barbadian tenantries, coupled with the assembly's unwillingness to take adequate public health measures against typhoid, assured the presence of the disease in Barbados throughout the early years of the century. Occasionally typhoid flared into epidemic form as in 1906–7, when 507 cases were recorded throughout the island, an outbreak traced to the almshouse in St. Lucy parish.⁶³

Typhoid also was particularly "partial" to black Barbadians in the early twentieth century just as it was to United States slaves (rather than to whites) in the antebellum South.⁶⁴ During a severe outbreak of typhoid (3,070 cases) in Barbados in 1921, disease data were compiled by race: only 0.86 percent (89 cases) were reported among all of the island's white population, 2.24 percent (2,508 cases) among the black, and 1.31 percent (449) among those counted as "mixed."[65] In contrast, among the 86 yellow fever victims in the epidemic of 1907–9, fully 32 were white (from a small population) and only 54 "Blacks and Coloured."[66] Doubtless public health officials in Barbados in 1900 did not understand fully the relationships between disease incidence and race (just as these relationships are not fully understood in the late twentieth century). But it seems safe to assert that in 1900 official indifference toward typhoid, dysentery, and other diseases was partly because they were associated almost exclusively with black working-class Barbadians and rarely, if ever, afflicted the whites.

A combination of poor nutrition, crowded and unsanitary conditions, and a lack of control over any but the tiniest parts of their island meant disease and early death for many black Barbadians at the turn of the century. White officials of Barbados insisted that black laziness, stupidity, or indifference toward one another "explained" their high disease rates. But one needed to look no further than the differences in living conditions between blacks and whites to find the real reasons for disease. The Reverend J. Sutton-Moxley, for years chaplain to the British troops in Barbados, noted the good health of the soldiers garrisoned there, described Barbados as a health spa, and "powerfully urged its charms on the attention of the travelling public."[67] Rev. J. Sutton-Moxley might have added that in order to enjoy the invigorating, salubrious environment of Barbados, upper-class white travelers would also need the stomach for occasional glimpses of diseased, ill-nourished black children residing in the dank plantation tenantries on the same healthy island.

A surrogate measure of the general ill health among Barbadian blacks at the start of the twentieth century was the high infant mortality rate. Compared even with the similarly depressed sugar cane colonies of the Commonwealth Caribbean, Barbados stood out. The average number of deaths of infants under one year per 1,000 live births for the years 1900–4 was 282. Comparative data for other places were Jamaica, 171; Nevis, 197; Dominica, 185; Trinidad, 162; British Honduras, 139; British Guiana, 185; St. Kitts, 247.[68] In the middle of the decade, Barba-

Table 3. Barbados Infant Mortality per 1,000 Live Births

Parish	1905	1906	1907
St. Michael	391	499	335
St. Philip	390	457	340
Christchurch	284	423	294
St. George	267	464	331
St. John	216	359	227
St. Thomas	268	483	300
St. James	275	442	323
St. Peter	223	344	280
St. Lucy	218	317	249
St. Andrew	148	197	219
St. Joseph	198	230	214
Average	301	420	302

Source: Data from John Hutson, "The Half-Yearly Report of the Poor Law Inspector, July-December 1907," *OG*, Oct. 11, 1909, p. 1719.

dian infant mortality rates increased (table 3) islandwide, with those of the Bridgetown area and St. Michael parish usually the highest on the island. In 1906 half the infants of St. Michael parish died before they reached twelve months of age. The death rate for Barbados as a whole had increased noticeably in the latter decades of the nineteenth century, as the bounty depression lowered wages and, apparently, life chances for black Barbadians. The average islandwide death rate per thousand was 21.5 for 1861–70, 23.6 for 1871–80, 27.0 for 1881–90, increasing to 29.7 for the four years 1891–94.[69]

The very high infant mortality rates on Barbados invited comparison. Public health inspectors submitting annual reports noted often that the Barbadian infant death rate was markedly— as much as threefold—greater than in England and Wales, where death rates in general and child death rates in particular had plummeted in the latter half of the nineteenth century.[70]

"Reasons" for the high incidence of infant deaths on Barbados were not difficult to find. Africans, despite the civilizing influences that the New World plantation system had bestowed upon them, really had not "evolved" as rapidly as the whites. Poor living conditions and malnutrition, to be sure, were factors, but much of the responsibility—according to official sources—lay with the blacks themselves. "Promiscuous illegitimacy, involving general inexperience and neglect of mothers" were considered major causes of high death rates.[71]

Not every public official was so cynical. Parish doctors making their rounds through the unsanitary black living quarters spoke out from time to time, pleading for official action against the conditions creating inevitably high infant death rates. On the recommendation of the parochial medical officer, Dr. N.L. Boxill, St. George parish instituted a novel, if short-lived program to save sickly infants. On April 30, 1912, the parish vestrymen allotted $300 to hire two nurses and to provide milk for malnourished babies. The following year the special relief program was discontinued "on account of a decision of the Vestry to withdraw the grant." During the year, the "neglectful" mothers of the parish had brought 971 infants for treatment at the parish clinic.

The brief experiment in actually attempting to help materially the infants of St. George parish was part of a heightened consciousness among colonial officers in 1912 with regard to the relentlessly high death rates of black babies. Governor Leslie Probyn called a conference on infant mortality on March 6, 1912, summoning representatives from every parish, members of the central poor-law board, and some of the poor-law inspectors and parish medical officers. The significance of the conference's proceedings was what was considered and *not* approved: free milk for the neediest cases, parish nurses in order to advise new mothers, and "day nursery" programs. Rather, the only agenda proposal passed was an agreement to register more carefully the infant deaths themselves.[72]

The recasting of mortality data into new categories by Barbadian health officials, as a result of the 1912 conference on infant mortality, provided a classic case of using "objective" and "scientific" numbers and method in order to satisfy existing prejudices.

The conference had called for the causes of infant deaths to be recorded in registering child deaths, but discerning single reasons for a death was difficult if not impossible, and even parish doctors could only guess as to whether malnutrition, lack of fresh water, or a particular disease had "caused" a baby's death. What could be done and was done, however, was to classify the dead infants either "legitimate" or "illegitimate." One of the semiannual reports of the Barbados poor-law inspector in 1913 thus began with a triumphant "Table of Illegitimacy and Infant Mortality," demonstrating "scientifically" that (black) infants born from immoral unions had a two to three times higher chance of dying during the first year of life. "[T]his comparison demonstrates a close connection between illegitimacy and a large infant mortality," began the report.[73] The crowded, unsanitary estate conditions imposed by the white plantocracy could be ignored if one were willing to seize the opportunity to blame high death rates on black indolence and immorality.

Blaming high infant death rates on black immorality doubtless also allowed white Barbadians to shrug off the frequent, tragic sight of small coffins being buried in the ground or to avoid contemplating the obvious absence of tiny black children who recently had been playing in a given tenantry house yard. "Ordinarily, the death and burial of children attract no attention" announced a 1905 Barbados newspaper.[74] Indeed, the routine of infant death seemed to influence the fatalistic nature of accepting the grief by black parents. "When a baby died, it was taken for granted. It was regarded as a natural thing. They didn't have funerals until children were seven or so," recalled an old man in St. Thomas parish. But fatalism was not indifference. By deluding themselves and each other that black parents maintained a casual attitude toward a child's death and by referring continually to "bastardy" or "concubinage" in order to explain the high infant death rates, Barbadian officials deliberately misinterpreted "that stoicism toward the death of an infant which appears in all societies with high infant mortality, especially among the poor."[75]

The Bridgetown Area

The squalid conditions in the rural Barbadian tenantries at the turn of the century probably were even worse in the pockets of lower-class black housing scattered throughout Bridgetown and the suburbs of St. Michael parish.[76] In 1890 a special committee, chaired by the colony's secretary, assessed the overcrowding in Church Village in the heart of Bridgetown by sampling firsthand the conditions existing "in a great many parts of the City and suburbs" and constituting "a menace to the whole community." At Church Village the committee found no fewer than 266 small wooden houses on only three acres of land. The dwellings were packed together, creating narrow alleyways, the widest of which was only thirteen feet. Sanitation facilities consisted of latrine holes that were covered over when filled with excrement. The entire village area was pockmarked with these shallow pits, all of which emitted an unimaginably foul stench in the heat of the rainy seasons. The committee deplored the overcrowding and filth at Church Village. In particular, there was a need "to keep the Island sanitary since it is now becoming a health resort for Americans."[77]

When rural black Barbadians spoke of heading for "town" in 1900, they were referring—as they do late in the twentieth century—to Bridgetown. Small urban centers, Speightstown on the west coast and Oistins on the south coast, existed, and some of the larger sugar cane estates provided a quasi-urban atmosphere. But the urban agglomeration of Bridgetown in the southwestern corner of the island overwhelmed any other urban centers on the island by far, typical of the single, primate cities that exist throughout the Commonwealth Caribbean.

The best known of the black urban settlements in the Bridgetown area besides Church Village were Carrington Village, the notorious "Golden Square" zone of Lower Bay Street, and the New Orleans area north of the downtown area. But small clusters of lower-class housing could be found in unlikely places in town, sometimes juxtaposed with residences of the well-to-do. The lack of a clear delineation in housing quality in parts of Bridgetown made the city "a place of striking contrasts, a region of surprises."[78] Generally, the houses themselves of urban blacks were the same chattel houses as in rural areas. But urban dwellers had little access to rented subsistence plots. In the Bridgetown area, a black family's net financial worth usually was confined within the walls of a house on a rented house plot. In the Golden Square fire of July 20, 1910, which destroyed twenty-seven small dwellings and several commercial buildings, James Earle lost everything he owned: an eighteen-by-ten-foot boarded and shingled house and a quantity of shipwright's tools, all valued at twenty-five pounds.[79] Overcrowding in the poorer districts, moreover, pertained not simply to house density but also to the numbers residing therein. In August 1902 a Roebuck Street resident refused isolation for his smallpox-stricken daughter. A police constable was stationed at the front door of the house in order to prevent the twenty-one others who lived inside from mingling with the public.[80]

Public officials attempted to control the chaotic spread of the black urban tenantries (the term for small-scale settlements in town) through legislation.[81] Section 41 of the Barbados Public Health Act of 1898 required that formal plans be submitted to and approved by the St. Michael parish health commissioners before land was subdivided and rented for housing areas. According to one source in 1906, only one such plan ever had been disallowed. Worse yet, the surveyors' drawings and the conditions on the ground usually bore little resemblance to one another. The diagram submitted for subdividing part of Bank Hall Plantation, just north of Bridgetown, into more than one hundred house plots, each measuring thirty by fifty feet, bore the reassuring advice that the land in question enjoyed "natural drainage" into nearby gutters.[82] In reality, many of the subdivided areas suffered badly—as they do in the late twentieth century—from poor drainage, a condition compounded by the sudden presence of many houses, paths, and latrine pits within small and restricted areas.

Not all of the small land parcels in the urban and peri-urban districts of St. Michael parish were rented. Parts of Bank Hall, Bay, Black Rock, Bush Hall, Jackmans, Jacksons, Kensington, Mount Clapham, Salters, and other estates in St. Michael parish were sold as small land parcels to more prosperous black Barbadians as the bounty depression persisted.[83] Nor were rented and freehold house plots necessarily separated within particular tenantry areas. In some cases, black tenants themselves subdivided small rented properties and sublet them—often to relatives—so that the tiny houses seemed to proliferate on progressively tinier house plots. Jointly owned land parcels and the rental of plots of land of odd shapes and sizes compounded the settlement and land-tenure confusion in the urban area.

Competition among urban tenantry landlords combined with the mobility of renters added spatial instability to the complexity of black urban residential patterns. Large-scale tenantry owners, who stood to gain considerable profits from monthly rents, occasionally tried to lure renters to their property with the enticement of a month or two of rent-free occupancy. Occasionally, renters literally "had been induced to leave one side of the road and go to the other," creating a fluid pattern that had small portable chattel houses continually being carted about and "scattered all over the length and breadth of the parish."[84] The resilient, picaresque character of "squatters" that has been noted in Third World cities in the late twentieth century—particularly in lower-class urban dwellers' ability to pick up everything and move on short notice—had ample precedent in the Bridgetown area in 1900.

Urban blacks' residential mobility was similar to that in outlying parishes, an unsurprising similarity because urban dwellers or their parents often had come into town rather recently. As one eighty-six year old in St. George parish answered, "Well, let's face it, most of the people in town is people from the country." One way for rural blacks to escape rural hopelessness according to the 1878 Poor Relief Commission was to "troop to town" for casual employment or even for begging. Young black men and women often came into town, stayed with relatives and friends, worked at odd jobs, and sometimes were sent back to their own parishes if they tried to obtain poor relief in St. Michael parish. Sending an individual back home did little good though because "in a few days he finds his way again to town."[85] If they were successful in finding anything even approximating full-time employment, then they often sent for their families in the countryside to join them. The "migration" from country to city in Barbados was by no means a sharp, irrevocable break.

Bridgetown's appeal for black rural Barbadians went beyond

seeking work and sustenance. The excitement, variety, and bustle of the city fairly sparkled in comparison with the drab monotony of wooden shacks surrounded by endless cane fields. Young people who had spent time in Bridgetown were said to have acquired urban habits and even speech accents that distinguished them from country cousins. A ninety-year-old retired school headmistress of St. Lucy parish recalled her visits to Bridgetown in the first decade of the twentieth century, the terminus of a bicycle trip from Swampy Town, St. Lucy, to Speightstown followed by a ride on the "horse bus" to Bridgetown: "The differences between Bridgetown and the countryside? Why, it was like chalk and cheese! In Bridgetown there was piped water, trams, real stores, and nice houses. People in town had the benefits of lower prices over people in the country. But in Bridgetown they had to buy everything. There was no exchange like in the country."

The seasonal slack period and low wages inherent in the Barbadian sugar cane industry brought some rural blacks to town in the autumn, but there was as little job permanence for lower-class black workers in the city as in the country. The Bridgetown tenantries were reservoirs of semiskilled, redundant, black laborers who competed with one another for urban wage jobs that were more varied but as similarly short-lived as plantation work. The construction of the dry dock at the Bridgetown pier had, for example, lasted from 1889 to 1893, and at the dock's grand opening Governor James Shaw Hay acknowledged the importance of the project for such a "heavily populated" labor market.[86] His observation was reinforced two years later during repairs at the same facility when mounted police were called to manage the crush created by an estimated five hundred applicants seeking only two hundred temporary wage jobs.[87]

Loading and unloading ocean vessels at the Bridgetown docks absorbed the activities of hundreds of black longshoremen when vessels departed and arrived. But, again, dock work was not steady, and longshoremen clamored for available work. The surplus of black laborers, moreover, allowed white steamer agents and dock bosses to depress workers' wages by paying them with "credit" at particular stores and shops.[88] The necessity to be available immediately for any possible dock labor kept numbers of black men continually waiting near the wharf in order to secure a day's work. And self-appointed black "tour guides," willing to carry luggage for a pittance, hounded shipboard visitors. The ever-present crowds of black men desperate for some kind of work produced the inevitable condemnations of quayside "idlers, loafers, and loungers" in newspapers and from colonial officials.

The intense competition among black working men for niches within the Bridgetown laboring system led them to render extraordinary physical efforts in their search for wages. As in the rural sugar cane estates, an oversupply of labor in Bridgetown depressed its market value, so black men in the city hauled goods through the streets, acted as messengers, and vied with one another to perform nearly any service in exchange for money. The effects of labor abundance were obvious even to casual visitors to Barbados, who noted the remarkable profusion of "Stalwart negroes, dragging heavy, two-wheeled 'spiders' loaded with hogsheads of molasses—for the negro is an important draught animal in Bimshaw land."[89] The profusion of laborers in town and the depression years affected black urban artisans as well. During the 1890s, coopers at the wharfside who earlier had been employed to trim wooden hogsheads and puncheons for forty cents apiece suddenly found the rates halved in light of labor oversupply. And skilled laborers—carpenters, masons, and others—could "be seen on the wharf and elsewhere ready to do anything as a means of employment."[90]

Whereas the 1891 census of Barbados characterized nearly 800 males as "Porters" in Bridgetown and St. Michael parish, the most common female occupation—530 in Bridgetown and 974 more in the parish—was categorized as "Hawkers and Pedlars."[91] Market women of St. Michael parish, whether formally registered with parish officials or informally selling goods from house to house, extended themselves into the interstices of the island's system of interpersonal exchange just as black men routinely labored beyond normal job expectations. A woman in Bridgetown dealt in tiny, diverse commodity arrays reflecting both her supply and demand.[92] Sometimes she sold produce—a few beans, tomatoes, root crops, one or two fresh eggs—from her own garden plot, but more often she purchased her goods either from rural people who had brought them to town or by traveling herself into the countryside. Her many customers, all with insecure cash incomes and very little money to spend, prevented her from specializing in one commodity or in maintaining stocks in any quantity. The small numbers and varied assortments of items within each of the many window-front shops in the city—"a few small bundles of chipped firewood, a dozen bottles of aerated drinks, a mysterious collection of empty bottles, some greasy-looking fish cakes, a box of cigarettes and such sundries, all to the value of about ten dollars."[93]—were additional evidence of the fine-grained system of commodity marketing that served and was operated by the men and women of the black working class in Bridgetown.

Throughout Barbados, the shopkeepers—who were mainly men—and the market women of Bridgetown and rural parishes represented the principal commercial links among the black workers of both town and country. By walking back and forth between the city and the rest of the island, hucksters exchanged the cash in Bridgetown for the variety and quantity of rurally produced foodstuffs. The concentration of buying power in Bridgetown inevitably tied all of the island's market women to the urban retail network. And the relatively flat topography and small size of Barbados allowed women, literally, to walk all over the island, thereby representing a nearly continuous circulation of people, goods, information, gossip, and money between city and country. Black shopkeepers, who often were small landowners as well, transported imported goods into the countryside for purchase by plantation tenantry dwellers. Most shopkeepers possessed their own wooden carts, and throughout Barbados in the first years of the twentieth century black rural tenantry dwellers were accustomed to seeing "tough little ponies haul the carts to town and haul them back the same day, freighted with goods, toiling up stiff climbs with a splendid pluck and a superb exhibition of stamina."[94]

Families and friends, moreover, maintained ties between black Bridgetown and the estate tenantries in the countryside. Visits, marriages, and holidays brought relatives into town and city dwellers back "home" to the country, thereby blurring distinctions between the two. Often, black folk from the country brought gifts of food—a few fowls, sacks of yams or potatoes—when they visited relatives or friends in St. Michael parish. Urban dwellers, however, learned to be wary of gift-giving exchanges because it seemed as if relatives from the countryside always carried back home about "twice as much" in gifts from their city cousins as they themselves had brought to town.[95]

For many black Barbadians, the differences between "city" and "country" really represented a diversity of opportunity in the same way that cash acquisition and subsistence gardening together composed total livelihood. In the last years of the nineteenth century the suburban tenantries of St. Michael parish seemed attractive settlement alternatives when compared with, say, a remote part of St. Andrew parish. Moving closer to town by no means involved a full-time commitment to urban life; if an individual was willing to walk long distances into town from a peri-urban tenantry, he or she could compensate for the one to two days of work per week given out by estate managers. Moving their houses to rented spots just outside the city, moreover, gave many black Barbadians a completely new experience, namely "the privileges of labouring anywhere they please."[96] Living in the suburbs, rather than inside Bridgetown itself, allowed black workers to maintain vital access to the land—even rented land—that could sustain a family during the lean depression years. Providing typically succinct and shrewd commentary, Lizzie and Joe remarked that access to a small land plot "outside the town" afforded sustenance, cash possibilities, and even self-respect:

> An little way oukside de tung wha yuh kin raise uh pig,
> An raise yuh ducks an fowls an got yuh piece uh lan fuh dig,
> Ess yuh wan tea enny mawnin yuh kin alwuz sell uh egg,
> An wen uh man kin help heself he en got cause fuh beg.[97]

Mutual Assistance

Lord Olivier, who had been in Barbados with the 1897 commission, returned three decades later to chair public hearings dealing with the local consequences of the latest lowering of sugar prices. At an open meeting in Bridgetown on October 21, 1929, Olivier sought historical perspective in attempting to understand better the particular plight of the black working class of the island. At emancipation, he asked, were there no villages laid out for freedmen as in Jamaica and British Guiana? And, as a result, was there "no district in this island to be known as the small planters' district?" The respondents replied in the negative. Unlike in some of the larger colonies in the Commonwealth Caribbean, black agriculturalists on Barbados controlled no extensive parts of the island, no real "village" areas that they could call their own.[98]

Landlessness and a shared poverty had led black Barbadians of the plantation tenantries to adapt in several ways. One way had been to initiate and maintain an extraordinary reliance on each other. Besides the reciprocal food sharing in rural parishes, black Barbadians—in both town and country—developed and sustained rotating credit associations, burial groups, "class clubs," and friendly societies; all of these associations helped to spread food assistance, social support, and money as widely as possible. As in lower-class mutual-assistance groupings everywhere, individual survival and the expectation of the group to honor mutual obligations were bound up with one another. In Barbados these mutual-assistance groupings were local in character, hardly ever extending past the immediate settlement or neighborhood. Local mutual-assistance groups had had their beginnings during slavery and thus carried with them the spatial limitations that had been fundamental constraints to any of the earliest institutions developed by the slaves.[99]

The widespread institution of "meetings" or "meeting turns" in 1900 resembled community-level banking systems among black Barbadians and represented at least partial local control over individual savings and spending in an impersonal monetary system.[100] While friends, neighbors, and kinsmen shared food on a reciprocal basis, small groups of blacks also made regular contributions of tiny fixed sums of cash to a "banker" who was a trusted friend or neighbor. The "meeting" (the small group of usually less than ten participants) together contributed a sum, all of which would be awarded to one of the individual contributors at periodic intervals. The group's sum contributions were thereby distributed weekly, fortnightly, or monthly until each participant had received the total sum. After each contributor had received the group's lump sum, the "meeting" would "turn" again. Meetings existed throughout the tenantries and black districts of Bridgetown early in this century. "My mother always counted on the meetings during those hard times. They helped plenty," remembered a seventy-two-year-old shopkeeper in St. James parish.

The meeting's main benefit was in providing a periodic sum of cash for a variety of expenses—ranging from school fees to food purchases—but within a communal setting. By participating in one or more meetings, black individuals avoided indebtedness to shopkeepers and planters. Nor were they obligated to entrust their savings to the formal colonial banking system controlled by whites. Although meeting turns were informal institutions lacking written rules, a code of individual reliability and interdependence underpinned each meeting group and thereby reinforced community cohesion. An individual failing to contribute his or her meeting sum was subject to being "stigmatized by the community" and stood to lose much more than money through the devastating consequences of gossip networks that ranged well beyond the tenantry grounds.[101]

Colonial officials were dimly aware of meetings. As early as 1878 members of the Poor Relief Commission described "the system of class clubs or turns, which is described as being very popular among the agricultural labourers and mechanics." Black Barbadian men and women, according to the commissioners' report, donated weekly not less than sixpence and occasionally as much as five shillings apiece to the sums collected by the "clubs." The commissioners paid grudging compliments to the meetings because they represented "a somewhat clumsy method . . . to force . . . thriftiness and to practice compulsory saving." At the same time the system was said to be subject to the potential misorganization of "dishonest scamps," community bankers who might depart with the sum total of a group's contributions.[102]

While Barbadian meetings were adaptations to shared poverty, they also had African origins. Remarkably similar systems of rotating credit and short-term savings—the "Susu" in Trinidad,

"Partners" in Jamaica, the "Box" in Antigua—were found throughout the British Caribbean. All of these informal institutions almost certainly had derived from the Yoruba "Esusu," a short-term savings institution of West Africa that had been transplanted to the Caribbean during slavery and had since been adapted to the particular characteristics of each West Indian island.[103]

Community "friendly societies" also were black mutual assistance institutions, although they differed from meetings in several important ways. Friendly societies were vaguely church-based associations to which black Barbadians contributed sums for "sharing out" (as in meetings), sick benefits, and burial funds. Friendly society antecedents could be traced to England, but their widespread popularity among blacks of the Commonwealth Caribbean also had African roots. By 1900, moreover, local friendly societies were registered with the Barbadian government and thereby subject to formal government control.

Possibly owing to chronic landlessness and the resultant need for mutual assistance, friendly societies always had been more popular among the poor blacks of Barbados than in the other colonies of the Commonwealth Caribbean.[104] Friendly societies perhaps had been introduced to Barbados by the Moravians, but it has also been suggested that William Hart Coleridge, the bishop of Barbados and the Leeward Islands, first had founded friendly societies in Barbados between 1825 and 1834. In any case, the functions and popularity of the friendly societies among black Barbadians seem to have ebbed and flowed throughout the latter half of the nineteenth century, tracking periods of economic depression and relative prosperity. Barbadian newspapers of the nineteenth century paid somewhat more attention to friendly societies than to other community-level organizations, possibly seeking information with which to convince British authorities that local Barbadian self-help groups precluded the need for an islandwide poor law. But official understanding of local friendly societies was slight. The Barbados House of Assembly passed its first Friendly Societies Act in 1880, and in 1901 there were 167 Barbadian friendly societies registered with the government.[105]

Similar to meeting turns, members' cash contributions sustained Barbadian friendly societies. In most cases the school headmasters, with both an acquaintance with rudimentary accounting and a need for extra income, acted as society treasurers for small fees. An estimated "Working Man's Weekly Budget" before World War I assumed a payment of twelve cents each week into a typical Barbadian friendly society, although members paid varying amounts down to six cents per week and even less.[106] Sometimes friendly societies paid out cash "bonuses" to members, thereby assuming a function similar to meetings.

But friendly societies satisfied spiritual needs as well. As among the British working class, the most important benefits paid by Barbadian friendly societies in 1900 were for funerals.[107] Although colonial officials insisted that the laborers generally were indifferent to high mortality rates, no one could ascertain such apathy in the extraordinary efforts that Barbadian blacks made to honor their dead. The local friendly societies provided community, as well as family, support for the bereaved during wakes and funerals, and the death benefit money from the society paid for coffins and church fees. In many cases, the real funeral service was held at one's home or at a small revivalist church in the countryside, then a formal "second service" followed at the Anglican church.[108] Local funerals, a principal reason for a friendly society's existence, allowed black Barbadians at the turn of the century to celebrate death in a West African tradition that had been modified by three centuries of West Indian plantation oppression.[109]

Friendly societies paid sick benefits of varying amounts and durations, depending upon how much the sick member had paid in dues, and they also paid maternity benefits. Those claiming sick benefits were likely to receive an unannounced visit from the society's "sick visitor," an investigator dispatched—often at odd hours—from the friendly society's meeting place to ascertain whether or not the member in question was feigning illness. Few black tenantries were unfamiliar with the stealthy sick visitor from the local friendly society. The visitor, on the other hand, often met his conspiratorial match in the family children, whose job it was to warn of the visitor's approach so that the applicant for sick benefits could appear to be as ill as possible.[110]

At the turn of the century Barbadian friendly societies monitored their members' activities and exerted a certain moral authority over their subscribers. Excessive gambling or drinking could bring expulsion. Friendly societies emphasized biblical teachings and conduct, and society members commonly referred to one another as "brother" or "sister." Joining a friendly society carried obligations to attend members' funerals, and an annual parade and church service emphasized mutual religious obligations. Although some members of friendly societies doubtless took the group's religious formalities more seriously than others, community friendly societies fostered considerable moral influence throughout the island's black districts.[111]

Contrary to their social and religious virtues, not every friendly society was blessed with sound and honest accounting. The Barbados Friendly Societies Act of 1880 was repealed by the act of 1891, which stipulated that each society be registered and little else. Without auditing or accounting rules, some friendly societies flourished just long enough to extract payments from gullible applicants, at which time officeholders disappeared with or simply misused the funds. The colonial government initiated investigations in 1896, and in 1901 and 1902 the registrar of friendly societies reduced the number of societies on the island from 167 to 97.[112] Much of the registrar's initiative was inspired by Governor Hodgson, who considered the number of societies excessive, suggesting one or two per parish as sufficient for subscribers' needs. In particular, the governor objected to members' donations being "frittered away paying a crowd of officeholders."[113]

Mismanagement notwithstanding, the Barbadian friendly society movement—symptomatic of the plight of the island's black working class in general—was in a seemingly stagnant state at the turn of the century. Community friendly societies really could do nothing about lowered wages or the bounty depression. An underpaid black laborer had little if any personal savings and could fall back only on his family, neighbors, and friendly societies before incurring indebtedness or shame in dealings with shopkeepers or poor-law officials. Meeting turns and friendly societies provided mutual support and assistance, but these groups' lifeblood, money, was in extremely short supply among friendly society donors. When a Barbadian newspaper article in 1901 reported "the falling away" and "indifference" of friendly society members toward their associations because of the remote prospects of receiving financial benefits, the statement really was recording one more dimension of the dismal economic prospects of the island's black workers.[114]

"The Manners of the Masses"

While members of the Barbadian plantocracy assumed an attitude of careful indifference toward the miserable living conditions imposed on black families, they took an absorbing interest in any changes in the group behavior of the plantation workers themselves. This interest was unrelated to sociological curiosity but, rather, was a symptom of the planters' continuous fear of insurrection. In 1900, throughout the Caribbean, planter families still whispered about the inferno of Haiti, barely a century old. Closer in time and right at home, the Federation Riots on Barbados in April 1876, had spread alarm throughout the homes of the island's planters. And now the sugar bounty depression, entering a third decade, had exploded into bloodshed, riot, and property loss elsewhere in the British Caribbean. In Dominica in 1893 and 1898, St. Kitts in 1896, Montserrat in 1898, British Guiana in 1896 and 1903, Jamaica in 1902, and nearby Trinidad in 1902, worker unrest had flared into violence.[115] Even worse, immigrant cane cutters from Barbados had been shot during the riots in Georgetown, British Guiana, in late 1905.[116] What if disgruntled troublemakers were to return to Barbados and attempt to instigate similar anarchy? The question nagged and stuck in the backs of planters' and officials' minds. "Supposing we had a riot?" queried W.K. Chandler during a discussion of the Public Health Act in the Legislative Council in November 1906.[117] Chandler's concerns, like those of others, involved the possible spread of urban tenantries throughout the Bridgetown area so that white planters and administrators might have potential rioters living, literally, right under their balconies.

The Barbadian planters, pressed hard themselves in the midst of depression and badly outnumbered in case revolt ever occurred, could not rely entirely on the set of harsh colonial laws to prevent general disorder. Furthermore, the withdrawal of British troops from the Barbados garrison in 1905–6 left the island with only a skeleton volunteer reserve force of 9 officers and 125 men.[118] Publicity-oriented preventive measures appealed in general to older black workers of Barbados to dissuade youthful wrongdoers and to condemn, as ill-mannered and incorrect, any misbehavior. For example, noticeable rudeness among plantation laborers early in 1901, followed by a spate of rock-throwing incidents in the countryside, inspired a newspaper article entitled "The Manners of the Masses." The article deplored the general disrespect, breakdown in social standards, and shiftlessness among a few of the modern, twentieth-century workers. Young men and women of 1900, according to the article, showed little of the respect that their parents and grandparents had displayed back in the 1850s and 1860s.[119]

Of course, general insurrection in Barbados—at least in the first decade of the twentieth century—never occurred. Barbadian planters counted themselves fortunate that riot had not visited their island. And, despite the public scolding for rudeness and rock throwing, relieved estate owners generally credited their workers with good behavior and admirable attitudes during economic crisis. Barbados, it was claimed, fortunately had been blessed with decent, respectful workers, especially in the rural parishes. Their pleasant behavior stood in direct contrast, for example, to that of the insolent "quayside niggers" of Roseau, Dominica.[120] Accounting for the stereotype of the good Barbadian worker occasionally inspired explanations such as the image of the "happy laborer in the tropics" that Inspector Lawrance divulged to the 1897 Royal Commission. But more thoughtful observers knew that any answer had to be more complex. Those same pleasant Barbadian laborers sometimes experienced personality transformations when working abroad. Planter George Carrington had visited British Guiana, for instance, and there he had witnessed normally civil Barbadian laborers who had emigrated there for work and with whom he was personally acquainted "stand and look at the manager and whistle in his face and 'cheek' him in any kind of way."[121]

The paternalistic character of Barbadian plantations of 1900—especially in contrast to the factory atmospheres in Trinidad and British Guiana—gave individual workers the latitude of coping with familiar owners and managers rather than facing the frustrations of corporate impersonality. Small acts of benevolence by individual Barbadian planters such as allowing workers' animals to graze estate grounds, giving away potatoes, or overlooking petty violations of estate rules went far in defusing the potential for violence. Moreover, in Barbados individual laborers were known personally and could be traced to their particular tenantries. Wrongdoers could lose access to their land plots or worse for becoming involved in public disturbances.

Whether viewed in the context of resignation or accommodation, the generally acquiescent attitude on the parts of individual Barbadian workers in 1900 had to be intertwined with a lack of alternative options. A black man toiling in the sugar cane fields had long-term interests at stake in keeping his wife and children alive through the judicious combination of subsistence gardening and wage labor. However satisfying a frontal assault on the estate system might be—by attacking a manager, for example, or expressing rudeness to an owner's wife—the reactions almost certainly would lead to even worse conditions for the laborer and his family. And those potentially worse conditions were exemplified with chilling regularity by estate officials against troublemakers for all to see: dismantling a laborer's chattel house, allowing him very little work, hauling him before a parish magistrate for contract violation. It was obvious that "good" behavior paid dividends to black workers. Tipping the hat when the owner's carriage passed, maintaining a smile in adversity, remembering "Sirs" and "Ma'ams" when conversing wth whites, all could be interpreted as sensible tactics in light of the existing socioeconomic system. On a broader scale, the bloody quashing of disturbances on nearby islands by police and British bluejackets gave black workers on Barbados little hope that rebellion or riot on their own island would lead to anything else. In discussing his father's relationship with white estate managers early in this century, a seventy-year-old tailor from St. Peter parish recalled: "We were lucky. My father never got sick. He always got along well with the manager because he never complained and worked hard. He had the right attitude."[122]

Deferential and good-natured behavior, however, was by no means the same as really accepting existing conditions. Black Barbadians simply lived as best they could with what they knew were unjust conditions. Not a single elderly black Barbadian I interviewed ever hinted that he or she had been treated fairly or equitably when compared with whites. Lizzie and Joe's published mockery and satire in 1903 continually underlined, in oblique fashion, the fundamental inequities in Barbadian society at the turn of the century. Dr. J.F. Clarke, testifying before the 1897 Royal Commission, pointed out the difference between image and substance in black attitudes and behavior:

> Through all the hardships the labourer endures he assumes a pleasant demeanour, and which is mistaken by his employer for comfort and happiness. . . . he is often taken to the magistrate of his parish and punished for breach of contract, or for taking a few points of sugar-cane from the plantation . . . and yet he returns to the very plantation and resumes his work peaceful and quiet.[123]

The stoicism and good manners of black Barbadians were also reflected in the deeply religious nature of the laborers. The Anglican church represented a powerfully conservative force in preserving the existing social order, despite its ambivalent and potentially subversive messages of submission on the one hand and individual equality and the glorification of the human spirit on the other. Sunday sermons could draw the hatred from within black souls while nurturing the hope of individual salvation by doing good deeds. Immersion in prayer services and devotion, moreover, provided a spiritual respite from the stark material conditions of the estate tenantries. Black Barbadians, on at least one day per week, could feel a pride and self-respect that were denied them otherwise. The religious feelings of black Barbadians at the turn of the century were genuine and unhypocritical, and few old Barbadians today, in the 1980s, can recall the past without suggesting that his or her successes in life are due largely to God's good graces.

These points, however, are not made to suggest that religious fervor among black Barbadians represented a blind submission to the white man's religion. Black workers shared enough obeah-related convictions and customs of African origin, supported by folktales and folk medicines, to make their belief systems anything but unmodified versions of British religion. A Caribbean Christianity provided a social context for black Barbadians that reinforced a spirit of community. The intense Barbadian interests in friendly society wakes and private funeral services indicate that, as among Afro-American slaves in the United States, the "real religion" and the "real preaching" took place among the blacks themselves, outside the parish churches that had been established during and were interrelated with plantation slavery.[124]

Evidence of a special, black Barbadian Christianity was clear enough in the popularity of fundamentalist sects that had gained widespread followings among the island's black working class in the 1890s. Dr. F.B. Archer provided a simple answer to a complex issue when he attributed the large numbers of black Barbadians being attracted to recently introduced religious sects as indicative of an increase in lunacy.[125] Foremost among the new religious groups, coming mainly from the United States, were the Pennyites. Later known as the Christian Mission, the Pennyites began their proselytizing in Barbados in 1891, and they were followed by such movements as the Church of God, Pilgrim Holiness, and the Salvation Army. Different from the Anglican church of the elite (which required perfunctory homage from all) and the middle-class Wesleyan and Moravian churches, the fundamentalist movements of the black working peoples of the plantations represented the first attempts to form a genuine "people's ministry," a sincere religious thrust designed for and by black Barbadians.[126] White planter families of Barbados in 1900 could chuckle and gossip among themselves about the unsophisticated black families trekking to the tiny roadside churches to render lusty chants of praise in their gaudy finery. But they also could be secretly grateful that so much black energy and emotion was being poured into religion.

Few black workers really could forget a residual anger and indignation, however, and when planter reprisals seemed remote, blacks settled scores. Barbadian workers were civil and courteous "especially in daylight" to planters and managers.[127] But at night or when detection was impossible, disgruntled black workers indulged in countless acts of minor sabotage, from destroying plantation equipment to poisoning a planter's favorite dog. The most damaging, widespread, and symbolic act of revenge was the cane fire. Burning the fields did not automatically ruin sugar cane crops, but it did necessitate immediate harvesting of the burned cane to lessen sucrose loss. In this regard, cane fires sometimes solved short-run rural employment problems because usually they forced planters into hastily recruiting cane cutters to reap the recently burned canes.

Yet everyone knew that cane fires, as old as sugar cane plantations themselves in the Caribbean, were nearly always malicious acts of vengeance designed to destroy planters' crops. Moreover, the beacon of a cane fire on a neighboring estate provided a spontaneous and irresistible suggestion to others. So cane fires often came in clusters, sweeping across the ripened canes of contiguous estates in a single parish. "Canefires, canefires, night after night and week after week is a burning disgrace to the labourers of this colony," a 1901 Barbados newspaper reported indignantly, attributing the blazes to "vicious firebrands" who roamed the countryside.[128] Occasional fires, it was supposed, had been set accidentally in the St. George valley from the sparks and embers of the passing railway engines. But a cane fire that had begun by chance might easily lead to other, less innocent blazes in the repressive atmosphere that existed on most of the plantations of Barbados at the turn of the century.

"Vicious firebrands" was more a vague slogan than it was a condemnation of specific individuals, because the incendiaries were seldom caught. The ubiquitous closed-mouth solidarity among black workers, exemplified by their only rarely informing on arsonists, modified the "pleasant laborer" stereotype considerably. Posters throughout the countryside routinely offered rewards of up to £50 (or $240) to impoverished workers for turning in those responsible for cane fires, but they produced few results "beyond providing work for the printers."[129] The authorities were incredulous. Even in 1901, when the torched cane fields cost cane cutters their jobs, no informants appeared. In that year one report noted, "it is curious that, in this thickly peopled place, the many-handed, and ubiquitous incendiary can hide safely in the mass of the people, and, except in rare instances when caught red-handed, defy detection. Undoubtedly the population hides him contrary to its own interests."[130]

What Barbadian colonial officials failed to comprehend was that working-class "interests" were a good deal more complex than those of possibly meeting short-term material needs, even in times of incredible hardship. To satisfy needs for money, few estate workers were willing to collaborate with the white establishment of which all blacks held a deep and overriding suspicion. Even when someone did inform, the promised money just might not all be there. In April 1907, for example, when Wilfred Bovell turned in Jestina Morris for lighting a field of canes at Haggatts plantation, he was given only $100—less than half the announced reward.[131]

The suspicion that black Barbadians held for white Barbadians, as well as for those who worked to maintain the existing social order, had been learned through years of plantation slavery and later. Planters, magistrates, and police constables attempted to control nearly all phases of black workers' lives. One means of resisting was to maintain a mutual solidarity that, in some cases, could overcome or at least blunt official control. Daily examples of black suspicion of and antagonism and resistance to this control occurred at points where petty officials interacted with individuals of the black working class. Police constables and black market women, for example, engaged in endless skirmishes over the market licenses or badges required of hucksters to sell their fruits and vegetables. Even the fee of a penny or two was considered outrageous by the market women who were trying to raise cash to help pay family expenses. When police accused a badgeless market woman and asked for her name and address, the woman cheerfully responded with false information, accompanied by smiles and nods from her associates. During the first half of 1902, of the 189 market women accused, police later located only 56. The remaining 133 had given to the police fictitious names and addresses within earshot of the others. Just as common, a huckster would register with police authorities and then give the badge to another person outside town so that one badge might serve "the whole family."[132]

Suspicion of whites and its corollary, mutual assistance and friendship with fellow black workers, helped also to explain a further dimension of the personalities of black Barbadians at the turn of the century. Although affable and deferential in outward display, black workers were quiet, tight-lipped, and withdrawn toward whites who attempted to penetrate the black circle of family and friends. This mild hostility was the "sullen" attitude so often noted by Caribbean colonial officials about the region's laborers. When black workers of Barbados were together—even when performing work mandated by white planters—they could enjoy a certain camaraderie and thereby a certain social distance from immediate white supervision. If white planters or managers intruded into the group, animated exchanges among workers then suddenly became "surly," opaque silence. A particular case, which doubtless repeated itself many times in Barbados in the first decade of the century, exemplifies the point. A white man approached a laughing, chattering group of black Barbadian women picking cotton. Upon his approach the noise ceased and they cast "looks on the intruder which [said] as plainly as words could, 'Please go away.' "[133]

The Nineteenth-Century Migration Outlet

During the latter half of the nineteenth century, not all of the money helping to sustain black Barbadian families had been locally derived. Ever since emancipation, working-class Barbadians, mainly men, had been emigrating, mostly to Trinidad and British Guiana, to escape local conditions and to seek higher wages. The voyages had been mostly on sailing schooners until the last decades of the century, when many Barbadian men traveled as seasonal "deckers" on steamships, usually to harvest sugar cane in British Guiana. Not all Barbadians returned; it is likely that in the six decades between emancipation and the turn of the century, tens of thousands of working-class Barbadians had departed permanently. The potential for interisland movements of black West Indians to redistribute regional laboring populations and thereby to relieve economic distress in some territories received attention from the 1897 Royal Commission. During the commission's hearings in Bridgetown, Dr. C.G. Gooding remarked about the large numbers of Barbadians residing in the neighboring islands. Gooding suggested that, from Barbados, "about 1,000 persons, most of them men, emigrate permanently every year."[134]

Similar round figures, rough estimates, and an almost complete absence of official data confounded any efforts to determine precisely how many Barbadians emigrated, stayed away, and returned during the nineteenth century. In May 1842, less than four years after emancipation, the Barbadian planter George Carrington had estimated that "between 3,000 and 4,000" black Barbadians had emigrated, mainly to British Guiana and some to Trinidad, and probably 300 to 400 had returned.[135] During the decade 1861–71 the "gross emigration . . . might have been as much as 20,000" from Barbados.[136] The only official accounts of Barbadian emigration were compiled for the years 1873–78, providing precise numbers that may or may not have accurately represented emigration from the island. During 1873, a total of 2,830 Barbadian emigrants were counted, heading for British Guiana (2,793), Trinidad, Nevis, and Surinam.[137] By the 1880s Barbadians of unknown quantity were traveling to Trinidad and from there onward to laboring destinations in Venezuela and Panama.[138]

Barbadian planters of the nineteenth century were not anxious for members of their abundant workforce to travel away, but they also saw emigration as a possible means by which parish relief roles might be reduced. The Barbadian government's various emigration acts and policies of the nineteenth century that attempted to resolve the conflict were never effective in establishing real control. Especially in the decades following emancipation, planters routinely complained about clandestine migration by black workers. The Barbados House of Assembly passed its first restrictive acts against worker emigration in 1839, attempting to curtail the activities of recruiting agents from Trinidad and British Guiana.[139] Recruiters from the latter colony sought Barbadian workers with varying intensity and success throughout the nineteenth century; and black Barbadians were attracted by the free passage usually offered by the Guianese planters to and from the South American coastal mudflats.[140] The British government monitored and modified colonial emigration laws in the nineteenth-century Commonwealth Caribbean. In general, the Crown wished to prevent planters from either restricting free black mobility or using neighboring colonies as dumping grounds for the young, weak, or infirm—those unfit for estate work.

A principal complaint against laborers' emigration by Barbadian planters of the late 1800s was that it always seemed that the "able bodied males" were those most likely to go. Beyond such vague assertions, there is only slight evidence about which types of persons among the black working class really left the island. In general, a disproportionate number of artisans or "mechanics" seem to have emigrated, such as those going to British Guiana in 1864, although "the bulk of the emigrants was of those accustomed to the use of the hoe."[141] Emigration, it seems, was never a livelihood strategy pursued by the desperately poor. It was not an activity that would have recommended itself to those destitute Barbadian laborers on precarious cash-subsistence treadmills trying to keep their families alive, families with neither savings nor extra time to risk emigrating. Rather, nineteenth-century emigration from Barbados seems, more than likely, to have been accomplished disproportionately by those members of the working class with skills as coopers, masons, windmill repairmen, carpenters, and the like. These occupations were higher paying than field labor and would have allowed minimal cash accumulation to finance emigration or to purchase food in a father's absence. Also, these same occupations already involved travel for seasonal construction and estate repair projects within Barbados itself and would have thereby conditioned individuals to consider personal mobility a necessary adjunct to earning a living. In the course of Dr. Gooding's travels to the other British Caribbean islands in the late nineteenth century he noted that the jobs Barbadians held in those places—policemen, grooms, butlers, porters—usually were of a nonagricultural nature.[142] Of course, a person's agricultural background in Barbados did not mean that he or she could not do other kinds of work, and Gooding might simply have been noting a sea change tendency among some of the black Barbadians who chose to emigrate and reside elsewhere.

By the late nineteenth century, substantial Barbadian minorities, both transients and permanent residents, lived in British Guiana and Trinidad. Some Guianese planters preferred Barbadian estate workers, who usually were willing to work for low wages. But Barbadians in British Guiana also tended to form friendly societies as they had at home, and planters feared these groups' goals of mutual assistance might be redirected into incipient antiestate labor coalitions.[143] In Trinidad, Barbadians were, on occasion, stereotyped among planters as having a troublesome sense of independence. Barbadians in Trinidad often became police constables, railway workers, artisans, and small land proprietors. By the 1890s sizable Barbadian enclaves existed in San Fernando and also in the suburban corridor running east from Port of Spain.[144] In Trinidad, British Guiana, and also throughout the other colonies of the British Caribbean, black Barbadians—with names like Alleyne, Braithwaite, Codrington, and Cumberbatch—were settling with their families, intermarrying with the local black populations, and creating informal networks of families and friends that transcended the region's fragmented insularity.

Overseas, Barbadians maintained a pride in their home island as they do in the late twentieth century. A group of the "more prosperous Barbadians in Trinidad" exulted in the cabled news of a cricket victory of a Barbadian team against the English in 1895.[145] Much more important, individuals and families kept in touch by letter and through occasional visits. An old man born in St. Andrew parish, Barbados, in 1886, recalled that his older brother had emigrated to New Amsterdam, Berbice, in British Guiana, eventually becoming a policeman, before the turn of the century: "He sent small amounts of money back home. I used to write to him for my mother, and I can still remember writing 'N.A., Berbice' on the envelopes." So an incipient social network for at least some black working-class Barbadians extended beyond the home island at the turn of the century. And it represented a potential outlet, at least in theory, for the landless tenantry dwellers. But emigration usually meant leaving friends and loved ones behind, perhaps permanently, and black laborers of Barbados were understandably ambivalent about the prospects. For those administrators favoring emigration from the island "the reluctance manifested, by even the poorest, to relinquish their squalid and uncomfortable surroundings" in Barbados for possibly better economic prospects abroad was an irrational impediment to grand colonial design.[146] That these unsophisticated creatures, innocent of the overriding importance of colonial planning strategies, might fear never seeing their parents, friends, or children again usually went unnoticed among administrators obsessed with matching "excess" peoples with "underdeveloped" lands.

A better understanding of the social impact of emigration on the black Barbadian working class of the nineteenth century awaits further research. It is likely, however, that few, if any, of the tenantries were without individuals or families who had departed or who had close relatives living overseas. Occasionally, officials remarked that the migrations of black workers had negative local social effects. As early as 1841, Robert Schomburgk had suggested that the high infant death rates in the tenantries followed the migration of parents who had apparently left the children with uncaring relatives.[147] But individuals had emigrated not simply for themselves but to maintain their families at home as well. From 1868 to 1875, for example, when a postal money-order system linked Barbados and British Guiana, 5,654 money orders sent home from Barbadians in the South American colony had totaled nearly £10,000.[148] If, in 1900, a Barbadian official or planter doubted the propensity of the island's working class to travel away in order to improve the impoverished conditions they had left behind, they needed only to witness what would occur in the ensuing decade.

CHAPTER 4

"Hit de Manager in de Head, and
Come Along wid We!"

In the first few years of the twentieth century, Barbadians also were traveling to places other than neighboring British Caribbean territories. As the desperation and impoverishment of the sugar depression entered yet a third decade, some black Barbadians responded with outbursts of travel to seek wage labor anywhere. Hundreds (accurate records never were maintained) accepted job contracts in South American countries, mainly as railroad construction laborers. Many never returned, some came back with money, and a few reported lurid tales of Latin American despotism and even conditions of slavery. These stories, enthusiastically reported in Barbados newspapers, made the planters back home seem positively benign, a comparative image the Barbadian plantocracy did nothing to discourage.

But the emigration outlet that would irrevocably change Barbados and forever widen the horizons for the black Barbadian working class appeared in 1904. In that year the United States renewed the construction of a canal across the Isthmus of Panama that the French had earlier discontinued. Accordingly, United States officials sought thousands of workers throughout the Caribbean and beyond. Early in 1905, the United States Isthmian Canal Commission (ICC) established its principal labor recruiting office in Bridgetown. During the next decade 20,000 young black Barbadian men traveled to Panama under ICC contract. Probably that many more Barbadian men and women went informally (and therefore uncounted), joining husbands and fathers and also working in a variety of capacities.

The Barbadian plantocracy monitored the emigration to Panama closely. As the first black estate workers from outlying

105

Barbadian parishes signed contracts and departed for Panama, the island—according to some planters—had rid itself of its "idle" and "shiftless" element. And in the first few months, as the initial reports of disease, death, and construction difficulties drifted back from Central America, the planters of Barbados must have considered the Panama phenomenon simply another ephemeral wage destination for a few itinerant emigrants. But as more Barbadian men departed for Panama, wrote home, and returned with money to spend, what had been a trickle of migrants suddenly became a flood. By 1905, monthly steamers each were carrying away hundreds of the island's most capable workers. Regular, fortnightly steamer runs from Barbados to Colón were established by March 1906. Now, clusters of young black men wearing suitcoats were commonplace sights on the highways of the rural parishes and the city, all headed to the wharf and eventually to the Panama Canal. This recurring scene was unsettling, to say the least, for the planters. The legislature attempted to resurrect old antiemigration legislation and to pass new laws in order to "protect" the emigrants from being exploited abroad. On July 16, 1907, by which time well over ten thousand contract laborers from Barbados already had emigrated, J. Challenor Lynch—the owner of one of Bridgetown's largest import commission agencies—joined the heated discussion in the chambers of the Legislative Council: The local labor market might be "upset" if emigration continued at such a rate. Already, money remittances from Panama had transformed some members of the working class into "thriftless idlers." Furthermore, the "excitement . . . engendered in the minds of the ignorant labourers" as crowds of departing migrants marched through the populous areas of Bridgetown might reach inflammatory levels. Just recently, Lynch had heard of an absolutely intolerable incident that had occurred as a crowd of young men bound for Panama passed a field where a gang of sugar estate workers were being supervised by the plantation manager. One of the young men in the passing crowd had shouted: "Why you don't hit de manager in de head, and come along wid we!"[1]

"Hit de Manager in de Head"

Pre-Panama Emigrations to Africa and South America

Barbadians, particularly those who travel or reside abroad, are fond of explaining to strangers that "You find a Barbadian wherever you go." And while the literal interpretation of this saying may not always hold, it is true that Barbadians have traveled to some very unlikely places. In the years just before and after the turn of the century, black men and women of Barbados traveled out in groups, as contract workers, and independently on ocean steamers to tropical destinations far from the Caribbean realm. None of these movements ever closely rivaled the Panama Canal exodus in terms of either numbers of people or money earned. But they did condition the black working class of the island to risk traveling far afield in search of wages. Moreover, some black Barbadians had found their way to Panama itself even before the Americans began their construction efforts there. A few Barbadians had worked for the French in Panama in the late nineteenth century. Later, in the first years of the twentieth, a small number of Barbadians became acquainted with Panama on their way to work in Ecuador.

In September 1892, an estimated 270 Barbadian men, augmented by 23 others from Martinique and St. Lucia, were responsible for a disturbance aboard a German steamer at Boma, a tiny downriver port town of the Belgian Congo. The Barbadian men, after having agreed at home to work in a faraway place called the Congo, had traveled to the Canary Islands on an English vessel. From there, they proceeded south along the African coast on the German ship *Gertrud Woermann*. As the voyage continued, the Barbadians began to grumble about its length. Their dissatisfaction intensified when some African carpenters, who had boarded the vessel at Accra, warned them that they would become slaves in the Congo. The *Gertrud Woermann* ran aground at the mouth of the Congo River, and the Barbadians threatened to murder the steamer captain if he did not take them back to the Canary Islands. Eventually, at Boma, the Barbadians cut the steamer from its mooring ropes, but their mutiny was aborted by Belgian troops who shot and killed two blacks and sent the rest upriver to Matadi for railway work, a job from which they presumably never returned.[2] This incident was isolated, although it possibly dampened any enthusiasm for emigration to Africa, at least as far as working at white-imposed jobs was concerned. In 1904, Governor Hodgson of Barbados briefly considered sending Barbadians for work in the Transvaal Gold Mines as a means of "disposing of some of the surplus . . . population" of Barbados, but the Transvaal authorities at the time opted to employ only Chinese workers.[3]

Surinam was an emigration destination for a few Barbadian laborers, although it was considered an exceptionally unhealthy place. As early as 1890, large numbers of Barbadians in Surinam and Cayenne were reported in a destitute and diseased condition. Railway work there in 1906 prompted the British consul in Paramaribo to request black rather than "colored" workers because mixed-blood workers there from the dry Dutch Antilles had suffered disease and, according to Dutch colonial authorities, had become ineffective workers because of the heat and humidity. Shortly thereafter, a detachment of 150 Barbadian laborers answered the call, although they too were soon affected by a combination of disease and what was reported as a most unhealthy climate.[4]

Traveling black Barbadians in 1901 received a forewarning of the kind of welcome many more of them would soon receive from native Panamanians. In May 1901 a contingent of 190 Barbadian men and women left Bridgetown via the steamer *Catania* to work on the railway between Guayaquil and Quito, Ecuador, for an agreed-upon three shillings per day. The *Catania* took them to Colón, Panama, from which they traveled to Panama City by rail before completing their journey via another steamer. Between the steamer and the railroad in Colón, a guard of police was assigned to the Barbadians to ensure that none slipped away and stayed illegally. While the Barbadians were debarking from the steamer, one policeman threatened a Barbadian with a rifle, whereupon the Barbadian cracked the policeman over the head with a piece of wood. The Barbadians then were "hurried aboard the train, which steamed off for Panama [City]," local officials wishing to avoid further trouble.[5]

Barbadians at the turn of the century were described to be "in the habit" of finding employment as butlers and servants in northern Brazil, mainly in Belém, a principal stop along the steamer routes. Because their work involved no signed contracts, Barbadians in several cases were stranded in Brazil without either a passport to prove their identities or enough money to pay for return passage.[6]

Barbadians also traveled up the Amazon River from Belém. Within a decade, black Barbadian men—perhaps as many as two thousand—were engaged as railroad construction workers on the Madeira-Mamoré railroad, more than 2,000 miles upriver from Belém near the border of Bolivia. From 1907 to 1912 more than twenty thousand workers of many nationalities worked on the railroad. Probably most were black West Indians, and all West Indians on the rail construction project—regardless of island of origin—were described as *Barbadianos* in the Upper Amazon at the time, a probable indication of Barbadians' numerical superiority among West Indians working there.[7]

Unlike earlier emigrants to the mouth of the Amazon, black Barbadians destined for the Madeira-Mamoré project were recruited at home and should have had written work contracts. But in 1910 the steamer *Oteri*, with 160 laborers aboard, left Barbados for the Upper Amazon although no contracts had yet been signed in Bridgetown, a clear violation of the current Emigration Act.[8] The recruiting agent of the *Oteri*, who probably took other boatloads illegally from Barbados, was W.B. Spiller, a particularly unscrupulous labor procurer. Promising extravagant wages throughout Panama and the Caribbean, Spiller—who owned a gambling casino in Colón—was wanted by United States and Cuban authorities for illegal labor recruiting.[9] Once in Brazil, Barbadian laborers discovered that the railroad company stores overcharged for the cassava-based food and that workers had to build their own makeshift camps. Also, medical facilities were inadequate and fever rampant. Barbadian officials at home publicly chided those who had chosen to work in territories governed by capricious and cruel South Americans, a miscalculation that had led some unfortunate Barbadians in Brazil to be "sold into bondage."[10]

But laying railroad track while attempting to cope with both fever and unfair labor bosses was child's play compared with the conditions encountered by a few Barbadians deep in the Amazon in the disputed area between Peru and Colombia. In April 1906, the *Barbados Advocate* published a letter from Barbadian workers whose location was specified only as "Peru":

> Sir—We are sorry to trobble you But pleas to put this in your papers about the labours that left barbadoes On the Second of march 1905 for peru South America they have not delt with us according to the Contract they took us from Barbados as labours. after we reach there they refuse to give us any wages according to the Contract saying they pay to the Government of Barbados a Sum of £150 for each head of us and now we are Suffering day by day as Slaves we thought that we was going there as labours but we found out afterwards there is Slaves where we are. We cannot get away for there is soldiers guarding us. That is because they carry us where there is no Council that we can apply to.
> So we ask you kindly Sir to Drop it in the papers for us.
> We Remain yours Obedient Servants,
>
> John Clarke
> Joseph Dawson
> Isaac Conliffe
> Joseph Nurse[11]

Almost certainly the letter had come from the Putumayo River district east of Iquitos and far west of Manaus. Since the turn of the century, unconfirmed rumors had circulated from priests and other travelers in the area of Indians enslaved, tortured, and killed by the infamous Arana brothers and their armed guards who had terrified aboriginal tribesmen into collecting and processing native rubber. In 1904, Julio Arana recruited and sent two hundred black Barbadian "wardens" from Bridgetown to supervise and guard the Putumayo labor force. Two years later, forty of the Barbadians were repatriated to Bridgetown through Iquitos after reporting that they themselves had been beaten and abused. Amid continuing reports of murders and other atrocities directed toward British subjects, the British consul-general at Rio de Janeiro, Roger Casement, traveled officially to the Putumayo rubber camps in September 1910. Casement interrogated several Barbadians who reported floggings and murders. He eventually brought fourteen Barbadians downriver, nine of whom decided to stay in Manaus to look for work. The remaining five came home to Barbados.[12]

Roving as individuals to far places seeking jobs and also traveling under contract, black Barbadians at the turn of the century

"Hit de Manager in de Head" 111

sometimes encountered inhumane conditions, particularly in the brutual colonial atmosphere of the Congo and the isolated anarchy of the Amazon headwaters. Barbadian officials and planters were doubtless correct that black laborers traveling far afield, without any legal protection whatever, were vulnerable to insults and injuries worse than at home. Terrifying reports of atrocities committed by rubber barons and murderous soldiers, moreover, were ammunition that planters, estate managers, and newspaper reporters passed on to Barbadian laborers with a clear conscience. After that, it took little imagination for any individual considering travel abroad to assume that all places outside the British realm were haunted by murderers and slavedrivers.

After the first few hundred Barbadians had tested the conditions in Panama, however, a planter or manager could do little to arrest the flow of migrants there, even with the shocking stories of horrible conditions "abroad." A Barbados newspaper cartoon in February 1905 showed two black men conversing. The first commented that advice from his manager ("mangah") suggested a conservative attitude toward heading for Panama. The second, doubting that a manager had any notion of the problems black workers faced, had already made up his mind to sign up with Mr. Brewster ("Brusta"), the emigration agent who was the local representative for the Panama Canal authorities:

> Thomas: Bwoy, wah yu gwine to Panama fuh? I allus hare muh mangah seh, bettah fuh bare de ill we hab, dan fuh fly to dem we duzzn no nuffin bouk.
> Jones: Da is berry good tawk fuh a mángah, but ess he bin hah uh wife, seben childun an a mudder-in-lah, an no wuk fuh do he wudda fly heself sumwa. Ta, ta man Ise gwine fuh se missa Brusta nung, muhself fuh I is orf to Panama.[13]

William Karner and the Bridgetown Recruiting Station

The decision to locate and maintain the Panama Canal's main labor recruiting station in Barbados was affected by the attitudes of both United States officials and those of the colonial authorities of particular Caribbean territories. Isthmian Canal Commission officials knew that they would need West Indian laborers for the job, but they did not know how many or which islands they would come from. American officials initially had hoped to recruit the great majority of their workers from nearby and populous Jamaica. But early in 1905 the Jamaican governor forbade the establishment of an ICC recruiting station in Jamaica because so many Jamaicans had died earlier in Panama while working for the French. The commission authorities were sorely disappointed.[14]

The ICC officials then began systematically to consider other Caribbean islands as potential labor sources, encountering problems in several of the places. The British Windwards and Leewards were considered unsuitable by ICC authorities because of the relatively low populations, recent officials' hostility toward American advances, and what the Americans perceived as direct rule from the British Colonial Office. Populous Martinique was important initially as a source of laborers, but the Continental French government subsequently discouraged labor movements to Panama from all the French Antilles. Haiti and the Dominican Republic were dismissed as "Negro republics" whose inhabitants "lacked incentive to work." By late 1906, only Barbados, the Bahamas, the Danish West Indies, and the Dutch West Indies were considered attractive areas for worker recruitment by ICC-authorities, and on the last islands Venezuelan railroads competed for labor.[15]

The ICC eventually decided that Barbados was the most attractive. The island was relatively close, densely populated, its inhabitants spoke English, the government was somewhat independent of direct British rule and not unfriendly, and it was served by reliable, adaptable steamer lines. But nearly as important as Barbados's objective characteristics in its becoming the principal recruiting center for the Panama Canal were the activities of a single individual.

William J. Karner, an American engineer in the Canal Zone, left Colón via the Royal Mail Steamer on December 23, 1904, with instructions "to arrange for laborers to assist in the construction work of the Panama Canal."[16] On January 3, 1905, Karner called on Governor Gilbert T. Carter of Barbados at Government House in Bridgetown, where he submitted a sample contract for Barbadian laborers that was subsequently modified by the local attorney general. Carter agreed to support a labor-recruiting campaign in Barbados, although he warned Karner of the "home loving" nature of the island's people and their wary attitude toward emigration in light of recent experiences some of them had had abroad.

Karner then began to plan for both short-term and long-term enrollment of Barbadian workers for Panama. He hired S.E. Brewster, one of two local licensed emigration agents, on January 11 as the ICC's official representative on Barbados. Brewster had formerly published a newspaper in Bridgetown and had acted locally as an assessor, sanitary inspector, and road inspector; he was reputed to be honest and reliable by several Bridgetown businessmen.[17] Karner and Brewster then arranged for the immediate publication of service contracts, medical examination forms, and press notices so that as many men (no women were contract workers) as possible might ship out on the RMS *La Plata* sailing for Colón on January 18. Disappointed at the relative lack of enthusiasm among the local black populace about the prospects he offered to them, Karner wrote a letter to the *Barbados Advocate* that was published on January 23. Karner's letter, addressing rumors circulating about unemployment in the Canal Zone, carried assurances that the construction effort was sponsored by and under the direct supervision of the government of the United States and that there was "plenty of work" in Panama "at good wages."[18] After laborers' ships left the Bridgetown wharf bound for Panama, the workers' passage and food to Colón would be paid by the United States government, according to Karner. Furthermore, the transportation itself would be aboard the Royal Mail Steam Packet Company vessels, which had been contracted for by the United States.[19]

William Karner, whose Barbados recruiting effort would soon be very successful, often left the gathering and processing of workers to others because of other recruiting sojourns that took him, unsuccessfully, to Jamaica and France. Nevertheless, he returned frequently enough to ensure an efficient operation in Bridgetown. He was conscientious and, from all reports, treated everyone with honesty and fairness. Karner was sensitive to local laws and allowed Barbadian officials the final decisions about the wording of contracts. He possessed none of the tactlessness that British and Barbadian officials had learned to dislike in other

Americans, but he did have the Yankee resourcefulness and push that they admired. During the 1907-9 yellow fever quarantine period, for example, when the Royal Mail line refused to dock at Barbados, Karner engaged private steamers and directed them to cruise about for six days with laborers. Then, if no yellow fever appeared on board, the ships proceeded to Colón.[20]

It is worth speculating briefly what might have happened had the ICC's other recruiting agent in the Caribbean, S.W. Settoon, been assigned to Barbados. Settoon resided in the French Antilles for most of 1905-7, journeying to Grenada and St. Lucia early in 1906 to arrange for the shipment of a small contingent of laborers to the canal. Settoon's tactless behavior in Grenada had inspired the local governor to write to the Canal Zone to ask if he was indeed an official representative of the United States government.[21] In the French islands his inability to converse adequately in French, his inattention to instructions, and the rudeness he displayed in correspondence with steamship officials created confusion and even hardship. On Martinique in January 1907, hundreds of prospective emigrants had to walk up to thirty miles back home from an overcrowded vessel because of Settoon's miscalculations. The following August, Settoon complained from Guadeloupe of being "awfully tired of this place," and he subsequently moved on to the Danish islands. In December 1907, Settoon contacted Governor Cold of the Danish West Indies for permission to establish a recruiting station in Charlotte Amalie. When Cold requested that Settoon produce his credentials and observe local laws, an angry Settoon threatened the governor that he would "skin" the Danish islands, not leaving him "a messenger boy." Settoon's indelicate remarks, which he subsequently attributed to the Danish governor's imperfect English, were the subject of an official complaint by the Danish ambassador to Elihu Root, the American Secretary of state.[22]

Without Karner as the ICC's representative to Barbados, Barbadians still would have seen the Panama Canal as a source of money, and—as so many Jamaicans did—probably would have traveled there by the thousands without contracts. Furthermore, the changes in American perceptions of the abilities of West Indian laborers on the canal—from initial contempt to an eventual (yet grudging) appreciation—would have occurred. But had an individual like Settoon been the agent sent to Barbados, the island's colonial officials, with ruffled feathers, quite likely would have denied the siting of a recruiting station and the cooperation they gave Karner. Most important, the magnitude of both Barbadians emigrating and money coming back home likely would have been much less. Without Karner, Barbadian history early in the twentieth century might have been considerably different.

The Exodus to Panama

The initial hesitation of black Barbadians about emigrating to Panama came from Central America's despotic image, perceptions embellished and magnified by warnings from local Barbadian planters and managers. More important was Panama's deserved reputation as a worker's graveyard. Augmenting the fear of disease were the warnings of an overabundance of labor already in Panama as reported by Barbados newspapers. In November 1905 the *Barbados Advocate* described the experiences of sixty-two Barbadians who had just returned from Colón. They said that jobs were available and money was there, but they "practically stole away from the place" in fear of losing their lives. Besides having to cope with the "trillions of mosquitos" in Panama, they had grown accustomed to seeing the corpses of fellow workers "interred almost the same place that the drinking water had to be taken from." The recruiting agent Brewster lost no time in composing a rejoinder about the squeamish attitude of the returned workers. In any country, explained Brewster from the security of his Bridgetown office, one could find "timid men" who could be expected to return home at "the first convenient opportunity."[23]

But black Barbadians did not always have to rely exclusively on conflicting newspaper reports for information about conditions in Panama. Besides those who traveled to South America and beyond in the late nineteenth century, some had gone to Central America. By 1885 probably well over a thousand Barbadians had traveled to Panama to work on the French canal, and many had subsequently appealed officially for Barbadian government assistance to be repatriated when the French effort failed.[24] Reliable

ble data do not exist as to exactly how many Barbadians had gone or stayed in the late nineteenth century. By 1904, however, at least some black Barbadians had had family members living in Panama for years and also writing home. I located an old man in St. Michael parish who went to Panama as a contract laborer in 1907. In Colón he stayed with an older brother who had already been there "quite a few years."

Personal contact with families and friends already in Panama, however, was an experience limited to only a few black Barbadians in 1904, and these contacts lacked the contagious effect of actually seeing the recently returned Panama veterans coming home to the estate tenantries and hearing firsthand of the opportunities and prospects on the isthmus. Brewster had predicted to Karner that the Barbadians' wary attitudes about work on the Panama Canal would change in time, and he was right. It is unnecessary, even if it were possible, to establish exactly when the reluctance and fear of the unknown was overcome by the sights and sounds of money and success. But it must have occurred within months after Karner's first attempts in January 1905 to fill the *La Plata*'s decks with laborers.

The change of attitude came suddenly, and it electrified the black workers of the rural parishes of Barbados. *Craze* and *frenzy* were terms used commonly by contemporary observers to describe the black workers' enthusiasm to head for Panama where "money was like apples on a tree." This saying, which I was told at least twenty times while interviewing old Barbadians, suggests the infectious, exciting atmosphere that must have swept the black tenantries. By early 1906, it was "hardly possible to go ahead with the crop" in St. James and St. Peter parishes because men "have returned [from Panama] with money which they are spending in sight of those who did not go," and the latter were leaving for Panama themselves. In the same year, the increase in cash carried home by the "hundreds of men" who had returned from Panama was noticeably reflected in more money being spent by the black working class at Christmas.[25] The recruiting for the Panama Canal, begun by Karner with public pronouncements and newspaper advertisements, had achieved its true success through the informal verbal and visual chain reaction among the black working peoples themselves:

After the stream of men was started, and the influence of the returned men on their friends and neighbours became fully felt, the state of affairs became gradually modified, and finally entirely altered. The returned men have been practically recruiting agents of the most effective sort, using their influence in every parish of Barbados, and with the result that now the voluntary applicants for labour contracts are five or six times as numerous as the needs for men.[26]

The excitement of actually seeing men leaving the rural parishes for Bridgetown, with their eventual destination Panama, was a further source of enthusiasm, and it inspired the kinds of exuberant shouts and boasts as those reported by J. Challenor Lynch in the Legislative Council. The departure from rural parishes also gave families and loved ones cause to weep for the young men they might never see again. Departing men walking to Bridgetown from the farthest points of the island stopped en route at the chattel houses of friends who also were going, and their numbers swelled accordingly as the groups of walking men approached town. In 1907, Beresford Skinner, of Checker Hall, St. Lucy, departed on foot with others bound for Bridgetown and eventually Panama. As the group snowballed in size, they stopped to collect a departing friend whose wife was crying and holding him. Finally, even after the waiting men explained to him that they had left their wives home crying as well, the man decided to stay. Skinner himself eventually returned from Panama and bought a small land plot in St. Lucy parish with the money he had earned. And, the story goes, the same wife who tearfully had kept her husband from going never tired in later life of nagging her husband for not going away to earn money "the way Beresford Skinner did!"[27]

The sights and sounds of the Panama craze also included the extraordinary attention given to the postman's arrival in the black tenantries. Most of the emigrants were literate and could write home, according to elderly informants, and those who were not had friends write on their behalf. A retired school headmaster at the eastern end of St. Philip parish in 1982 remembered clearly "the postman coming down the road and all the people who had men in Panama running to meet him." But the letters home often brought sorrow, and thousands of black Barbadian families learned through the mail of a son's or father's death. An elderly woman who can barely remember when she was a child at Pie Corner, St. Lucy, does recollect that the postman's arrival left some of the people in tears: "Once as a small girl I heard some moaning and sobbing, and we went to the house it was coming from. There I saw a mother holding an envelope with a black border on it and crying. That meant that her son had died in Panama."

William Karner's main problem of locating enough men to fill the decks of Panama-bound steamers early in 1905 soon became a problem of managing the crush of applicants at the ICC office in Bridgetown. By 1908, Karner always had three to five times the number of applicants he needed for any one sailing, and when calls went out for contract laborers, up to three thousand men crowded Trafalgar Square. Canal officials routinely engaged a score of policemen to control the throngs. The police sent the men to the upstairs recruiting station in groups of one hundred, where some were dismissed for being either too young or too old. A doctor examined the remaining applicants for trachoma, heart trouble, and rupture. The medical examination was rigorous; of the original one hundred, usually twenty "fine and fit" men passed. When they were told they were bound for Panama, the men began to sing and congratulate one another. Then they received vaccinations, signed their contracts, and "went prancing down-stairs to spread the good news among their friends in the square."[28]

The service contract itself was a one-page document signed by S.E. Brewster and the individual laborer and witnessed and signed by a police magistrate. The contract declared the ICC's willingness to accept the worker in the Canal Zone "as a first class laborer, for five hundred days actual labor" at the rate of one dollar per ten-hour day in U.S. dollars or the Panamanian equivalent. The commission further stipulated in the contract that the laborer would receive free "transportation to Colón, medical attendance, medicine, and quarters without furniture," while employed by the ICC and return passage to Barbados after the five hundred days. The contract also served as the laborer's identity card. It carried his contract number and was to be shown "at any time on demand" to an ICC representative so that a laborer's identity might be established and checked.29

In addition to his contract, the worker received a pink vaccination slip. When the emigrant eventually boarded the ship for Panama he exchanged the slip for a meal ticket while his name was checked on the official list. This routine was intended to discourage and prevent stowaways, but it was often unsuccessful. Men who had passed the physical examination were occasionally known to sell either their vaccination certificate or contract document to those who had not, thereby hoping to create two places for Panama with one set of documents. Swindlers with bogus documents frequently duped those anxious to go to Panama. Moreover, when contract workers actually were boarding vessels, stowaways accompanied them and attempted to disappear into the crowd amid the confusion at the top of the gangplank. In replying to complaints from Panama about Barbadian stowaways arriving in Colón along with bona fide contract workers, Karner expressed surprise, not that there were stowaways, but that so few had gone illegally. Karner assured ICC officials in Colón that he was doing everything possible from his end to prevent illegals from boarding the steamers, but controlling near-desperate individuals among crowds leaving for Panama was a good deal easier prescribed than carried out. Karner himself had seen men paddle into Carlisle Bay on fishing sloops and wooden lighters and then scale the sides of the steamships, dangling from ropes and chains and asking for a hand from those already aboard.30

On sailing day for Panama, black workers of the rural parishes, as well as from Bridgetown, often walked all the way to the wharf to see friends and kinsmen leave. The ever-enlarging groups of people heading toward town therefore not always consisted only of those departing. Even at the height of the cane harvest, when black men of the tenantries could count on a full day's wage work, many chose instead to see friends and loved ones depart. In May 1908, throughout parts of St. Joseph parish, many of the canecutters did not report for duty on a Monday when parish mills were grinding and the crop reaping was in full swing. Planters prosecuted the absentees for a breach of contract, although they knew that the workers had gone to Bridgetown to witness "the departure of their relatives and friends for Panama."[31]

The actual steamer departure usually took place within a week after a prospective emigrant had passed the physical examination. An old man who had been a contract worker to Panama told of walking to the wharf from Black Rock, St. Michael, with his mother. He had never owned shoes, but he had bought a pair after receiving a Panama contract. He carried a canvas satchel containing his clothing and, in the other arm, a wooden deck chair. Some men carried guitars, and a few brought accordians.

The scene at the Bridgetown wharf captured the essence of what Panama meant, and would come to mean, for the black working class of Barbados. The loading of cargo and laborers began at dawn, but the steamer itself did not leave Carlisle Bay until late afternoon. "[I]t seemed that the whole population of darkest Africa was there," recorded Arthur Bullard, an American observer on a sailing day in Bridgetown. The departing men had been accompanied by mothers, wives, and sisters, all of whom crowded the dockside in their Sunday best. Each contract worker left the crowd as his number was called, displayed his vaccination slip and the mark on his arm to an ICC official, and then departed by lighter with others for the waiting steamer. As each lighter slipped away, parents, wives, and children pressed forward for a final wave.

The partings of families at the dock were accompanied by an array of emotions. Leave-taking and farewells among the men "for the most part . . . were light heartedly exchanged, as if the men were going on a brief holiday trip." But mothers found it difficult to hide their grief, and they wept openly when their sons left. Wives and sisters sobbed as well. Throughout the day the lighters carried the emigrants from the waiting crowd to the anchored steamship until only those who had come to wave good-bye remained at the wharf. Then the steamer drew up its anchor and started west for Panama. Those left behind stayed at the dockside and watched until the ship disappeared over the horizon.[32]

Arthur Bullard accompanied a boatload of black Barbadian contract workers from Bridgetown to Colón. He noted that, as the men clambered aboard in Barbados with baggage and deck chairs, they grouped together into religious clusters amid the strange shipboard surroundings. The Anglicans took to the port side of the vessel and the "Nonconformists" (who subsequently split into smaller subgroups) the starboard. To compensate for the unnerving combination of excitement and sorrow that each young man must have felt, the rival groups began to sing different religious hymns. As the steamer left Carlisle Bay, the men all collaborated in a secular song that they apparently had learned from those who had preceded them:

> Fever and ague all day long
>   At Panama, at Panama,
> Wish you were dead before very long
>   At Panama, at Panama[33]

The dramatic wharfside scene of the Barbadian men with their luggage and deck chairs leaving the women behind was begun in 1904 and repeated over and over until 1913, when the last contract laborers left Barbados for Panama. But nearly as soon as the all-male contract workers had begun traveling to Panama, black Barbadians—both male and female—had begun to pay their own passages to Colón in order to join the men and also to find their own jobs. In early June 1908, the *Thames* was delayed in its departure from Carlisle Bay to Colón because an estimated 300 stowaways had to be retrieved and brought back to shore. Finally, the *Thames* took leave, carrying with her 250 contract workers and roughly the same number who had paid their own passage, "about one third being women."[34]

Without legal requirements to register with any official before departure, the noncontract women and men left Barbados—and many returned—unrecorded. Steamer passage cost $14, and Panamanian authorities required another $15 in gold for "show money" (plus quarantine and varying vaccination fees) before one could land in Colón.[35] The show money was required of all incoming migrants, even those who arrived occasionally by sailing schooner rather than taking the six-day steamer trip. On July 13, 1909, for instance, the schooner *Viola* arrived at Colón from Barbados, one of three sailing vessels that had come from Bridgetown in the past month. Aboard the *Viola* were black

Barbadian men, women, and children as well as sacks of Barbadian yams and other vegetables. The port authorities at Colón were impressed that the Barbadian migrants, as was their habit, nearly all possessed the required sum of money necessary to be allowed ashore.[36]

Almost certainly most of the money carried by the passengers on board the *Viola* had been sent back home from men who had already gone ahead to Panama. But as soon as the newcomers arrived, they too began to earn their own money, in both Panama and the Canal Zone, in a variety of ways. Men worked as waiters, butlers, policemen, hospital orderlies, tailors, shopkeepers, cobblers, and in nearly any other skilled or semiskilled job imaginable. It was, moreover, rare for one individual to hold a single job or job type while in Panama, and many black Barbadian men who had traveled to the Canal Zone as contract workers soon found positions other than laboring on shovel crews. A number of men acted as vegetable "speculators," carrying large bags of yams, sweet potatoes, and other homegrown staples via sail and steamer from Barbados to feed the workforce in Panama.

Women traveled to Colón and joined their husbands and sweethearts, using remitted money to pay for the passage, and they also traveled to Panama on their own. Women were shopkeepers and worked as laundresses and seamstresses. The Barbadian newspapers and official government publications attempted, almost certainly to no avail, occasionally to regulate and control the movements of Barbadian women to Panama. The notice in 1908 that it was "inadvisable for girls" to journey to Panama because of a surplus of domestics looking for work there, for example, probably discouraged few black Barbadian women who already had planned to go to Panama to look for either work or their husbands.[37] Children too were brought to Panama by relatives after both parents had become entrenched in the isthmian labor force. A seventy-seven-year-old Barbadian who now lives in St. James parish was born one month after her father departed for Colón as a contract laborer. Her mother then left in 1909 and took a job ironing clothes in a laundry run by the ICC. By 1912 the mother had saved enough to send money home for her little girl and godmother to travel together to Panama by steamer. Eventually, in 1924, the elderly St. James resident returned

"Hit de Manager in de Head" 123

"home" as a young woman to Barbados—a place she could barely remember.

Enumerating the Emigrants

A total of 19,900 Barbadian men emigrated to the Panama Canal as contract workers recruited by the Isthmian Canal Commission between the years 1904 and 1913. The breakdown by year for Barbadian contract workers was 1904:404; 1905:3,019; 1906:6,510; 1907:3,242; 1908:2,592; 1909:3,605; 1913:528.[38] (From 1910 to 1912, the ICC recruited only 1,100 men altogether, none from Barbados.) The ICC officially declined to recruit anyone under twenty years of age, although S.E. Brewster simply took the recruits' words for their ages, and as a result, many teenagers signed up. "They never asked for proof of age. If you were big enough and strong enough, they took you," reminisced one old man who had been in Panama.

Beyond the lower age limit and the physical examination, ICC authorities placed no official requirements on its contract workers for particular work experience or background. It is therefore not possible to delineate with any accuracy the "type" of individual who left as a contract worker versus the "type" who stayed home. The conventional wisdom that black Barbadian tenantry residents were the contract workers while "middle-class" artisans of mixed blood paid their own way to Panama can never really be confirmed or denied, even if it were a testable assertion. Of course, the large number of contract emigrants alone, combined with old peoples' recollections and surviving photographs of canal-bound "deckers," tell us that the overwhelming majority of contract workers were black Barbadians. But whether they had all formerly been plantation field workers or mill mechanics and carpenters in disproportionate numbers would, among other problems, involve the construction of typologies of very doubtful quality. Nor do the recorded American perceptions of the character of the black Barbadian workforce help to clarify the issue, because the American supervisors, as old Barbadians remember, were egalitarian only in that they treated all black West Indians with equal contempt and disrespect. Occasional reports about the West Indian workforce in Panama, such as the comment that "many experienced artisans" numbered "between 4,000 and 5,000" among the black West Indians, probably can never be confirmed.[39] Nor can these artisans be differentiated on the basis of either home island or contract versus noncontract emigrants from such vague scraps of evidence.

Almost certainly those few who already were relatively successful stayed in Barbados rather than emigrating, but beyond this vaguest of generalizations, the Panama emigration seems to have taken field laborers, shopkeepers, and schoolteachers alike—even as contract laborers—if elderly informants' recollections are accurate. In questioning old Barbadians about who went and who stayed, the unvarying response was that "everybody went who could." The contagious character of the rush to Panama doubtless touched all black Barbadians, and the obvious financial success that returnees displayed reduced the caution about Panama that the preceding generation had had toward emigrating. It is not difficult to imagine, moreover, how attractive Panama must have been to groups of young, unattached, adventurous, and unemployed men of the Bridgetown area who had seen so many others leave. A note from a 1909 police report, for example, gave the names and addresses of stowaways, all of whom received two weeks' hard labor for attempting to sneak aboard a steamer headed for Colón: "Lance Corp. William Cole charged Charles Flemming of Beckles Hill, William Parris of Brittons Hill, Clarence Harding of Nelson Street, George Bynoe of Hastings, John Brewster and Cephas Brewster with boarding the RMS *Solent* without first obtaining leave from the master of the said ship."[40]

Although the number of contract workers from Barbados were accounted for, in all likelihood, with relative precision, the noncontract emigrants were not counted at all. "There is no proper record kept of the emigration from Barbados to other countries" noted Henry W. Lofty, the compiler of the 1921 census of Barbados.[41] Lofty was mindful of the net decrease of 15,671 between the 1911 census (171,983) and the 1921 census of the island (156,312), but he had no way of knowing the magnitude of emigration that had contributed to the decline and even less knowledge of the unenumerated emigrants' destinations. The 1911 census recorder, E.P. Boyce, had troubled himself to compare the 182,306 people of 1891 (there was no 1901 census) with the 171,983 of 1911, calculate the natural increase from annual births and deaths, and thereby to arrive at a net loss of 48,625 people during those two decades "attributed to emigration."[42] But the destinations of these people could be, of course, only suppositions.

The number of Barbadians who emigrated to the Panama Canal can therefore only be estimated; 25,000 noncontract emigrants added to the 20,000 contract workers for a grand total of 45,000 seems to me reasonable.[43] Fragmentary returnee data are of some assistance in attempting to quantify the magnitude of the exodus. The Bridgetown harbor master counted slightly more than 20,000 Barbadians returning from Colón between 1906 and 1915, an issue discussed further in chapter 5. But how many returned before and after? And how many emigrants (and returnees) were counted two or three times going each way? Contract laborers were not unknown to return to Barbados and then to ship out again for Panama a year or so later. A 1907 newspaper cartoon of "Janie" depicted two Barbadian market women conversing after not seeing each other for months. Janie's friend, noting her lengthy absence from the market, asked if Janie had been ill:

> No darling sweet love uh has bin down pun de Canal Zone
> Fuh look aftah Petah welfare as well as me own
> An uh now tek a bus back up fuh look fuh Aunt Jane
> Fuh bring sum money fuh she an uh den gwine back agen.[44]

Emigration data for 5,728 individual contract workers who went from Barbados to Panama during 1906–7, apparently the only surviving data at the microlevel that exist for this period, are available in handwritten "emigrants' registers" at the Barbados Department of Archives. Nearly every entry includes the emigrant's name, reported age, address (village, tenantry, or Bridgetown street), and mother's or wife's name.[45] The information from these registers is arrayed by parish in table 4. If St. Michael and Christchurch together are considered the urban parishes of Barbados, then one interpretation from table 4 could be that urban residents, who constituted 45 percent of the total Barbadian population in 1911, contributed decidedly fewer (37

Table 4. A Portion of the 1906-1907 Contract Laborers to Panama by Barbadian Parish

	Contract Laborers	% of Total	Total Population 1911 Census	% of Total
St. Andrew	221	4	8,159	5
St. Peter	515	9	9,423	5
St. George	597	10	14,329	8
St. John	306	5	10,137	6
St. Lucy	415	7	8,951	5
St. Michael	1,757	31	57,382	33
St. Joseph	227	4	7,837	5
St. Philip	467	8	17,023	10
St. James	507	9	10,615	6
St. Thomas	360	6	7,921	5
Christchurch	356	6	20,206	12
Totals	5,728		171,983	

Source: Data from Emigrants registers, Barbados Department of Archives; Boyce, *Report on the Census of Barbados 1911.*

percent) emigrants than expected. The relatively high white and mixed-blood populations of these two parishes probably best account for these observations. The relatively higher than expected numbers of emigrants for Panama among the populations of the Leeward parishes of St. James and St. Peter also are interesting and might be explained by the proximity of these two parishes to Bridgetown and Carlisle Bay, and therefore the actual site of departing Panama steamers. It is doubtful, however, that on an island as small as Barbados, where pedestrian locomotion already was the dominant mode of personal travel and where market women routinely walked to town from the farthest parishes, that distance between Bridgetown and a laborer's cottage played an important role in influencing the decision to travel to Panama.

"Hit de Manager in de Head" 127

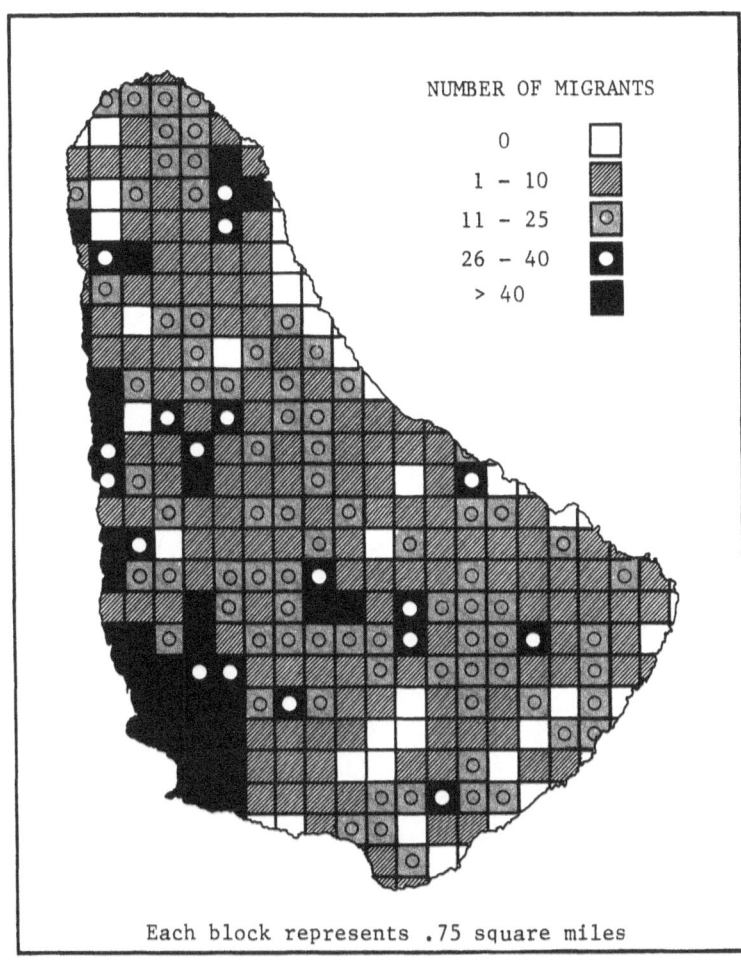

Figure 2. Contract workers to Panama, 1906–1907. Data from "Emigrants' Register, 1906–1907," Barbados Department of Archives, Black Rock, St. Michael.

Figure 2 displays a finer-grained portrayal of the home locations of the 5,728 contract workers. This map, of course, in large part reflects the population density of Barbados in 1906–7 because absolute numbers of emigrants are shown, and the more densely populated areas, as expected, sent more people. As well as Bridgetown and surrounding St. Michael parish being the obvious leading area for sending emigrants to Panama, however, parts of St. George and St. Lucy parishes display extremely high numbers of emigrants. These observations highlight the extraordinarily high rural population densities in some parts of Barbados in the first decade of the twentieth century.

Figures 3 and 4, both showing St. Michael parish, magnify the scale further. The data from the emigrants' registers were plotted

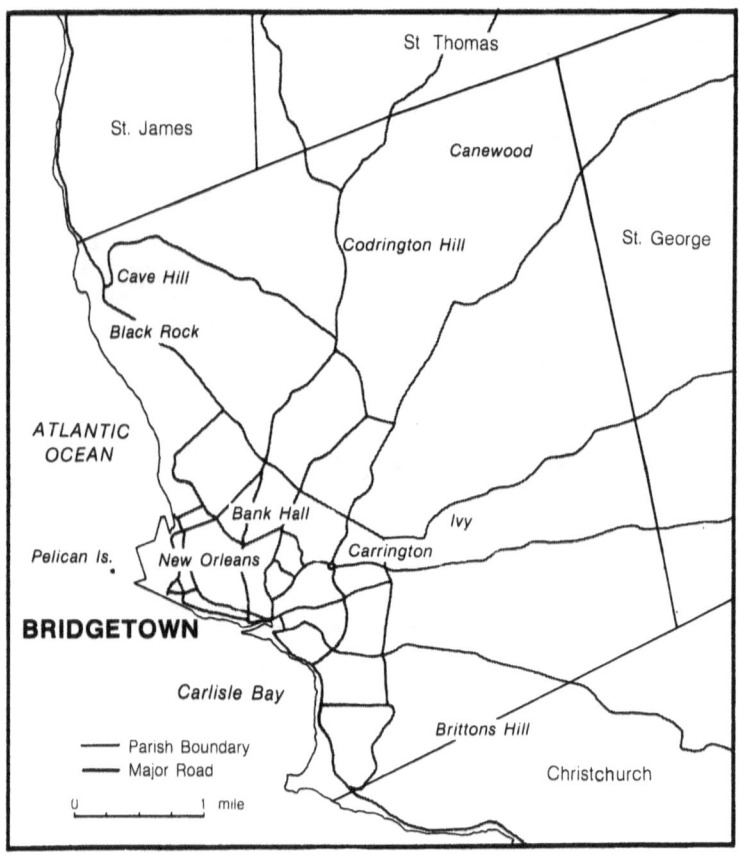

Figure 3. St. Michael parish, Barbados, in 1920.

"Hit de Manager in de Head" 129

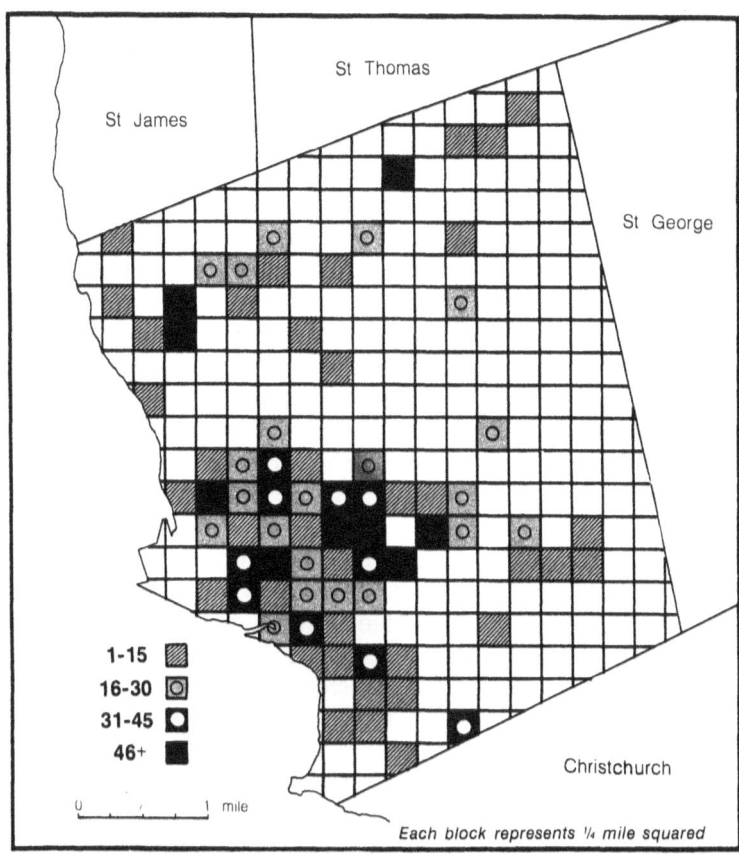

Figure 4. Contract workers from St. Michael parish to Panama, 1906–1907. Data from "Emigrants' Register, 1906–1907," Barbados Department of Archives, Black Rock, St. Michael.

onto a 1920-vintage base map, and the contemporary street map of the Bridgetown area was used to help in locating emigrants' residences.[46] The Black Rock-Cave Hill area of the northwestern part of the parish emerges as an extremely important sending area. These data may have been plotted into too confined an area, because "Black Rock" probably was a more vague term, meaning roughly the northern end of the parish, given by departing emigrants filing past a seated record keeper who was writing names and addresses very quickly. Nonetheless, figure 4 portrays the incredibly high population densities of the black urban tenantries of the time—the New Orleans, Carrington Village, and Ivy areas—whose tiny alleyways and even smaller, closely packed houses were remarked upon at the time by so many government officials.

Further observations from the handwritten emigrants' registers render a clearer picture of the workforce and of the emigration from Barbados in general. By far the most common age given to the ICC record keepers was "twenty," and often six or seven emigrants in a row announced their age as "twenty," presumably teenagers suddenly adding a year or more to their real ages in order to meet the ICC age standards. Teenagers could emigrate as contract laborers to other destinations with impunity because along with the lists of Colón-bound contract workers were a sprinkling of mainly teenage emigrants bound for "Brazil" (presumably the Madeira-Mamoré railway) and also to St. Croix as cane cutters. In a few cases, departing contract emigrants for the Panama Canal gave two different home addresses on Barbados, usually one in the Bridgetown area and one in a rural parish, listing both wife *and* mother as next of kin. Although government officials at the time insisted that a person be assigned to a single parish for possible poor-relief purposes and the located laborer statutes also sought to immobilize individual black Barbadians, there seems to have been a good deal more intra-island residential mobility among members of the black working class than is normally pointed out.

The emigrants' register data also remind us that a few non-Barbadians also left Bridgetown as contract workers. Other West Indians traveled to Barbados via steamer deck passage as well as sailing schooners and fishing sloops. Then they signed on as contract workers with the ICC and left for Panama from Barbados. Almost all of the non-Barbadians listed in the registers for the 1906–7 period, besides the 5,728 from Barbados, were from other Commonwealth Caribbean territories: Antigua, 36; British Guiana, 20; Grenada, 19; Montserrat, 6; St. Kitts, 5; St. Lucia, 49; St. Vincent, 103; Trinidad, 105. An intriguing characteristic of the non-Barbadian emigrants whose names appear on the register is that so many of them had Barbadian names, particularly those from Trinidad and the Layou district of St. Vincent. Apparently the extraisland network of families that had been established by Barbadian emigrants late in the nineteenth century had been activated during the Panama Canal era. And former Barbadians, or even children of former Barbadians, then traveled back home, probably staying with kin in Barbados, in order to take advantage of the recruiting station there.

Black workers of Barbadian heritage even came back from non-British territories, further suggesting the attraction of the possible Panama emigration and also the extent of earlier migrations away. Beresford Lashley, age thirty and presumably a former resident of Barbados, was the only contract worker, among the nearly 6,000, from Martinique. Lashley apparently had traveled back home to stay with relatives until he could leave again for a new destination. He sailed to Colón with hundreds of fellow Barbadians and other West Indians on February 6, 1907.

The Planter Reaction

J. Challenor Lynch, who had passed on to his colleagues in the Barbados Legislative Council the story of hostile shouts from crowds of young blacks headed for Panama, was only one of many among Barbados's white elite dismayed by the Panama exodus. In the short run, the loss of a few workers posed no problem and might even reduce parish relief roles. But the loss of many thousands would destroy the labor redundancy underpinning the low wages which, in turn, supported the antiquated character of the Barbadian sugar industry itself. Even with the recent agricultural grant from Britain and the availability of planter loans, many more estates soon would tumble into Chancery Court receivership if planters had to raise wages because of a thinned-out labor force. More immediately, some of the workers already had begun clamoring as individuals and in small groups for more money, threatening to leave if wage increases were not granted. For the first time, black Barbadians could exert at least slight leverage at home for better living conditions. In 1982, eighty-seven-year-old Douglas Gay of Niles Corner, Christchurch, could still recall a laborers' song that he had heard as a young boy in St. Thomas parish:

> We want more wages, we want it now,
> And if we don't get it, we going to Panama
> Yankees say they want we down there,
> We want more wages, we want it now.[47]

Although the threats to emigrate did not lead to wage increases, the rousing marches of black estate workers to sign up at the Bridgetown ICC office preoccupied white Barbadians. At first the planters were unable to agree whether they were losing their most capable workers to Panama or the lazy types who were better off gone anyway. A planter newspaper in August 1907—well after the emigration craze had taken hold—asserted that the emigration had doubtless taken away "a much greater proportion of the lawless and idle than of the industrious."[48] But probably that assertion was as much spiteful rhetoric as anything else, because just as many observers bemoaned that the laziest and least competent were the ones staying behind.

Most planters did agree, however, that with the thousands of men already in Panama and the prospects of others following them, many of the traditional male agricultural activities would have to be done by women. As early as August 1905, a newspaper report described a sign of the changing times: a gang of women in St. James parish were "trenching and moulding up a field," a task normally accomplished by men. The women, moreover, were performing the job ably. Six months later, women in St. Thomas were preparing the new sugar cane crop and using "the fork as cleverly as their brothers who have gone to Panama would have done."[49] In early 1907, a newspaper cartoon depicted women doing police work, cutting cane, and performing other traditionally masculine tasks; its title was "When All the Men Go to Panama."[50] A happy aspect to women's taking over plantation duties, as far as the owners were concerned, was that women's wages—regardless of the tasks performed—were lower than men's.

But optimistic observations about the growing female component in the island workforce was simply another reminder of the serious complications for the Barbadian sugar cane estates if most male workers left. What if Panama attracted contract workers for another decade or two at the 1906 rate of 6,510? Inevitably, the plantocracy began to consider legally restricting the exodus. In 1904 the House of Assembly had amended an existing Emigration Act in order to specify more accurately the obligations of recruiting agents not to allow emigrant Barbadians to become stranded abroad. Recent employers of Barbadian emigrants to St. Croix, for instance, had reportedly not honored the written contracts. In 1905 the assembly debated controlling the movement to Panama and other non-Commonwealth destinations. In 1906 a bill to that effect reached the floor of the house before it was defeated.[51]

In July 1907, the two houses of the Barbados legislature amended the Emigration Acts of 1891 and 1904 to give the Governor's Executive Committee the authority to curtail Barbadian emigration to non-British areas.[52] Ostensibly drafted to protect British subjects from captivity by undesirables such as the Peruvian rubber barons, the law really was aimed at eventually closing off the Panama outlet, and everyone knew it. Debate raged in the assembly accordingly. Before the House of Assembly passed the emigration amendment by a vote of eight to five on July 2, members were reminded of the workers' "frenzy" about going to Panama and therefore the very delicate, even dangerous, piece of legislation being contemplated. In the conservative Legislative Council, J. Challenor Lynch met the issue head on. He considered that it might be "advisable, even expedient" for the governor and his committee to stop the movement to Panama, at least for a while. The migration outlet, after all, was "upsetting the labour market and creating excitement" among black Barbadians. On the general topic of excitement, the colonial secretary, E.T. Grannum, added that recent unrest in Bridgetown probably was simply a sympathetic reaction to disturbances of late in the other Commonwealth Caribbean territories.

The unrest Grannum was referring to, however, was a direct protest against the legislation that the House of Assembly had passed on to the upper house for ratification. On the evening of July 15—the night before the Legislative Council passed the restrictive legislation—a torchlight mass meeting had been held in Bridgetown to protest the legislative action. "An enormous crowd" at the lower green had condemned "any undue interference" with black workers' emigration to Panama. The meeting was peaceful, although the size of the boisterous crowd was indeed unsettling.⁵³

The captain of the RMS *Solent* took the disturbing news of the Barbadian planters' attempt to stop the migration to Colón to the ICC authorities in Panama. He informed them of the legislative action in Barbados as well as the public protest in reaction to it.⁵⁴ Furthermore, the captain complained, Barbados port officials had begun to require him to abide by the letter of the "old Emigration Act" of Barbados, which specified a certain square footage for each deck passenger and entailed other restrictions that would reduce the number of deck passengers on any given ship.⁵⁵ If he had to comply with all of these artificial restrictions, the *Solent* would be unable to carry more than four hundred men per voyage from Barbados, and it was therefore unlikely that the Royal Mail Company would be interested in continuing its service contract with the ICC.

The Americans' fears were short-lived. The ICC experienced little further hindrance from the Bridgetown harbor authorities. Much more important, the Executive Committee never did use the power given it in July 1907 to curb emigration from Barbados to Panama. Amid a flurry of heated and contradictory rhetoric by legislators, newspapers, and doubtless most everyone else on the island over what the legislation would or would not do, Acting Governor S.W. Knaggs finally made a public pronouncement in September. Knaggs wished "specifically and emphatically to deny" that the Executive Committee had any intention "of preventing further emigration to Panama." Knaggs continued that it was obvious to anyone that the emigration had benefited materially the black working class of Barbados, although its members had paid a high price for it in the mounting Barbadian death toll in the Canal Zone. In light of the death and danger there, Knaggs could only suggest caution. The planters' legislation therefore had been a meaningless triumph. The governor and the Executive Committee knew that closing the door to Panama—although they now were legally entitled to do so—might lead to a revolt.⁵⁶

Those who advised against the restrictive legislation had done so more in fear of riot or insurrection than they had in championing the causes of the black workers. And doubtless the possibility of riot had preoccupied the Executive Committee. As Gordon Lewis recently has written, a pan-Caribbean antislavery ideology earlier had ranged through a spectrum encompassing both nonviolent and violent resistance, the latter expressing itself in open slave revolts.[57] It is not improper to suggest that this range of theoretical responses to plantation repression persisted in Barbados well after emancipation, extending into the early twentieth century. Simply put, the workers could be pressed just so far. And that limit might very well be reached if the government closed the emigration outlet that had given many black workers a ray of hope. The blunt, immediate character of a governmental decree, moreover, might ignite riots in Bridgetown and throughout the countryside. A worker might put up with earning pitiful wages, tilling a tiny subsistence garden, and even seeing his children sick and undernourished when the ultimate causes of these conditions were complex and vague and obscured by a history of economic and legal oppression. In contrast, a placard at the wharf or at the ICC office declaring that emigration to Panama was suspended, might very well provide the spark, if not the target, for violent reaction.

The Panama outlet had given the black workers an advantage they had not hitherto possessed. But this advantage, from the planter viewpoint, could be absorbed into the calculus of the Barbadian sugar cane economy. Many planters seemed to realize that overt restrictive measures on their part might lead to destruction, or at least irrevocable damage, whereas slight modification of existing policies at home could ward off disaster and even lead to planter benefits in the long run. "Keep his food cheap; grow provisions and plenty of them" advised the *Barbados Agricultural Reporter* in September 1905 in prescribing how the best laborers could be induced to stay home. "And let us keep the located and other attached labourers constantly employed. . . . give them no time to think of Cayenne and Colon." When the emigration amendment passed in July 1907, the same newspaper cautioned that this new weapon in the hands of the plantocracy "would have to be handled judiciously, so as not to antagonize the labourers."[58]

Accommodations and adjustments would have to be made at the parish and islandwide government levels as well, not just by individual planters, in order to reestablish the equilibrium of a plantation society that had been destabilized by a migration outlet. But there too, intelligent and cautious planning to make homelife better for the black working class could lead to eventual payoff for the planters. This attitude of accommodation toward the Panama exodus by Barbadian officials, moreover, allows us to understand better why they made some seemingly anomalous decisions. Two years before the St. George parish vestry established the baby clinics temporarily, for example, the parish medical officer had advised that immediate measures would have to be taken "to stem the devastating torrent of infant mortality and keep our supply of cheap labour plentiful enough to stand the constant stream of emigration."[59]

From the workers' viewpoint, any restriction of their emigration to Panama would have justified violence because it would have violated their legal and informal right to emigrate. Migration was one of the few ways black Barbadians could cope with the crowded impoverishment of the estate tenantries, and going away to work elsewhere—and often to return—had been carried out by their parents and grandparents for decades. In other words, migration was both a customary and a legal right possessed by black Barbadians in the first decade of the twentieth century. At the height of the furor over the impending restrictive legislation in July 1907, and two days before the public gathering in protest of the impending legislation, a letter published in a Bridgetown newspaper captured the essence of the black workers' fears and frustrations. Black workers, the letter explained, should not be prevented from taking "the only commodity they possess to the best market they can obtain. As their labour is the only commodity which our poor peasantry have, it would be manifestly unjust, cruel and impolitic to play or tamper with *the rights and privileges of the people*" (emphasis added).[60]

The legal right to emigrate had come at emancipation or, more accurately, in the years immediately following freedom. The British Colonial office had overturned the first restrictive acts against migration that were devised by the Barbadian plantocracy. But individual planters of the nineteenth century possessed a number of informal means which they could employ to attempt to thwart emigration, such as not allowing an emigrant's family to occupy a plantation-owned house plot in his absence or not giving him work when he returned.

The informal or customary right to emigrate, however, was quite different from formal legalities. An informal right to migrate had to be carved out of a coercive system of plantation oppression by Barbadian estate workers. Thousands had resisted heavy-handed attempts to keep them at home after emancipation. Despite threats and coercion, black men and women had doggedly traveled away and returned in the latter half of the nineteenth century in attempting to solve the unending problem of having too little money at home. By the turn of the century, recurring migrations had established a migration precedent for black Barbadians, and this precedent had become a hard-earned, informal right to migrate. White Barbadian planters of the Panama Canal era, whether they liked it or not, recognized this informal right and were obliged to accept it. Planters and officials not honoring this obligation, furthermore, risked becoming targets of violence.

The interdependence between Barbadian planters and their labor force, even during slavery, had involved mutual obligations and informal rights. The slave's obligation, to labor for the planter, was relatively straightforward. And the planter's obligation, as in the system of slavery in the United States, "to behave like a decent human being . . . had . . . become the slave's right."[61] The relationship between planter and worker in Barbados, obviously, had been altered in the decades between emancipation and the early twentieth century. One may argue that the located laborer contracts and the array of legal entanglements devised by the plantocracy had replaced any of the interdependence and mutual understanding that might have persisted from earlier days.

But unspoken reciprocal obligations and a system of informal rights did characterize the relationships between planter and worker in Barbados in 1900.[62] For one thing, the planter expected the "good Barbadian worker" behavior from his laborers, although expectations of this attitude, of course, were not stipulated legally. In return for this accommodating behavior and punctual labor, the tenantry resident had come to expect the paternal benefits that the Barbadian planters prided themselves in and never failed to advertise as the benign qualities of the island's special owner-worker relationship. Access to land plots, toleration of petty vegetable thievery during drought, and extra provisions and gifts of meat at Christmas may have been considered kindnesses by the planter, but the tenantry workers expected them as their just due. The old woman from Orange Hill, St. James, who remembered receiving the periodic gifts of sugar and breadfruit from her white mistress (whom she considered a "pig") accepted the gifts as part of an ongoing reciprocal transaction, not as benevolent acts of kindness.

In a broader sense, the black Barbadian tenantry dweller expected his planter, and the Barbadian plantocracy in general, to provide access to the two interlocking halves of his total livelihood, subsistence gardening and wage labor. The subsistence part was available locally. Most black workers were guaranteed, both legally and informally, a rented land plot as part of the Barbadian plantation system. But wages posed a different problem because they were subject to external control, such as the impacts of low sugar prices that were, in turn, the effects of economic depressions. And if planters could persuade Barbadian workers during the bounty depression, as they did, to accept wage decreases because of an externally imposed economic downturn, then the black workers could not, in fairness, be prohibited from traveling to external destinations as their forefathers had done in order to earn the money that was not locally available.

The grudging acknowledgment through toleration by the planters that black Barbadians were informally entitled to travel away did not mean that planters liked the arrangement any more than they liked supporting the parish almshouses with their land taxes. On the other side of the coin, the assertion that black Barbadian tenantry residents of 1900 expected material benefits from the planters and claimed rights under a system of plantation repression can in no way be interpreted to mean that the blacks enjoyed the estate tenantry system, which all of them considered to be unjust.

Nor did a social system of mutual expectations and reciprocal rights mean that rights on either side could not be expanded or withdrawn at the other side's expense. And planters' attempts at

"Hit de Manager in de Head" 139

expansion, and workers' fears of withdrawal, were at the core of what was eventually the absence of real restrictions placed on Barbadian emigration to Panama in 1907. The black Barbadians saw a fundamental right threatened and thereby a step backward to an earlier and even more repressive period in their history.

On August 15, 1914, the pulling of the steamship *Ancon* through the Culebra Cut marked the official opening of the Panama Canal. The completion of the excavation and construction phases of the project meant that thousands of black West Indians were no longer necessary as laborers in the Canal Zone. The Isthmian Canal Commission authorities had long anticipated the completion of the canal and had recruited no contract laborers during the latter half of 1914. Furthermore, the Americans had notified labor-recruiting officials throughout the British Caribbean islands that workers were no longer necessary in Panama. Numerous warnings to this effect had appeared in Barbados newspapers and official government publications since 1912. Of course, thousands of black West Indians would eventually stay on in Panama working in other capacities. But repatriation or relocation elsewhere were at hand for the rest. On Thursday, October 6, 1914, the RMS *Magdalena* left Colón with 140 deck passengers bound for Trinidad, Barbados, and the islands north to St. Kitts. After that, fortnightly steamers left Colón for various destinations throughout the Commonwealth Caribbean, and during the last three months of 1914, a total of 3,355 West Indian blacks were returned from the Canal Zone to their home islands. Two weeks after the *Magdalena* had left, the RMS *Orotava* took 323 Barbadian deck passengers from Colón to Bridgetown. Back home in Barbados the repatriated migrants greeted those they had formerly left behind, and they joined those others who also had returned from similar work sojourns in Panama.[63]

CHAPTER 5

Panama Men and Panama Money

> A Barbadian homeward bound from Panama, where he had been helping to dig the Canal, was heard to say to a companion, 'Wake up, man! Wake up! Dere is de world!' as the land of his birth appeared in the hazy distance like a faint smudge on the horizon.
> The remark was characteristic. Barbadians are intensely proud of their little island.
>
> Sir Algernon Aspinall, *A Wayfarer in the West Indies*

When official notices began to appear in Barbados that the end of the canal construction project was in sight and that no more workers were necessary in Panama, black Barbadian laborers were not the only ones with gloomy predictions about how the canal's completion would affect Barbados itself. Barbadian planters and officials, who had earlier feared losing their estate workforce to the isthmus, now reversed themselves, forseeing a post-Panama labor glut and severe unemployment in Barbados when all of the men came back home. These fears never materialized because thousands—certainly more than half—of those who had gone to Panama never returned.

Relieved at not having to face an expected oversupply of labor, Barbados sugar cane planters took even more satisfaction in the "era of unparalleled prosperity to Barbados" during the second decade of the twentieth century.[1] Local cane crops—despite drought in early 1912 and in most of 1914—were bountiful, but external variables were much more important than the Barbadian weather or even the introduction of new, drought-resistant sugar cane varieties. World War I had driven prices upward for all commodities, including sugar. Furthermore, the combat in Western Europe had left much of the Continent's sugar beet acreage trenched, cratered, and untilled, thereby ruining—at least, temporarily—the environmental basis for European competition with Caribbean cane sugar.

Black, working-class Barbadians also were better off by the century's second decade. "Prosperity" was hardly the appropriate term, but thousands of black Barbadian families saw definite material improvements compared with the frightful poverty they had known earlier. The reasons behind these improvements, however, were only partly attributable to higher prices for sugar cane. Much—perhaps even most—of the money spent at home by black Barbadians early in the second decade of the twentieth century had come or was coming largely from Panama and, to a lesser extent, from other external sources. An introductory glance at fragments of postal remittance data gives some idea of magnitude. In 1900 only £27,700 in postal remittances came to Barbados from all external sources; in 1910, of the total £99,000 in postal remittances sent to Barbados from all sources, more than £62,000 came from laborers in the Canal Zone. And, as discussed later in this chapter, postal remittances almost certainly represented less than half of all the Panama money coming back home.

This unprecedented surge of money from outside increased spending in Barbados, thereby improving government tax revenues. As early as 1906, an extra £1,200 in duty from local rum sales was attributed to the presence of free-spending returnees from Panama. In December 1912, Governor Leslie Probyn prefaced his annual report to the Colonial Office with a cover letter happily noting the general increase in government revenue and suggesting that a primary reason was the "large amount of money remitted to the island by Barbadian emigrants, and especially by the labourers who are employed at Panama."[2]

Many among the Barbadian plantocracy had come to agree with Governor Probyn's positive assessment of the Panama Canal's effect on Barbados. The labor force, contrary to the predictions of those who had pushed through the restrictive legislation of 1907, had not rushed off in its entirety to Central America. And the money sent home had benefited the local laboring class in many ways. Of course, there were those who could find only negative consequences in any black activities that were not imposed by the island's planters. For example, Assemblyman Stanley Robinson of St. George peevishly (and incorrectly) noted during a discussion of the possible presence of yellow fever in Barbados early in 1909 that "this country never was attacked by these diseases . . . until the Panama Canal was opened and the labourers who were shipped thither from this colony began to return here."[3] But most observers were not inclined to Robinson's sour attitude toward the laborers' exodus. Buoyed by their own prosperity, individual Barbadian planters could afford to compliment their black workers in a condescending way for traveling abroad, leaving friends and family, and compromising their health in order to remit small amounts of liquid capital to those staying behind.

But planters' benign attitudes also carried the unstated and invalid assumption that black Barbadians would thereafter remain content with the near-feudal social arrangements in the plantation tenantries. On the contrary, the era of Panama money represented a turning point in Barbadian history. The money sent and brought home from Panama, an influx of external money that later would be sustained, and even increased, by remittances from the United States, would help to bring about socioeconomic changes, including the ability of black Barbadians eventually to seek new and more equitable adjustments to old problems.

These adjustments, in many ways, were related to the quantity of money brought and sent home. As early as 1910, the beginning of a shifting financial balance between the laboring class and the Barbadian plantocracy could be noted, in a very rough way, by inspecting the island's finances at the macrolevel. In 1910, Barbadian merchants advanced £80,000 to the island's planters to carry on the business of planting and reaping the sugar cane crop which was, of course, the core of the Barbadian economy.[4] In that same year, black Barbadians working on the canal brought back (officially) and sent back through postal orders a combined £83,000, a figure that would be much higher if all money remitted to Barbados from Panama ever could be determined.

How Many Barbadians Returned?

If an estimated 45,000 black Barbadians emigrated to Panama and the Canal Zone during the first two decades of the twentieth century, it becomes necessary—although ultimately quite difficult—to estimate how many came back home. Over and over again, throughout all of the Barbadian parishes, elderly men and women recalled that most of those who went to Panama never returned.

Seventy-three-year-old Kenneth Greaves of Boscobel, St. Peter, was much more precise.[5] As a boy, Greaves delivered newspapers, and thereby became acquainted with men who had returned from Panama. My wife and I were referred to Greaves as a possible source of information about "Panama men" from the eastern end of St. Peter parish. We located him on an exceptionally hot and humid morning as he was returning from working in his garden. He then obligingly studied our computer printout, which enumerated the thirty-eight emigrants who had left Boscobel as contract workers for Panama during 1906 and 1907.

According to Greaves, only ten of the thirty-eight returned, and of the eight others who left from nearby Collins estate in St. Peter, only three came back. Obviously, these recollections given in numerical form from one small portion of one parish cannot be extrapolated throughout the entire Barbadian population of Panama emigrants. But Greaves's recollections confirm, in a tiny sample, what other Barbadians remember for their communities and for the population as a whole.

The most comprehensive islandwide data for Panama returnees were kept by the Bridgetown harbor master from 1906 to 1915.[6] Empowered by the Immigration of Paupers (Prevention) Act to count the second-and third-class passengers on arriving steamers as well as everyone arriving aboard sailing schooners, the Barbadian harbor authorities counted 20,326 Barbadian returnees from Panama during this decade (table 5). These data were not further differentiated by age or sex. Neither are there any indications of how many of the 20,000 went back again to Panama or emigrated elsewhere after being enumerated as returnees. Nor have we any idea how many of these returnees, like "Janie"

Table 5. Barbadian Returnees from the Canal Zone and Their Declared Money

	Returnees	Declared Money (£)
1906	3,501	18,800
1907	3,525	26,291
1908	2,376	21,864
1909	1,552	14,820
1910	2,048	20,604
1911	1,559	14,032
1912	1,387	12,773
1913	1,910	19,342
1914	1,759	16,449
1915	709	6,666
	20,326	171,641

Source: Data from Annual Barbados Harbour Master Reports, *Official Gazettes.*

and other market women and vegetable speculators, were counted several times on their many returns.

If the majority of Barbadians who emigrated to Panama did not return to reside in Barbados, why did they not do so? The posing of this unanswerable question possibly could generate a facile typology contrasting the "types" who returned with those who stayed away, all of which would underestimate seriously the importance of the Panama emigration to the group as a whole. Individual Panama migrants were members of families and communities, and those families and the wider black society in Barbados benefited from the individuals who emigrated and then sent money home. The group at home, moreover, provided support and inspiration for the workers they sent to Panama. Those workers often sent money home to finance deck passages for marriage partners to come join them in Panama. Older Barbadians recall, moreover, that some migrants to Panama continued to send money and gifts home for years, although they themselves never came back to Barbados. In other words, the connections between Barbados and the isthmus in the early twentieth century were complex and cannot be captured by enumerating migrants versus nonmigrants or those who stayed versus those who returned. Black Barbadians as a group exploited the distant and short-lived source of Panama money, and most of them, including many who never left Barbados, benefited from it as well.

Thousands of Barbadians never returned because they died in Panama. The ICC records from 1906 through 1920 enumerated 5,893 Barbadians who died in the Canal Zone, and had records of death by nationality been kept for the first two years of the project—when West Indian laborers were becoming acclimated to a new disease environment as well as to the novel dangers of heavy construction—possibly the Barbadian death total would be in the neighborhood of 7,000.[7] The ICC records of 1906-20 enumerated all Barbadian deaths, not just those of contract workers, but the causes of the deaths were not specified. Many died in explosions, landslides, and similar mishaps; young Barbadian men, whose only industrial experience at home had involved occasional encounters with the gears, rollers, and canvas sails of sugar grinding windmills, soon learned the dangers of "a hole of dynamite with a bad temper, a scaffold that likes to play tricks, the uncertain steam shovel, the everlasting hustling trains."[8] But almost certainly many more died of disease, mainly malaria and pneumonia.[9] Old Barbadians tell stories about the inadequate measures against disease taken by the first emigrants to Panama. Black men often slept outside in hammocks in the same sodden clothing they worked in, and, especially in the early years, they took little if any precaution to guard their health.

The friends and co-workers of the Barbadian men who died in Panama sent home the black-bordered envelopes to the mothers and wives of their dead associates. The commission authorities, however, sent the official lists of Barbadian dead to Bridgetown, and all relatives of Panama emigrants throughout Barbados who had received no mail for an extended period could ask at the Immigration Office in Bridgetown if their sons, husbands, and fathers had been counted among the dead. The Barbados government did attempt to notify black families of deaths in Panama; the task of tracing local relatives of those who had died abroad fell to the detective branch of the Bridgetown police force. Sergeant Collins dispatched detectives and constables to the tenantry cottages in both urban and country districts to carry the sad news to next of kin.[10]

The collective term *Panama Men*, which was invariably used in Barbados to describe large groups of returnees, may provide a clue as to why many persons never returned. The harbor master noted that his counts of return migrants included women and children too, but the great majority apparently were men. When Barbadian women went to Panama and married there, the resultant nuclear family often had a tendency to transplant itself permanently in Panama. Young men without mates, in contrast, were more likely to return, according to elderly Barbadian informants. So the export of "Panama women" from Barbados to the Canal Zone often carried with it a good chance that neither men nor women would return. Of course, male Barbadian contract workers and other male emigrants sometimes found other West Indian and Panamanian marriage partners in Panama and never came back for that reason. And the considerable male majority in all aspects of the movement from Barbados to Panama was reflected in the preponderance of women, especially among black Barbadians, in the Barbados censuses of 1911 and 1921.

For many Barbadians who emigrated to the Canal Zone, the exodus to Panama was simply a first step for movements farther afield. Many veterans of the canal moved on to Cuba for sugar factory and cane-cutting jobs with the Americans there. Others migrated to the United States. Jobs in Central America and Santo Domingo attracted others. Two cases of Barbadian movements beyond Panama came to the attention of the Barbados House of Assembly late in 1918 and serve to exemplify the complexity of individual migration trajectories at the time. Two Barbadian women residing in Panama, Selina Sealy of Christchurch parish and Aletha Thompson of St. Joseph, recently had applied to the British consul in Panama for Barbadian government funds to pay for their passage home. Sealy's husband had moved on to Cuba from the Canal Zone in 1917 and had "taken up with another woman," stranding her in Panama. Thompson's husband, on

Thompson's husband, on the other hand, had joined the Jamaican contingent for World War I and had been killed in combat. The Barbadian House of Assembly considered the merits of each case, taking care not to establish precedent by repatriating "distressed widows from Panama, of which there may be many." In the end, Aletha Thompson was the only one of the two applicants repatriated at government expense.[11]

Other reasons—besides death, staying in Panama, or emigrating elsewhere—kept some Barbadians from returning. Some old informants suggested that many of the workers feared coming home penniless or were afraid that they would be considered strangers if they came back. Indeed, a few stayed away for decades, not returning to Barbados until mid-century. By that time they were estranged from wives and children in Barbados with whom they had not been in contact for years. Usually, their family's indifference was based upon the returnee's lack of remittances. Even some who came back soon after the opening of the canal were not taken in by the kinsmen they had seemingly forgotten while they had been away. An eighty-seven-year-old in St. Philip parish remembered that when one of her two brothers who had gone to work in Panama returned in "about 1925," the police came and asked her to take him in and support him. She refused, although he was ill, because "he was gone for so long, and he didn't send anything." Her brother eventually died in the St. Philip almshouse.

The Returning Men

As the exodus to Panama extended its influence to nearly every black Barbadian household, the planters began to realize that the behavior and expectations of Panama returnees probably would alter the character of the black community at home. The Americans at Panama, everyone knew, were businesslike and demanding. They expected punctuality, hard work, and accomplishment, and if a Barbadian could not do the work, they would find a Jamaican who could. So Barbados planters expected that the returnees, conditioned by this experience, would carry back with them "greater habits of industry . . . and greater discipline than constituted their habits . . . when they left." At the same time, a few thoughtful planters predicted that Panama returnees would "also have learned to place a higher value on what they have to offer." Anyone not willing "to believe in, or indisposed to accept, such changes" might find himself facing "considerable difficulty" in coping with the altered state of affairs in Barbados after the return of the Panama men.[12]

From the point of view of the emigrants to the isthmus, they were indeed obsessed with thoughts of returning home. Yet they were much less concerned about the changed images and attitudes they would convey to the planters than they were about the amounts of money they would carry back with them. If there was a single common aspiration among all of the young Barbadian men who had gone to work in Panama, it probably was to return home as soon as possible with money. As early as mid-1906 one observer in Colón found it "touching to see the people gather as the ship set sail for Barbados, looking with wistful eyes as she disappeared in the dim distance toward 'God's country!'"[13]

George McLellan asserted that it was precisely the "rose-tinted" dreams about Barbados and the money they would take back there that kept the young men working in Panama, often with inadequate food (to save on expenses) and too little rest (so they could earn more money).[14] McLellan's point probably was no exaggeration. When Barbadian men in the Canal Zone found that they could earn what was, to them, extraordinarily high wages, many worked double shifts or took two different jobs. Some Barbadians in Panama, inspired by dreams of taking money home, seem, literally, to have worked themselves to death. In late 1905 a Barbadian man known only as Prince was familiar to many persons around the Colón dockyard. Prince—apparently possessed by those rose-tinted dreams—was reported by returnees to Barbados "to have stiffened out and died after thirty days and thirty nights of uninterrupted labour."[15]

No single stereotype, however, captures successfully the many images projected by the Barbadians returning from Panama. Shiploads of Panama veterans returning to Carlisle Bay included the young and the middle-aged, the healthy and the diseased, the prosperous and the penniless, the talkative and the quiet, the roughneck and the family man. An assessment of the variety of stereotypes and characteristics of the returning Panama veterans, nevertheless, helps to delineate the variety of impressions they made on friends and relatives who greeted them upon their return.

The swaggering show-off was the most colorful stereotype recalled of Panama returnees by old Barbadians, recollections often accompanied by laughter. The strutting self-importance, distinctive dress, and jingling pockets of Panama veterans often set them apart from everyone else. In St. Philip parish the story is still told of "Moneytree" Alleyne of Six Cross Roads, a portly returnee who habitually lent money to others and always bought sweets for the children of the community. Alleyne was so anxious to advertise his prosperity by being generous that he never bought a house or a piece of land for himself. Observers at the time also recorded similar impressions of the Panama men in general, though perhaps not all were so generous as "Moneytree" Alleyne:

> The returned Panama Canal labourer is an uncommonly vain fellow, and his vanity feeds largely on his imagination, which is of a sprightly enough kind. As he struts along in all the glory of a gay tweed suit, a cylindrical collar and a flaring necktie, one can see him smiling complaisantly to himself now and then, as he glances down at this fine raiment. For once the characteristic Barbadian shrewdness seems to die out or sink into a dormant condition. . . . [he thinks] all Barbados is whispering admiringly, 'There goes Mr. Cudjo Hogg from Panama.'[16]

Returned Panama men, like their fathers and uncles who had earlier traveled away to British Guiana and Trinidad, had been "cheeky" and assertive abroad. At least that is what many of them told friends upon return. In the small rum shops and chattel houses throughout the Barbadian tenantries, ex-laborers from the canal explained that the Americans had had their hands full when dealing with the particular storytellers. "Whuh? I carry on like a rattlesnake," proclaimed the returnee to Barbados in *Tropic Death*, while describing to friends his behavior in the Canal Zone. "I let dem understand quick enough dat I wuz a Englishman and not a bleddy American nigger!"[17] Some listeners considered these braggadocios simply corollaries of the pretentiousness that Panama men often carried home; more believable stories about life on the isthmus suggested that the American bosses there never would have tolerated such behavior. The Americans, after all, were well known to "kick, clout, and swear at every Barbados labourer with a glorious impartiality" if ever he got out of line.[18]

The enhanced assertiveness of some returned Panama veterans, however, was not confined simply to recollections or to conversations within the tenantries. Groups of "ruffians," generally acknowledged to be Panama men, sometimes showed contempt for police constables by pelting them with stones. They also often threw rocks at passing railway cars or snatched other passengers' hats on the Bridgetown tramway lines. Their bullying, boisterous behavior even menaced innocent bystanders in the evenings of 1911 when the downtown buildings of Bridgetown were festooned with strings of colored lights to celebrate the coronation of George V.[19]

These types of behavior were indicative, according to some observers at the time, of the kinds of men who had been attracted to Panama in the first place, men who were not simply boisterous but prone to become "hooligans" and hardened criminals. In 1906, Lieutenant Colonel Kaye, the inspector general of the Barbados police force, hypothesized that a notable decrease in crime was attributable not only to the money being sent home but "also to several bad characters having left the Island."[20] A decade later, among the thousands who had returned, 142 had been deported from Panama and Colón to Barbados because of criminal activities. After these convicted lawbreakers returned, "many" of them were caught stealing in Barbados, turning out to be among the island's most dangerous burglars.[21] In 1917 the acting public health inspector suggested not that criminal types had been attracted to the isthmus in the first place, but that those who returned probably were "comparative failures." Their misfortune or lack of incentive in Panama had transformed them and sent them back to Barbados "as rogues and vagabonds with their wits sharpened by their residence abroad."[22]

Besides burglary, returned Panama men often were held responsible for the ruinous sugar cane fires, although—as in years past—the incendiaries were rarely, if ever, apprehended. In 1908 a series of damaging fires were thought to be the handiwork of "idlers" who had recently "returned from the zone with a little money in their pockets, and disinclined . . . to resume work, but ready for what to them is only a lark, to set a canefield in a blaze."[23] Six years later, the outbreak of cane fires had become epidemic. Between November 1913 and June 1914 a total of 217 fires had destroyed nearly 1,500 acres of growing sugar cane. A local commission was appointed to investigate, but the only substantive thing the commissioners could do, besides tabulate the number of fires and total acreage lost, was to offer possible reasons for the large number of fires. "Returned emigrants from Panama" was one of the prominent explanatory factors offered by members of the Cane Fires Commission.[24]

Although we will never know the actual extent of criminal activity and arson among returned Panama veterans to Barbados, it is not difficult to understand why such behavior occurred. Young men who had been abroad and who had seen the world were not always inclined to revert to a subservient existence in the estate tenantries upon return. Furthermore, the seasonal underemployment in the Barbadian sugar cane plantations, even for those men willing to take up again where they had left off, was irksome when compared with the year-round availability of wage labor in Panama. The association between returned migrants and increases in "criminal" activity, moreover, was not unique to Barbados in the early twentieth century. Throughout the Caribbean, planters and officials have long assumed relationships between increased rates of robbery and the return home of local migrant laborers.[25]

Not all Barbadians prospered in Panama. Some returned in a worse condition than before. Several old informants recalled broken men coming back who had spent all their earnings in the Canal Zone or carried home with them only a pocketfull of pennies. The stereotype of the impoverished returnee from Panama was common enough to be reflected in the lyrics of a Barbadian folksong:

Look de Panama man come home from sea
As skinny as a Church rat
An' all he had in he grip fo' me
Was a wide-brim Panama hat.[26]

Illness and accidents had weakened and disfigured many of the returning men. Residual malaria plagued numerous Panama veterans until they died. Industrial accidents, explosions, and machinery had taken arms, legs, and eyes. It was almost as if some of the returnees had been to war. Some of those crippled or losing limbs in the Canal Zone had received token compensation payments from the ICC, but usually it was not enough to replace future wages lost because of an inability to work. One man returned from Panama to Six Men's Bay, St. Peter, with only one hand. He had lost the other in the Canal Zone when his cloak had been pulled into a machine. He had received payment for his lost hand from the ICC, but back home in Barbados he could do nothing except occasionally "whistle birds" for white sportsmen in the swampy area north of Speightstown.

It is not surprising that members of the Barbados House of Assembly demonstrated little compassion for those who returned from Panama ill or crippled. Members of the house had for long resented those Barbadian blacks who emigrated in order to give their "best laboring years" to employers elsewhere and who then came back home to apply eventually for parochial relief. In March 1910, Dr. E.G. Pilgrim, representing St. James parish, offered that these "derelicts" had certainly learned their lessons by going abroad. "Derelict" was "not a bad word," explained Pilgrim, "for it pretty well fits them all—insane, diseased, and incapable."[27] One way to make it difficult for crippled, destitute Panama veterans to return was to invoke certain clauses of the Immigration of Paupers Act. But controlling the arrivals from Colón from leaving ship and disappearing into Bridgetown was as difficult as it earlier had been to curb the activities of potential stowaways trying to go the other way.

Many old Barbadians, when asked what distinctive characteristics the Panama returnees displayed, replied that they simply had resumed their estate jobs and, except for having saved small amounts of money for their families, they had changed very little. Indeed, it would be misleading to discuss ostentatious, rebellious, and crippled returnees as if they were the sole stereotypes applicable to returning Panama men. Probably the majority of those who came back to Barbados did so rather quietly, a bit older and more sober. Often they made subtle but important contributions around their houses and tenantry yards, such as improving drainage in their house plots or screening windows, and thereby improving local health conditions by implementing what they had learned in Panama.[28] Their presence, moreover, added to the local reservoir of wisdom and knowledge about the world outside, and, as in all Caribbean societies, they became the village elders, older and experienced men and women to whom everyone else in the community would take their problems as well as appeals for advice.

Thousands of Panama returnees achieved limited upward mobility by becoming small landowners at home with the money they had earned abroad, a subject discussed further in chapter 6. Others assumed better jobs when they came back. Among the ten returnees to Boscobel, St. Peter, three had saved enough money to purchase land plots nearby. Five others had elevated themselves beyond estate field work within a short time after their return to Barbados. Two became postmen, one an estate driver, one a blacksmith, and another a well-digger.

Often the "rose-tinted dreams" that Barbadians had entertained while working in Panama had included hopes to save enough money to buy a small shop upon return. Many achieved this dream, including Eric Walrond's fictitious (although eminently believable) country shopkeeper, Mr. Poyer, who came back from the Canal Zone minus a foot but with enough saved to establish a tiny country store. When Poyer was trapped inside the shop in a fatal fire, witnesses retrieved physical evidence of his past years as a labor migrant to Panama: "A straw valise, label spattered—deckers' luggage—an old shirt."[29] In a number of cases, returned Panama veterans established shops in Barbados, became insolvent, and then had to travel back for yet another sojourn on the canal before coming home again. The most successful shopkeepers seem to have been those who had earned enough money to combine shopkeeping and the ownership of an acre or two of land for "cultivation, affording him a small living apart from his exertions in other directions."[30]

The children (now in their seventies and eighties) of men who returned to Barbados from the Canal Zone often remembered their fathers with fondness and extraordinary pride. Asking elderly informants about recollections of their parents, many of whom died decades ago, hardly constitutes a search for objective evidence. But it was remarkable to encounter statement after statement expressing love and admiration for Afro-Caribbean fathers, men whose general importance to the family has been reported as relatively slight in the works of so many scholars who have emphasized the predominance of the mother-centered family in the region. "My father was a family man and a person of exceptional intelligence," "Daddy worked night and day as a tailor in Panama to support all of us," and "My father could do anything" were a few of the many glowing remembrances of fathers who had worked in Panama. One woman who lives in St. Michael parish was born in Panama in 1910 and moved on to Cuba with her family in 1917. She eventually returned to Barbados in 1937. Her father died in Cuba in 1960, but she has fond memories of him still: "I remember evening walks with my father. I really loved him more than my mother. He used to play with my sisters and me and make a lot of jokes. Sometimes he used to bring home coins—both gold and silver—and ask me which ones I thought were the prettiest. Then he would let me roll the coins on the floor."

Not all fathers returned from Panama, of course, and some of them stranded wives with small children at home and never sent money back. This "absent father" stereotype, not surprisingly, had been emphasized by those Barbadian officials who in 1907 had hoped to prevent laborers from leaving altogether. The quantitative extent to which desertion of family took place among Panama emigrants would be exceptionally difficult to determine. Needless to say, those members of families deserted by fathers who either stayed in Panama or moved on without them to Cuba or North America, had few of the glowing memories cherished by those whose fathers returned or who provided for their families in absentia.

An emphasis here on Panama men is not intended to ignore the contributions that Panama women made to the home society. Women sent home clothing and money from the Canal Zone to parents, offspring, and siblings, and they accumulated money so that they eventually could purchase land in Barbados. One lady, born in 1909, now residing in St. Philip parish had heard vaguely about her father going to Panama. He disappeared before she was old enough to know him. It was her mother who really was the earner and saver of Panama money. The mother—leaving the daughter with an aunt—paid her own deck passage to Panama in 1912 with money she earned through local plantation work. In Colón she ran a small fruit shop and washed clothes. She used to send back to Barbados "money, clothes, sheets, pillowcases, everything." In 1920 she came back to Barbados with enough money saved to buy a small land plot near her birthplace. Then she took her daughter, now eleven years old, back to Panama for a decade. "Be sweet and don't talk like a Bajan when you get to Panama," was the mother-to-daughter advice about getting along in strange places recalled from a conversation on the deck of the Panama-bound steamer more than sixty years ago.

The Returning Money

The type of money currency earned by blacks and whites working in the Canal Zone was the symbolic basis for the racial segregation on the isthmus, a point emphasized by all who have ever written about the Panama Canal. The skilled workers, who included nearly all Americans working there, were on the "gold roll," while the unskilled workers, including nearly all black West Indians, were "silver employees." "Gold" and "silver" therefore became the universal euphemisms for "white" and "black" in Panama and the Canal Zone, a distinction that extended to housing areas, dining halls, hospital wards, commissaries, and nearly every public facility down to drinking fountains. The Barbadian and other black West Indian workers actually were paid in standard Panamanian silver coins called balboas. The black workers sometimes referred to the coins as "spiggoty money," and they resented receiving "a whole hatful of this stuff" when a Spaniard, doing essentially the same work, was sometimes paid in gold. But then the black worker would stop to realize that he was receiving "far more than . . . in his native land, and that there is another . . . waiting for his job" if he were to quit in disgust.[31]

After putting aside enough cash for his own food and housing in Panama, a Barbadian worker usually sent money back to his family. Unlike at home, where money could be given freely from person to person, transferring money from one political realm to another usually involved confronting postal officials. Some observers at the time suggested that "ignorant" West Indian workers were suspicious of postal authorities in the Canal Zone and therefore reluctant to send postal money orders home. Almost certainly black Barbadians' suspicions, if such reports were accurate, were not because of ignorance; they and their fathers had known about money orders from earlier experiences in Trinidad and British Guiana. In any case, black Barbadians working on the isthmus exported money home in three different ways: through postal money orders; in the pockets of the laborers themselves; and as cash sent in letters to friends and families in Barbados.

Table 6 shows the amount of money, the value of which was recorded in Barbados in pounds sterling, sent from the Canal Zone to Barbados in postal money orders from 1906 to 1920. The first postal orders between Panama (then a province of Colombia) and Barbados had been sent in 1885, but it was not until August 1906 that arrangements were made for laborers to send postal orders directly to Barbados from the seventeen branch post offices in the Canal Zone itself.[32] From 1907 to 1915, postal money orders to Barbados from the Canal Zone exceeded any other foreign source of postal orders. In 1916, postal orders from the United States—perhaps many sent by Panama veterans—to Barbados exceeded those from the Canal Zone by £5,000, and the United States was more important as a source of postal remittances to Barbados in every year thereafter.

The data in table 6 are supported and brought to life by the recollections of old Barbadians. Those who used the postal money-order system in Panama recalled sending small amounts of money home "every six months or so." And those who received money in Barbados remembered getting "a few dollars" (one pound equaled $4.80). What did the recipients of the average five to ten dollars in each postal order do with the money? "It wasn't enough to buy land, but it made a lot of difference. My mother could buy food and also things for us children. Some years we could even buy a Christmas ham," an old shopkeeper in St. Joseph parish remembered. His answer was typical. Most people reported that the postal money they received from Panama "was just enough to live on."

Table 6. Postal Remittances Sent from the Panama Canal Zone to Barbados, 1906–1920

	No. of Postal Orders	£
1906	3,613	7,509
1907	19,092	46,160
1908	26,360	63,210
1909	31,179	66,272
1910	31,059	62,280
1911	24,968	51,009
1912	28,394	56,042
1913	31,851	63,816
1914	22,619	39,586
1915	14,210	22,874
1916	11,241	17,539
1917	10,430	15,194
1918	8,777	12,680
1919	7,747	12,591
1920	5,782	9,173
Total		545,935

Source: Data from Annual Postal Reports, *Official Gazettes.*

It is hardly surprising that Panama returnees brought home with them sums larger than in an average postal order; an individual returning to Barbados carried home a reported average of nine to ten pounds (table 5). But this average sum was a considerable amount of money in the first decade of the twentieth century in Barbados. With such a sum (not to mention the average forty or so pounds declared by a family of four), an individual could make a down payment on land, buy a chattel house, purchase a boat and fishing equipment, or invest in a small shop. Viewed another way, each person arriving from Colón declared an average amount of cash that was greater than the total financial worth of many individuals who resided in the Barbadian tenantries.

The amount of money carried home was certainly greater—possibly much greater—than the sums actually declared by returnees. During most of the Panama years, the Barbados Immigration of Paupers Act called for an individual to have at least nine pounds in his or her possession in order to be admitted back to Barbados without further complications. So the average returnee—fearing that white harbor officials would tax or even confiscate their repatriated cash—routinely under-declared the amount he or she carried. A 1911 newspaper article, derived from the Bridgetown harbor master's report, complained at length about the suspicion that black "people of the emigrant class" exhibited upon returning from Colón:

> We are of the opinion that the amount of money brought back to the island by emigrants who returned from Panama during the five years was greater than the £20,000 a year which they are said to have declared to the Harbour Master on their arrival. People of the emigrant class are not given to taking persons of the official class into their confidence. That there is a sum fixed as a minimum to be shown under the Immigration of Paupers Act we are of opinion that most of those making declarations to the Harbour Master about the money they possessed knowing of this minimum, named that amount, or a few dollars more, as the sum they possessed. There is good reason to believe, too, that the labourer returning from Panama is not without his suspicions that there is an ulterior motive in the Harbour Master's enquiry respecting the amount of money he is bringing back home.[33]

The actual amount of money brought home to Barbados by those returning from Panama, including the amount declared to the harbor master, can only be estimated. Was it twice the £172,000 declared officially between 1906 and 1915? One man now living in Christchurch parish was born in Panama in 1909 and came back to Barbados with his parents in 1922. He recalls that his father originally had lived in St. Philip parish and had paid his own way to Panama, where he had a small shop and also sold items from a mail-order catalog. The father brought $270 (over £56) back to Barbados, where he used the cash to buy a house with a shopfront on Roebuck Street in Bridgetown. Almost certainly thousands of others carried back similar sums or even more in their pockets, money that was largely underdeclared.

Prior to the establishment of the postal money-order system in the Canal Zone in mid-1906, Barbadian canal workers routinely mailed cash home. The practice involved the risk of having the money stolen by one of the several postal employees along the way. During the first eight months of 1906, the Bridgetown post office received twenty-nine official complaints of letters arriving from Panama minus the money discussed in the letter. A few local postmen were reprimanded, but much of the problem, upon investigation, apparently lay with the postal authorities in the Canal Zone.[34] Barbadian postal authorities announced the danger of sending cash through the mail, and the practice almost certainly diminished after the money-order system started. But it was nonetheless customary, even after the postal money-order system was established in 1906, to place a little money in a letter going home to Barbados. The enthusiasm that greeted the postman's arrival in Barbados was as much for the small bits of cash in the mail as it was for the letters themselves. And mail recipients in the Barbadian tenantries occasionally grumbled about receiving an "empty letter," if a son or husband had not included a dollar or two along with the letter that told of a recent bout with malaria or inquired about a new child in the family.

Another means by which canal workers transferred money informally from Panama was with relatives, friends, or with seamen who worked aboard the steamers. This means of sending money home, of course, avoided a confrontation with intervening and impersonal postal clerks, but it took extraordinary faith in friends and acquaintances to trust them with sizable sums. Some of the money disappearing from registered mail envelopes in the Canal Zone was attributed to the handling of the letters by "third parties" before the envelopes ever reached the post office.

The variety of methods, both formal and informal, by which Panama Canal workers sent money home and the under-declaring upon arrival confound any attempt to arrive at the total amount of cash repatriated from the isthmus to Barbados from 1904 to 1920. Keeping in mind that £718,000 was remitted through official sources during only some of the years (tables 5 and 6), the estimate that £1,000,000 came to Barbados from the Canal Zone by 1920 is probably much too conservative.[35] And money figures, of course, do not take into account the gifts and clothing brought home or the personal training and skills learned abroad which materially benefited the home island.

The anticipation among Barbadian blacks of receiving money and gifts from Panama was, obviously, felt most keenly by those with family members working on the isthmus. But the money from Panama represented an external source of cash that raised the hopes of every black Barbadian that he or she might benefit by luck or chance. Old Barbadians occasionally tell a tale, always about a vaguely known acquaintance they heard about in another village, that has a story line running roughly as follows. One night a person had a dream about an old uncle who had gone to Panama. The next day, he or she, inspired by the dream, wrote a letter to the uncle with simply his name and "Canal Zone" on the envelope. Somehow the letter reached him. Having no family with him and his kinsmen having died years before in Barbados, the uncle sent the niece or nephew a thousand dollars (or a similarly large sum) by return mail. These fantasies (inspired, perhaps, by an event or events that actually happened) seemed to have been common throughout the Barbadian tenantries early in the twentieth century and doubtless added to the excitement and group support at home for the Panama migrants who had ventured overseas.

Although the receipt of letters containing small amounts of cash were exciting events within each rural district of Barbados, they could not match the scale of exhilaration greeting the arrival of a mail steamer at Bridgetown that had come from Panama. In 1910, incoming steamers landed at the pierhead of the south side of the harbor. The confusion and anticipation together called for the establishment of "some kind of order" during the "pandemonium which prevailed on mail mornings [as] cabs drove up, passengers got in, and there were half a dozen donkey carts laden with wood meandering between the cabs."[36]

It took several hours, and often into the next day, to sort and deliver the mail addressed to those in the Bridgetown area and longer for that going to outlying parishes. Recipients of money orders could redeem them at the general post office during weekdays and for a two-hour period on Saturday mornings. For the first years of the Panama emigration, the Bridgetown post office was ill-equipped to handle the volume, much less the excitement, of cashing the money orders arriving from the Canal Zone:

> In the face of this continual increase the post office retains the same antiquated method in issuing and paying out money orders; in a small room scarcely large enough to hold a dozen people at a very small counter with four or five rows of perspiring, gesticulating and shouting individuals elbowing and squeezing each other to reach the wire netting, behind which there is *one* clerk . . . need we wonder that the gentler sex who have their dependents abroad dread the ordeal of facing this veritable "black hole" of the Post Office![37]

Before the postal authorities would cash money orders, the recipient's identity had to be verified, and usually rural people attempted to locate their postman to identify them if the postman was there. When country folk finally emerged from the "black hole" of the Bridgetown post office after having cashed their money orders, they often encountered swindlers attempting to sell them brass rings or fake jewelry at exorbitant prices. Pickpockets, moreover, abounded in Bridgetown on the several days after the arrival of a mail steamer from Colón.

The influx of Panama money to Barbados and the accompanying crush at the Bridgetown post office led to improvements in rural mail delivery on the island. In 1900 in St. Andrew parish the postmen used ponies to deliver mail to the settlements in the hilly areas. Sometimes the mail never came, and when it did it was often at odd hours of the night. Postal officials pointed out that the rugged terrain in parts of St. Andrew precluded efficient mail service; those complaining about it suggested that the government might improve the whole operation "if the interests of the public were considered more and the interests of the mail cart less."[38] Poor rural mail service was not simply a function of attempting to navigate through the few areas of rugged terrain in Barbados. An eighty-nine-year-old woman of Brereton Village, St. Philip, remembers that the postman's gig made only brief stops on the road—sometimes at night—and everyone had to be ready to go and meet it.

For thousands of black Barbadians, indifference in rural mail service threatened their financial lifeline to Panama. When the postal money orders finally did arrive, moreover, usually a walk to Bridgetown afterward was necessary in order to cash them. In 1903 for the first time, the post offices in Christchurch, St. John, and St. Lucy parishes had established money-order offices, from which postal orders could be issued and paid outside the capital city.[39] By 1910, postal recipients residing in St. Peter, St. Philip, and St. James parishes also could cash money orders from the Canal Zone at the post offices in their home parishes, provided the sender had specified that on the order itself.

Rural parish postal officials in Barbados kept track of the value and number of money orders paid. During the Panama years the average value of a postal order cashed in the rural Barbadian post offices was two pounds, a reflection of the Panama money data islandwide arrayed in table 6. Rural money-order facilities, however, provided only partial relief for the Bridgetown post office. During 1910, of the 43,279 money orders paid in Barbados from all places of origin, 29,490 were cashed at the general post office in Bridgetown.[40]

The trek to Bridgetown by recipients of postal money orders was not made simply because of the superior postal facilities. Cash coming through the mail provided unprecedented shopping opportunities. In Bridgetown an individual encountered greater variety and cheaper prices. The repatriation of Panama money to Barbados made "the stores in Broad and Swan streets hum with quickened trade," and not all of the customers came from the urban area itself.[41]

In terms of shopping visits and in other ways, the influx of Panama money increased rural black Barbadians' familiarity with Bridgetown and surrounding St. Michael parish. The momentous, tearful scenes accompanying the departure of men from Carlisle Bay had drawn individual rural blacks to town for infrequent visits. But the periodic cash remittances now brought them into Bridgetown more often. The circulation of goods and people between town and the rural parishes, heretofore the domain of shopkeepers and hucksters, now was more voluminous and more rapid. Postal and shopping errands were not the only reasons rural folk came to town. Better educational, recreational, and legal services brought them too. The purchase of a house spot any place on the island with Panama money, for example, called for a trip to town to meet with a lawyer.

The Panama money itself—originally earned as silver Panamanian balboas, sent via a United States postal system, and recorded as sterling equivalences by Barbadian officials—had financed these heightened rural-urban connections. At home in Barbados the repatriated money had been converted into both British coins and also the dollar notes issued by the commercial banks on the island. Lacking its own indigenous currency until 1938, Barbados traditionally had exercised little control over the money circulating on its streets. Instead, in matters of currency the island "had to make the best of what the outside world provided in these respects," a generalization that could, of course, be extended to almost all local economic matters other than currency. In 1893 the Barbados legislature banned the use of Spanish, Mexican, and Colombian coins as legal tender on the island and acknowledged formally that "the term dollar shall be . . . taken to mean the sum of four shillings and two pence of British money." Early in the twentieth century, private accounts in Barbados usually were kept in dollars and cents and government accounts in pounds, shillings, and pence, an ambivalence in accounting systems that reflected the parallel but integrated systems of making change in the streets and marketplaces of Bridgetown and rural parishes.[42]

In 1900 the island government estimated that £50,000 ($240,000) in copper and silver British coins were circulating in Barbados along with another £50,000 in commercial bank notes. This same figure was stated routinely for two decades as the amount of money available locally until an actual count in 1920 showed over $400,000 in bank notes alone being used as money on the island.[43] Every bit as important as the amount of money in circulation, however, was the heightened rate at which it circulated. These quantitative and qualitative changes in Barbadian currency, changes financed in large part with Panama money, were the monetary causes and effects of accelerating commercial exchanges between urban and rural sectors of the island, sectors linked by good roads on an island without rugged terrain:

The Managers of both Banks tell me (Royal Bank of Canada and Colonial Bank) that 90 percent of the paper money passed over their counters in any one week, is paid back into the Bank within the following week, so that the same notes go on turning round and round. This is due no doubt to the ease with which people can get to and from town as compared with some of the neighbouring colonies.[44]

But an annual inrush of thousands of postal money orders and thousands of small bits of cash from the Canal Zone to black Barbadian tenantries did not mean that all of the money would be spent. For the first time, many black Barbadians faced the happy problem of finding a use for small surpluses of cash. As discussed in the following chapter, they invested much of the money they received in land and also in friendly societies. But money from Panama poured into bank accounts as well. Although scrimping and saving on a tiny scale had long been a Barbadian preoccupation, the few coins put aside by black families often had been kept in jars or in hidden corners of the house. These hiding places were insufficiently safe for sums of ten or even fifteen dollars. So thousands of black Barbadians, overcoming their inherent suspicion of white bank tellers, deposited tens of thousands of pounds of Panama money into individual savings accounts.

Table 7 summarizes the individual savings accounts at the Barbados Savings Bank (the official government savings bank) in Bridgetown during the first two decades of the twentieth century. The "bulges" both in numbers of depositors and in total deposits during the years of the Panama Canal construction (1904 to 1914) seem to stand out. The sharp rise in deposits beginning in 1917 reflects growing local prosperity because of high World War I sugar prices and, probably as important, increasing cash remittances from emigrants to the United States.

The ledgers showing the names, occupations, deposits, and withdrawals for individual Barbados Savings Bank accounts for the years 1902 to 1913 are kept at the Barbados Department of Archives. These ledgers indicate the tiny amounts of liquid capital maintained by individuals who described themselves as "hawkers," "boatmen," or as in other distinctive black working-class occupations. Individual accounts of, commonly, one pound, or slightly more or less, were added to or deducted from,

Table 7. Barbados Government Savings Bank Accounts, 1901–1920

	No. of Depositors	New Accounts	Total Deposits (£)
1901	13,457	—	97,161
1902	13,566	1,308	105,226
1903	13,936	1,341	113,462
1904	14,212	1,625	—
1905	14,773	1,464	117,395
1906	15,308	1,764	138,839
1907	16,193	2,465	153,452
1908	17,793	2,212	195,745
1909	18,696	1,973	216,278
1910	19,576	2,124	233,010
1911	20,185	1,931	295,912
1912	20,683	1,909	261,602
1913	20,572	1,716	253,013
1914	20,881	—	209,339
1915	20,393	—	193,646
1916	19,973	—	203,731
1917	13,110	—	254,790
1918	12,639	—	262,270
1919	12,647	—	303,734
1920	13,057	—	496,479

Note: Dashes mean that data are not available.
Sources: Data from Barbados, Blue Books, and Savings Bank Ledgers, Barbados Department of Archives.

often monthly, by amounts as little as one or two shillings. This high rate of banking activity also is suggested in table 7 by the large number of new accounts, especially during the Panama years. In some years, account openings and closings nearly balanced one another, and the closing of a personal savings account quite possibly indicated an individual's emigration from Barbados—perhaps to join a husband, son, or father in Panama or Cuba. In 1907 the Barbados Savings Bank inaugurated a system whereby Barbadians working on the isthmus could deposit their earnings directly into the Barbados bank by sending postal orders to a Barbadian actuary acting in their behalf.[45] The savings bank registers themselves, however, suggest that few Barbadians in the Canal Zone took advantage of this opportunity, apparently preferring to send their earnings directly home to family members.

The administrators and bank tellers at the Barbados Savings Bank were no better equipped to handle the crush of customers than were the employees at the money-order window of the Bridgetown post office. In 1914, during the first few days after "big mails" arrived "from Panama, the United States of America and Canada" a person venturing into the savings bank always would "find a crowd of people there depositing money."[46] The cumbersome rules and bureaucratic inefficiency, however, were enough to inhibit all but the most determined savers from patronizing the bank. Unlike the commercial banks, the Barbados Savings Bank issued no checkbooks, and therefore an individual wishing to withdraw money from a personal account had to walk to the bank in town to do so personally. Worse, after arriving, a bank patron occasionally had to wait for as long as half a day to be waited on by a bank teller.[47]

Despite the inconvenience at the government savings bank, black Barbadians stubbornly continued to patronize it rather than the commercial banking establishments. Apparently their preference had little to do with blacks' confidence in the government officials themselves but rather because the local banking laws guaranteed the safety of all deposits in the government bank. In any case, the manager of the savings bank could remark in 1920 that the government bank enjoyed the loyalty of "a good many of the gentle-folk" in Barbados who patronized it rather than any of the four branches of the Colonial Bank or the Royal Bank of Canada, which had branches in Speightstown and Bridgetown.[48]

A profile of savings bank patrons identified by sex, parish of residence, and skin color, summarized in table 8, indeed supports the notion that the government bank was supported mainly by the black working class. These data are derived from a list in which "occupation" and "complexion" were recorded for what were apparently those persons establishing new savings accounts. "Complexion" on the manuscript register apparently was originally recorded by the particular bank teller enrolling new account holders. In some instances "complexion" was left blank, and these cases are not included in table 8. The overwhelming preponderance of bank patrons from the urban areas of Barbados is obvious here as is the predominance of female

Table 8. Depositors in Barbados Savings Bank, 1915–1917

	White		Mixed		Black		
	M	F	M	F	M	F	Total
St. Michael	38	23	39	65	158	184	507
Christchurch	7	4	3	3	24	32	73
St. George	2	4	1	2	43	43	95
St. James	1	2	1	1	17	14	36
St. Thomas	2	1	0	1	25	16	45
St. Peter	1	3	0	3	12	7	26
St. Philip	1	2	2	3	18	21	47
St. John	1	4	0	4	17	14	40
St. Joseph	2	0	1	0	9	13	25
St. Andrew	0	0	1	0	8	4	13
St. Lucy	1	0	1	2	5	5	14
Total	56	43	49	84	336	353	921

Source: Data from "Barbados Savings Bank Guide and Register," February 22, 1915, to August 3, 1917, Barbados Department of Archives.

bank patrons for black and "colored" Barbadians. The great majority of black bank patrons listed in the register identified themselves as skilled and unskilled workers to the bank tellers—seamstress, hawker, domestic, groom, porter, agricultural laborer, carpenter. Only one man, among the hundreds, identified himself as "mason in Panama," although much of the money deposited in individual Barbados savings accounts—especially a few years earlier—must have been earned by Barbadians working on the isthmus.

Panama money did not always go simply into Barbadian shops, stores, and savings accounts; it was also invested in other forms of small-scale capital improvements. In July 1910, the sailing schooners between Bridgetown and Speightstown were busy carrying lumber north along the Leeward coast of Barbados so that black residents of St. James, St. Peter, and St. Lucy parishes could make house improvements prior to the onset of the hurricane season. The money for the lumber "mainly comes from the remittances [sent] home by labourers at the Isthmus."[49] House improvements, however, were not accomplished with Panama money just during the hurricane season but all year round. The racket of hammers and saws and the replacement of shingles, doorsteps, and window frames on the wooden chattel houses in rural parishes of Barbados were familiar signals that Panama veterans from the neighborhood finally had returned.

The building of a new chattel house for his mother or his wife—or, for a bachelor, house construction to enhance his marriage prospects—was perhaps the first real goal of a returned Barbadian from the Canal Zone. And if he had brought too little money home for an entire dwelling, he sometimes left his half-finished house in order to spend yet another sojourn on the isthmus, eventually returning to stay when his house was finished. After his home was built, however, the desire to earn the money necessary to purchase the land on which it stood often pushed a Barbadian veteran of Panama back again to Central America or on to a new external labor destination. The sights and sounds of new building throughout the Barbadian countryside were as certain an indication of local success earned abroad as were the crowds of customers at post offices and the savings bank. In some rural parishes of Barbados, old people remember "Panama houses," dwellings that were covered with shingles or painted red, surface features that were less functional than they were public notices of the repatriation of money from the Canal Zone. Stone and stucco houses and even two-story structures—some of which can still be pointed out today—also were financed throughout Barbados with money earned on the Panama Canal.

Early in 1909 a white visitor to Barbados was enjoying a ride with his family in a horse-drawn buggy through the southern part of St. Thomas parish in the vicinity of Bridgefield Village and Rugby estate. The rolling countryside and the pleasant sights of ripening canes were, however, of less interest than the new, brightly painted chattel houses at the side of the road: "Why so many new cottages on the same hill top? we ask the driver of a dray in which we have taken passage. The answer comes curtly and shortly, yet it is an answer sufficiently explicit—'Panama Money'."[50]

CHAPTER 6

The Social and Economic Changes: "Money Is a Blessed Thing"

I made the acquaintance of eighty-two year-old Joseph King while he was waiting for the bus at the churchyard of the St. Thomas parish church of Barbados in January 1982. King was bound for the hospital at Rock Hall Village so he could play his accordion for "the old folks" there. Later I visited him at his house in Arch Hall Village and queried him about his recollections of the Panama Canal and the Barbadians who had returned from Panama to that part of St. Thomas parish. King remembered that several men from Arch Hall came back from Panama with enough money to purchase peri-urban house plots in the Bridgetown area. Moving their chattel houses down the road from Arch Hall into town had been relatively simple, overnight projects involving rented donkey carts and the help of a few friends.

What Joseph King remembered about his own community in St. Thomas parish exemplified a demographic trend for Barbados as a whole during the first two decades of the twentieth century. The population decrease throughout the island as a result of emigration—from 182,000 in 1891 (table 1) to 172,000 in 1911 (table 9) to 156,000 in 1921 (table 10)—had affected the several parishes in different ways. The rural areas had been thinned out, and the urban area as a whole had stayed roughly the same. (Between 1911 and 1921, Bridgetown's population actually decreased, but its suburbs gained slightly.) Internal residential movement had therefore represented a demographic shift toward the urban area. In attempting to provide perspective on the net Barbadian population loss between 1891 and 1911 combined with the increase in the suburbs of St. Michael parish in the same

Table 9. Population of Barbados, 1911

	White	Mixed	Black M	Black F	Black Total	Total
Bridgetown	2,701	6,514	3,027	4,406	7,433	16,648
St. Michael	3,309	12,245	9,972	15,208	25,180	40,734
Christchurch	1,579	3,923	6,053	8,651	14,704	20,206
St. Philip	891	3,588	5,207	7,337	12,544	17,023
St. George	411	3,271	4,559	6,088	10,647	14,329
St. John	788	1,570	3,329	4,450	7,779	10,137
St. Peter	494	2,175	2,781	3,973	6,754	9,423
St. James	304	2,006	3,417	4,888	8,305	10,615
St. Thomas	290	1,235	2,655	3,741	6,396	7,921
St. Lucy	303	1,925	2,687	4,036	6,723	8,951
St. Joseph	595	1,614	2,390	3,238	5,628	7,837
St. Andrews	398	1,467	2,730	3,564	6,294	8,159
Totals	12,063	41,533	48,807	69,580	118,387	171,983

Source: Data from Boyce, *Report on the Census of Barbados 1911,* 14.

two decades, the compiler of the 1911 census summarized the situation by proclaiming that "Emigration had really cleared the way, [internal] Migration had stepped in and filled the breach!"[1] The movement to the St. Michael parish suburbs from outlying parishes of the island early in the twentieth century continued a trend that had begun at emancipation. This rural-to-urban movement, furthermore, has continued and has assumed spectacular proportions later in the twentieth century.[2]

Although a townward drift of black Barbadians in the early twentieth century represented a continuation of a decades-old trend, the local plantocracy still was disgruntled by it. The efficacy of the vestry system lay partly in the unstated assumption of a static local residential pattern, and the parish-to-parish

Table 10. Population of Barbados, 1921

	White	Mixed	Black M	Black F	Black Total	Total
Bridgetown	1,891	4,848	2,633	4,114	6,747	13,486
St. Michael	3,389	11,219	10,345	15,795	26,140	40,748
Christchurch	1,506	3,155	5,570	8,032	13,602	18,263
St. Philip	680	2,732	4,521	6,337	10,858	14,270
St. George	357	2,176	4,191	6,065	10,256	12,789
St. John	715	1,340	2,920	4,039	6,959	9,014
St. Peter	397	1,503	2,740	3,861	6,601	8,501
St. James	245	1,905	2,939	4,305	7,244	9,394
St. Thomas	240	1,120	2,292	3,519	5,811	7,171
St. Lucy	219	1,557	2,368	3,629	5,997	7,773
St. Joseph	483	1,414	2,222	3,058	5,280	7,177
St. Andrew	307	1,247	2,616	3,556	6,172	7,726
Totals	10,429	34,216	45,357	66,310	111,667	156,312

Source: Data from Lofty, *Report on the Census of Barbados 1911–1921*, 23.

mobility of black Barbadians defied this assumption. While the Barbadian planters grudgingly acknowledged the right to emigrate (an acknowledgment encouraged by prodding from the British Colonial Office), many planters longed for stiffer controls over intraisland movements. The landed taxpayers of St. Michael parish were particularly resentful when "worn-out" older black folk from rural zones moved to town and applied for poor relief, because these applicants "never did the parish any service in their working days."[3]

Perhaps of even greater demographic importance than the noticeable urban drift was the remarkable female preponderance among black Barbadians, especially in Bridgetown and St. Michael parish, where females counted for over 60 percent of black residents in both 1911 and 1921. A majority of women—

typical of a populace partly dependent upon external migration—had been common throughout black Barbados since emancipation. Many of the absent men were maintaining wives and children in absentia with remittances, but not all mothers were regular recipients of money from abroad. This situation pressed "a very large number of women" into the labor force, and by the 1920s the presence of women in the Barbadian workforce, observed as a novel trend during the early years of the Panama exodus, was ubiquitous and considered necessary to run the island's sugar cane industry.[4]

The availability of jobs in St. Michael parish, as domestics, seamstresses, hawkers, shopkeepers, and estate workers, attracted black Barbadian women from rural parishes to suburban tenantries. But some of the women came into the city and the suburbs not simply begging for hand-to-mouth wage positions but as prospective buyers for the small land plots around Bridgetown. The cash down payments they offered for small holdings had been sent home to them probably more often than not by "emigrants to Panama [who] have not been forgetful of those left behind."[5]

Central Milling and Remitted Money: "Things Have Changed Very Much"

The census data of the early twentieth century simply bore out what each Barbadian planter or manager had experienced on his own sugar cane estate ever since the laborers had begun heading for Panama. The availablity of female workers notwithstanding, the shortage of robust estate workers had gone beyond the nuisance level. The perceived lack of laborers, in an archaic sugar cane industry whose very lifeblood had been the presence of an overabundant labor force, led some planters to contemplate agricultural reorientation. "[T]hings have changed very much within the last few years. Labour is no longer cheap or efficient" proclaimed Stanley Robinson to fellow Barbadian assemblymen on March 7, 1911. Although Robinson and the other planters disliked even to contemplate the economic dislocations that would open the door for outside financiers to enter the Barbadian picture, they convinced one another that they had no other choice. "[W]e must have central factories on a cooperative basis" continued Robinson.[6] In other words, the eventual acknowledgment by the Barbadian sugar cane plantocracy of the need for twentieth-century sugar-milling techniques was directly influenced by the exodus of the laborers to Panama.

One way Barbadian planters could have responded to the loss of so many laborers was to offer higher wages, but they did not. As discussed in chapter 3, the average wage per Barbadian field worker was raised from eight pence to one shilling per day in 1911–12, a rate that then continued unchanged into the 1920s according to the annual *Blue Books*. The meager wages offered at home, obviously, continued to push more and more black Barbadians to external destinations for wage work and reinforced the local importance of money sent home from elsewhere, mainly from Panama.

The social history of Barbados during the second decade of the twentieth century is partly the story of the subtle yet discernible shift away from the old-fashioned, individually owned, paternalistic, sugar cane estate of 1900 toward the modern factory that eventually replaced it. The change did not occur overnight, and windmills and vestiges of paternalism persisted into the 1930s, but the direction was unmistakable. "[S]omething approximating central factories" was established in Barbados early in the twentieth century according to Sidney Greenfield.[7] His remark is less hesitant than it is a reminder that subtle economic dislocations can produce momentous changes that cascade throughout socioeconomic systems.

The changes in the Barbadian sugar cane industry in the second decade of the twentieth century were noticeable in any number of ways. At perhaps the most obvious level—among the physical contours of the industry—the elimination of inefficient mills, the inevitable substitution of steam for wind, and the replacement of subsistence acreage by sugar cane all created far-reaching transformations. For Barbadian society as a whole, moreover, the central milling act passed by the Barbados legislature in 1911 delineated an entirely new social agenda as far as many Barbadian planters were concerned. A day's work for a day's pay, minus the traditional, paternalistic social buffers, would be the rule from now on. H.A. Vaughan has explained the planter position thus: "[A]s between themselves and the labourers, paternalism vanished from the plantation."[8] Perhaps most important, it was at the level of personal relationships that the changing Barbadian plantation would create irrevocable changes. Examples of such changes were cataloged by a Barbados planter newspaper as early as 1910:

> The old-time planters managed . . . their business very admirably. They kept in the closest possible touch with their labourers, knew them all by name, took some interest in their domestic life, and enjoyed their fullest confidence. The ladies from the "great house" . . . also found many means of introducing rays of sunshine into the lives of their people. For, in the days referred to, the system of settlement prevailed and the labourers on a plantation were really an institution of that plantation. Their lives were intimately bound up with the fortunes of the farm. There are but few and faint traces remaining of this healthy spirit of mutual confidence between the planters and their labourers. There is instead an air of aloofness everywhere prevailing.[9]

The transformation of the Barbadian sugar cane industry in the early twentieth century was by no means unique. During the nineteenth century, plantation agriculture in the Caribbean and in other tropical colonial areas had responded to the demands of a widening world market. The intensification of European and North American capital investment in tropical staples, a tendency to spread these investments over more acreage, and concerted efforts to lower costs per unit of production together created an atmosphere in which modern sugar-grinding factories outcompeted old-fashioned muscovado mills; this competition took place in particular places and also internationally for the growing world market. Therefore, it was simply a matter of time before the anachronistic family-owned estate of Barbados, "possessed of limited access to capital and wedded to outmoded patterns of production," would change or die.[10] The imperial free grant of 1902 had simply financed the last gasps of a socioeconomic system that had not really changed since slave emancipation, and neither it nor Joseph Chamberlain's benign attitude toward the outdated sugar industry of Barbados could sustain it any longer.

Sidney Mintz has discussed the ways in which North American capital transformed the traditional sugar cane haciendas of the Greater Antilles at the turn of the century. Within a brief period of time, the paternal, family-owned estates of Cuba and Puerto Rico became "factories in the field," transformations that created socioeconomic changes throughout the local societies.[11] George Beckford, moreover, has shown that the fall of the individuals of the planter class relative to corporation control was not simply a West Indian phenomenon but the result of an international surge of investment capital that eliminated old-fashioned planter-worker social ties from South America to Asia during the late nineteenth and early twentieth centuries.[12] Barbados changed in similar ways. Despite the Barbadians' traditional and special relationships with London, the colony could not resist being swept into the orbit of international finance early in this century. Thereafter, local conditions in Barbados would be determined even more by decisions made in distant commercial centers than they would by local planter-worker accommodations. Barbadian workers' demands and Barbadian planters' counteroffers soon would be expressed in the now-familiar parlance of increased wages, specified work weeks, threatened strikes, and negotiated benefits for worker groups; conversely, needs and expectations no longer would be governed by promised access to subsistence plots, implicit grazing rights, and Christmas gifts of pork, breadfruits, and potatoes, all reciprocated by the local workers' quiet dependability to plow, to weed, and to harvest each year's sugar cane crop.

Appealing as a comparative macroanalysis of economic change can be, however, it nearly always gives the real people in question—in this case the Barbadians themselves—a good deal less credit than they deserve. The residents of Barbados, planters and workers alike, in the early decades of the twentieth century were not simply passive recipients of economic signals from afar pointing in new directions that they followed mindlessly. Rather, the attitudes and aspirations of the Barbadians would influence greatly the timing and the character of economic change. Although the local planters had been aware of modern methods and equipment and the financial attractions of modernization for decades they had resisted it and had been willing to pay the price of outmodedness by reducing wages, forgoing higher profits, and emphasizing local pride and satisfaction in traditional techniques. The local labor force, the group forgotten most often by those macroanalysts who imply faceless masses responding listlessly to external economic decrees, was, in the Barbadian case, the real catalyst of change. Individual black Barbadians of the plantation tenantries withdrew their labor from, and thereby undermined, the character of the local sugar industry. Furthermore, the money they sent and brought back home to Barbados forever altered the social conditions that had underpinned the Barbadian sugar cane industry since slave emancipation.

The persisting, vigorous, and successful emigration of black Barbadians to compensate for low domestic wages not only reduced the local labor supply but also created new expectations in those who emigrated and, in turn, in those who had stayed behind. The impersonality undermining the traditional plantation of Barbados in 1910 was therefore not simply a vanishing paternalism decreed by the owners. The growing spirit of aloofness had been fostered in part by black migration experiences abroad and the cumulative success—expressed in sums of money earned elsewhere—of those experiences. Despite his propensity to migrate, the Barbadian laborer of 1910 was "profoundly patriotic. . . . But there are also other objects for which he entertains a liking. One of these is money; and in order to obtain money, he is prepared to work."[13]

The Barbados legislature's central sugar milling bill of 1911 represented more an institutionalized consensus toward the need to modernize the industry than it did a finite goal or plan buttressed by powers of taxation. Nevertheless, the total number of Barbadian sugar-grinding mills decreased substantially as smaller, less-efficient mills were forced to cease operations during the following decade. The number of factories fell from 329 (220 powered by wind, 109 by steam) in 1911 to 263 (178 wind, 85 steam) by 1921.[14] Perhaps more important, by late 1911 fourteen sugar mills in eight of the island's eleven parishes had adopted improved production techniques.[15] By installing modern vacuum pans, these large sugar factories could produce the desired dark sugar crystals that were easier to refine and commanded generally higher prices on world markets. The number of modern sugar factories in Barbados increased to nineteen by 1921. Throughout the Barbadian countryside the tiny, inefficient windmill operations were giving way to large neighboring factories whose higher quality product and increased capacity attracted canes from surrounding estates. For example, the central factory at Locust Hall, in the northwestern corner of St. George parish, was grinding not only its own canes but also those from neighboring estates in St. George, St. Thomas, and St. Michael parishes by 1921. The two largest estates of the island, Foursquare and Carrington, both roughly a thousand acres in extent and both in the western part of St. Philip parish, also were served by modern, vacuum-pan refining equipment.[16]

The trend toward central sugar milling, in part an agroindustrial adaptation to an emigration-induced labor shortage, further decreased the number of sugar mill jobs in Barbados. Hundreds of windmill repairmen and carpenters, many of whom already had emigrated to Panama or to Bridgetown, would no longer be necessary to maintain the wooden beams or the sails of now-defunct windmills. A smaller number of factories required fewer but more highly trained mechanics and technicians, including the skilled black boilermen from British Guiana who came to Barbados as vacuum-pan operators. Mechanical cane hoists, introduced to Barbados in about 1923, eliminated much of the handling at the mill sites and further reduced labor needs. For those workers kept on as factory employees, the regimen in modern grinding factories demanded more punctuality and a heightened sense of routine. During grinding seasons in the old windmill days, factory crews often had waited around the mill or even had slept there at night in case the breeze stirred, thereby activating both the mill's canvas sails as well as the factory crews. These environmental uncertainties, which meant differentiation in the timing and intensity of factory labor requirements from one part of the island to another, were gradually being eliminated by 1920. Now estate regimens were being standardized throughout Barbados by coal-powered steam.

Unlike in the Greater Antilles where the Americans had transformed lightly settled, frontierlike lands into oceans of sugar cane with imported equipment and imported labor, the modernization of the Barbadian sugar cane industry involved the painful relocation and reorientation of a dense human settlement pattern that had been in place for decades. The high rate of black Barbadian emigration and the demographic drift to St. Michael parish had helped cause these changes and had also made agricultural reorientation somewhat easier, but labor redundancies and job losses created hardships for thousands of workers. In general, the rural Barbadian labor force, like the means of grinding the sugar cane, was becoming more homogenized. Earlier, in the windmill era, carpenters, boilers, blacksmiths, carters, wheelwrights, and others had performed separate and related tasks. As the smokestacks of the central factories began to dominate the Barbadian countryside, however, plantation labor forces were becoming simplified into small and specialized factory crews on the one hand and large, undifferentiated field gangs on the other. Assemblyman S.C. Thorne was one of many who had foreseen these painful changes in the restructuring of Barbadian agriculture, but the insufficiency of labor, from his point of view, had caused them in the first place. As to the future economic roles played by displaced sugar factory laborers, as far as Thorne was concerned they probably "would be only too glad to be employed in the fields."[17]

The advent of central sugar cane milling in Barbados also increased the propensity for seasonal unemployment. The seasonality of planting and harvesting the canes always had represented the pulse and the continuity of Barbadian agriculture, and wages, of course, had been meager between harvests in the old days. But with workforces becoming more sharply defined into field and factory gangs and with factory jobs becoming more specialized, the possibility of bits and pieces of work becoming available to estate workers in the off-season, as they had before, declined severely.

The changeover from windmill to factory also affected Barbadian livelihood in more subtle ways. More efficient milling left less cane trash for manure, and vacuum-pan boiling left few of the impurities, in the form of skimmings from boiling tayches, that had heretofore supported a dense population of small animals within estate tenantries. Older Barbadians often recall a larger population of small yard animals, especially chickens and guinea hens, in the days before large-scale grinding factories. In 1916 a shortage of pork at the public abattoir in Bridgetown was attributed to "the establishment of sugar factories in districts where the windmill formerly prevailed," the latter milling technique providing by-products which were the traditional sources of Barbadian pig feed.[18]

A less-personalized plantation system no longer allowed an estate field worker to take his grazing animal into the plantation yard to forage during the cane harvest. This point was raised by the Reverend F.G. Stanton during the public hearings into the 1937 Bridgetown riots. Unlike in earlier days when estate workers' animals grazed plantation yards, a contemporary lack of access to grazing meant that "that man and his children do not get any milk nowadays." Besides the physical differences between small mills and large factories in the methods of grinding cane and in leaving different by-products, according to Stanton, the social differences between old and new were even more important "because [today] the factories are run by different people altogether."[19]

Between 1910 and 1920 the Barbados sugar cane industry was responding not only to long-term economic change but also to short-term price increases for unrefined sugar. From a low of seven shillings per hundred pounds on the London market in 1902, raw sugar's price had risen to eleven shillings in 1910, to more than thirty during World War I, and then to a dizzying fifty-eight shillings per hundredweight in 1920 before the price plummeted to less than twenty in 1921.[20] During the bounty depression, the price had dropped so low that marginal cane lands had gone untilled; between 1883 and 1895 the estimated acreage actually planted in sugar cane on Barbados had fallen from 79,500 to 50,000.[21] Planters also had experimented with sea island cotton at the turn of the century in the wake of depressed sugar prices, but as the price for sugar climbed, so, not surprisingly, did the number of Barbadian acres planted in sugar cane. Former grazing zones and poorly drained acreage, owned by estates but heretofore uncultivated by plantation managers, had been planted in canes by 1915. The managers of the larger cane-grinding factories, moreover, gladly processed canes not only from adjacent estates but also those purchased from the black smallholders in the neighborhood who had converted their one or two acres from corn and yams to cane. "My father came back from Panama with enough money to buy two acres of land," an old shopkeeper from St. Philip parish told me, "then during the war he planted it all in cane. At twenty dollars per ton, he couldn't afford to do anything else."

There were no official islandwide data compiled for the actual acreage planted in cane on Barbados during the sugar boom, although sugar cane's encroachment on marginal lands as well as on former subsistence plots was everywhere apparent. By late 1916, local observers warned that "nowhere in the island are as many vegetables planted as in past years, the result, it is supposed, of the present high prices of sugar."[22] The worrisome lack of homegrown foodstuffs, even within the context of Barbados's traditionally food deficit economy, led to the legislature's Vegetable Produce Act of 1917, which mandated acreage from each estate to be devoted to edible foodstuffs. More and more, bushes and leaves from formerly useless gullies and hillsides were being collected to plow into estate lands.[23] These measures, taken to enhance fertility and cane yields, provided further visual evidence that the island's entire landscape, including former subsistence buffers against monopolization by cane, was being affected by both higher sugar prices and central milling. An eighty-seven-year old man in St. George parish recalled the agricultural and related social changes of his youth. It seemed to him that "the self-sustaining life in Barbados ended when the estates started planting everything in cane."

Islandwide sugar production data for Barbados (table 11) tracked the London sugar price increases during the first two decades of the twentieth century in only the most general way. The exceptionally high output between 1916 and 1919 reflected World War I sugar prices, but the very low islandwide yields from 1911 to 1913 were because of recurring drought which affected Barbados severely in several years between 1910 and 1920.

During the decade, prolonged aridity desiccated subsistence plots, pushed up local food prices, and was the indirect cause of deaths and disease in black tenantry settlements. In St. Philip, the parish medical officer reported that during the third calendar quarter of 1912 the people "passed through a terrible ordeal of drought, pestilence, and famine, the like of which I have never seen before . . . even in the months succeeding the hurricane of 1898."[24] Dysentery, resulting from malnourishment, was epi-

Table 11. Barbadian Sugar Tonnage, 1901–1920

Year	Sugar Yield (tons)	Year	Sugar Yield (tons)
1901	56,912	1911	32,561
1902	45,576	1912	28,732
1903	33,795	1913	11,327
1904	55,785	1914	29,404
1905	41,210	1915	29,847
1906	50,630	1916	73,581
1907	33,033	1917	69,367
1908	31,353	1918	57,191
1909	15,571	1919	69,628
1910	36,389	1920	48,212

Source: Data from Deerr, *The History of Sugar*, I, 194.

demic in parts of St. Philip. Particularly hard hit were those with little money to buy food. Prices for food were inflated not only because aridity had reduced local crop volume but also because a greater volume of money on the island had bid up the prices of the fewer vegetables.

In the wake of technological change in sugar cane milling, extended dry periods—always a recurring feature of the Barbadian climate—precipitated the eventual demise of many of the remaining windmills. After the severe drought of 1908, a number of the smaller wind-powered mills on Barbados never even started up to grind the small 1909 crop. The few canes from their estates were instead shipped to the closest factories, whose owners' access to external capital ensured that these large, steam-powered mills would carry on regardless of local climatic perturbations. But even greater milling efficiency and extremely high prices could not control the overriding influence of climate on Barbados's cane output. An islandwide sugar cane shortfall in

1920—a year when the highest prices in a century were being paid on the London market for sugar—was the result of the near-continuous aridity over Barbados for the first six months of 1919.[25]

The years immediately following the Panama exodus in Barbados, highlighted by the growing importance of large cane-grinding factories, rising prices for sugar (and most everything else), and fading plantation paternalism, also may be interpreted as the period when the dual subsistence and cash character of black Barbadian livelihood became fully monetized. The volume of money coming home from Panama increased the likelihood that a money price would be affixed to food that had been formerly shared. The habit of purchasing food was, of course, one that thousands of young black Barbadian men had grown accustomed to in the Canal Zone. The encroachment of plantation canes on estate land formerly set aside for subsistence acreage meant that many tenantry dwellers could not cling to the old ways even if they wanted to. And smallholders of land—traditionally a basis of subsistence—now saw their acreage as a means by which they could realize larger sums of money than they ever had imagined. Jerome Handler has pointed out that land in Barbados has multiple meanings associated with ownership, prestige, and security but that its ultimate value in the minds of small farmers is that it is "a potential source of cash."[26] This attitude began to take hold firmly during the era of Panama money.

The unprecedented volume of money coming to Barbados early in the twentieth century, which put all sectors of the local economy on a monetary level, triggered an interrelated series of social changes. Money was by no means unknown to black Barbadians, for Barbados had been enmeshed in a money economy since before emancipation. Indeed, the Barbadian pursuit of money in times past has been described as "the colony's dominant avocation."[27] But Barbadian subsistence gardening, reciprocal food transfers, the access to land plots, and the tending of small livestock—economic activities bound up with social relationships within and among social classes—often had been carried on without exchanges of money. Much of the reason was that black tenantry workers, with a high percentage of their subsistence provided by access to provision grounds, received such low wages. While interviewing a very old lady in Christchurch parish, I asked her to recall as far back as possible and to describe what her father's estate wages had purchased. "And what did he do with the extra money?" I asked. "Extra?" was the stern and somewhat indignant reply, "There wasn't ever enough money until he and my uncles went to Panama!"

More money in a black Barbadian's pocket meant that he or she would be able to purchase more and better commodities and special ones, such as lumber, paint for the house, blankets, or even imported clothing. A retired school headmaster from St. Thomas parish remembered that, as a schoolchild himself, his classmates who had relatives in Panama or the United States always looked different from everyone else because of their distinctive clothing sent from abroad or purchased with money sent home to Barbados.

But upward social mobility and social differentiation among black Barbadians did not involve simply displaying the special commodities money could buy; it also could be achieved by having enough money to purchase all of one's economic necessities. White, brown, and some black Barbadians for decades had been involved in modes of urban-oriented livelihoods that involved money transfers for all economic necessities. Buying, not cultivating, one's own foodstuffs was a mark of the middle and upper classes. And now, with more money on the island, selling subsistence items that one previously had shared was an increasingly popular means to obtain money, even if an individual had not been to Panama. Therefore, just as the increased volume of Panama money financed the accelerating frequency with which rural Barbadians visited the Bridgetown area, it also tended to pull more rural foodstuffs—formerly exchanged or sold in rural areas—into town for the higher prices there. The presence of more money in Barbados tended to create a need for more money (and more shopping trips to town) because money was becoming the only medium by which an individual could obtain vegetables, which formerly had been cultivated by the family. In very general terms, the era of Panama money (associated with central milling and the World War I sugar boom) reoriented the economic geography of Barbados so that obtaining food for the family became partly an urban-oriented endeavor mediated within a cash nexus. An old man of Chalky Mount, St. Andrew, recalled to me his boyhood in rural Barbados: "At that time we didn't need to go to Bridgetown. Things were plentiful in the country. Things were different then."

The need to earn more money, the larger volume of money in Barbados, and the economic reorientation that now saw previously unsold items becoming market commodities, increased black Barbadians' vulnerability to price inflation controlled from afar. In a sugar-exporting economy, the necessity to import always had been fundamental, and externally influenced prices for locally sold items were anything but new. But during World War I, the prices of imported necessities, such as lumber for house construction, spiraled. In 1913, Canadian imported pitch pine, for example, sold in Bridgetown for an average of $44 per 1,000 board feet. By 1920 the price had risen to anywhere between $130 and $145. The prices for white pine and spruce, building lumber also imported from Canada, similarly had trebled within this seven-year period.[28]

But the most insidious feature of the treadmill of price inflation was that, by the second decade of the twentieth century in Barbados, it had pulled so many locally cultivated foodstuffs into its vortex. In January 1920, a hundred-pound bag of Barbadian potatoes—a traditional staple of the black working class—was being sold for $1.56. By May the price had risen to five pounds for $0.10. The price per pound of potatoes then soared to $0.06 in July, $0.07 in September, and $0.08 in October.[29] Those with little money had to starve or steal, especially when drought or the inflation-induced encroachment of sugar cane had taken over their subsistence grounds. The successful migration and return with Panama money thus had not meant unqualified success for all black Barbadians. The Reverend F. Godson, a Methodist minister in the West Indies since 1890, described the tragic scene in one part of St. Lucy parish in 1916, the local inhabitants being trapped between drought on the one hand and economic change on the other:

> In Crab Hill and neighbouring villages I came in contact with the worst poverty and destitution I ever saw up to then—except perhaps in one village in St. Kitts. It was a specially dry year, even for that

area; there was little work on the plantations around and very little money; the people's own gardens were bare; and the price of imported foodstuffs, together with sugar, were soaring. So I met with hunger, rags, dilapidated shacks, idling, and praedial larceny on an exceptional scale.[30]

The material prospects for the poorest black Barbadians also were worsening because the people were losing traditional social protection. The aloofness and vanishing paternalism were outward manifestations of dissolving social realtionships. The tide of Panama money returning to black Barbadians in rural parishes, for example, weakened the traditionally important roles of rural shopkeepers. Before, when money had been scarce to seasonally nonexistent, tenantry dwellers had depended on credit from shopkeepers in return for the patronage of the tenantry residents once they were paid. Afterward, with more cash in the tenantries, black workers and their families often bypassed, literally, the local shopkeeper if better prices were available in town.

The stereotype of the well-behaved Barbadian estate worker, not surprisingly, also began to break down in favor of vocal, demonstrative complaints by black individuals and working gangs for better pay and better working conditions. The passive, willing attitude of rural black Barbadians in years past was fast becoming anachronistic in the new scheme of things. And, as discussed later in the chapter, "lawlessness" in Bridgetown was reaching unprecedented levels.

In very general terms, the social changes in Barbados were pushing black workers in the direction of locating some kind of dependable cash source, whether it be a steady job, revenue derived from a piece of land, or upward economic mobility through nonstate work. Individualism and independence now were admirable personal qualities; depending on someone else, whether a planter or fellow tenantry inhabitant, was no longer a guarantee for subsistence and security. Indeed, such old-fashioned behavior was considered foolish, even hazardous, in a new era. Sidney Mintz described roughly similar attitudes among the rural peoples of southern Puerto Rico who were in a similar state of flux at the turn of the century: "The changes . . . led working people to look to themselves, rather than to those more powerful than they, for the solution of their problems."[31]

Individualism and independence, moreover, meant that cooperation and reciprocity among black Barbadians were no longer as important as before. By the 1920s, the increase in individualism among black Barbadians, when compared with other West Indians, was remarked upon and apparently very noticeable. For example, the Barbados government attempted to organize agricultural credit societies among local smallholders in 1924, but the attempt failed because of a lack of communal spirit. Unlike in St. Vincent and Trinidad, where similar organizations prospered, the black Barbadian was no longer "willing to risk his property for his neighbours."[32] These comparative observations, if accurate, could be interpreted in different ways. However, the varying interpretations probably all would lead back to the sudden yet massive importance of money on Barbados compared with the semisubsistence economies, based partly on greater access to interior Crown lands, prevailing on the other two islands.

The surge of money coming to black Barbadians heightened their interests in education, both for themselves and for their children, as a means to a better life. If a man worked hard and earned enough money, through the ownership of land and a small shop, for example, he might be able to send his son to the Combermere School in Bridgetown. Then his son would be eligible for white collar work or, very rarely, professional training abroad. Even rudimentary financial acumen, such as knowing basic accounting or possessing the ability to sum figures, now became an important attribute among Barbadian blacks. And financial success often became closely associated with intellectual prowess. A Bridgetown businessman remembered admirable qualities in his father: "My old man was educated, and he had good handwriting, so money naturally came his way."

Education would not become compulsory for all Barbadian children until the 1920s. Before then, a black child's education, though theoretically available for all and desired by almost every parent, often had required considerable family sacrifice. So in 1911 when the mandatory school-leaving age for Barbadian children was lowered by the legislature from sixteen years of age to fourteen, a vigorous protest was registered by parents of every social class. In 1913 the House of Assembly received a petition with 5,144 signatures (and "X's") from parents throughout the island appealing for the restoration of a higher school-leaving age. Particularly affected by the 1911 legislative act were children of emigrant parents, some of whom had, paradoxically, traveled away to earn enough money for their children's educations. A case in point was Mary Alleyne, a teenager who attended the St. Silas Girls' School. Her mother had traveled to work in British Guiana, leaving Mary to take care of younger brothers and sisters. Then she had been turned away from school for being too old upon her mother's return, after having spent so much of her adolescence caring for siblings in her parents' absence.[33]

Purchasing Land

In a comparative discussion about varying degrees of access to local lands among the working classes in the Commonwealth Caribbean, David Lowenthal points out that in Barbados "a peasant proprietary body . . . emerged . . . with the return of labourers from Panama and Cuba who could afford to buy lots carved out of estates in chancery."[34] This point has been generally understood and usually agreed upon as the most significant material benefit that black Barbadians back home derived from Panama money: it allowed them to purchase land and thereby to gain at least partial escape from plantation oppression.

Contemporary observers noted how important it was for returning Panama men to be able to buy land with money they had brought or sent home. But unlike shop goods or lumber, land in Barbados was not a commodity immediately available everywhere in small, affordable packages. The sugar bounty depression and the subsequent dislocations created by economic change had, however, generally loosened the private planters' grip on the land; and at the same time Panama money was flowing back to Barbados, economic necessity was forcing some planters to sell off their property to blacks. So, for example, in about 1910 when Dr. E.G. Pilgrim, an assemblyman from St. James parish, sold portions of his vast holdings at Carlton, Sion Hill, Westmoreland, and Reids Bay—estate lands tumbling down from the St. James escarpment right to the water's edge—Panama money bought up the land in small blocks.[35] Old informants in St. James who recall their parents' describing the land

The Social and Economic Changes   189

purchases, suggest that prospective buyers came from other parishes as well as from St. James. The demographic changes in Barbados in the century's first two decades therefore were often of a rural-to-rural character and influenced in some cases more by land availability than they were by the magnetic appeal of the city.

No known cadastral survey exists for Barbados at any scale which shows either the acreage or location of lands purchased with Panama money. Old informants throughout the island, not just in St. James parish, showed me property and deeds that they said had been bought with Panama remittances, although these incomplete and subjective reports hardly provide the basis for mapping land transfers early in the twentieth century.

The limited islandwide data that do exist for the period, however, substantiate the contention that a good deal of Panama money was devoted to land purchases on Barbados. From the estimated 8,500 small proprietors controlling 10,000 acres in 1897, the number of smallholders increased to 13,152 by 1912 (table 12), an estimated 15,000 by 1917,[36] and 17,731 by 1929.[37] No one really knew the total acreage involved in these land transfers. Seven estates of St. Michael parish totaling 970 acres were either being sold in small blocks or rented as such between 1912 and 1917, a figure that does not include small land plots held from an earlier date.[38] A 1917 map diagram dividing Barbados into various "oil mining" areas enumerates 8,557 acres (2,294 for St. Philip parish) held by smallholders among eight of the island's eleven parishes; the diagram gives no evidence for St. Joseph or the urban parishes of St. Michael and Christchurch.[39]

The varied and even informal means by which individuals (sometimes acting through relatives to whom they had sent money) purchased small blocks of land complicated any effort to maintain complete and accurate records of land transfers. Upon the sale and parceling out of the several Barbadian estates after the turn of the century, often there were no title deeds because they either had been lost or none ever had existed. And after having exhausted all of his or her saved earnings in acquiring a piece of land, a black Barbadian returnee from Panama many times had nothing left over with which to engage a lawyer in order to secure a clear land title. Occasionally, therefore, the

Table 12. Persons Owning Fewer than Five Acres of Land in Barbados, 1912

Parish	No. of Persons
St. Michael	1,125
Christchurch	1,802
St. George	1,494
St. Philip	1,811
St. James	1,855
St. Thomas	710
St. John	491
St. Peter	809
St. Joseph	737
St. Andrew	955
St. Lucy	1,363
Total	13,152

Source: Results from a return prepared by Parochial Treasurers, *Barbados Blue Book* (1915–1916), Y1.

buyer of a small land plot received only a receipt and sometimes nothing at all. Beginning in 1910, a means was devised to establish land titles for such plots whose legal status was hazy; it involved foreclosures on fictive mortgages—"selling" the land back to the owner—and is said to have benefited greatly small Barbadian landowners for whom this legal ploy probably was invented.[40]

The land transfer process was complicated further by intervening speculators, white men who bought up defunct estates, parceled them out, and sold them in small plots. The speculators apparently sold land plots in all Barbadian parishes, although their activities were particularly intense in the Bridgetown area. Speculators, after buying St. Michael plantations, established the Bush Hall Company and Bank Hall Company, dividing the land for sale into plots as small as one-eighth of an acre. Individuals like Athelstan Watson, who sold roughly 1,600 acres, mainly in Christchurch, profited handsomely from land speculation.[41] The combination of blacks' cumulative demand for small land plots and the rapid, unplanned division of estates into urban residential areas led to a proliferation of the inferior sanitation and water services that always had characterized lower-class housing districts in the Bridgetown area. In an assembly debate in April 1928, W.S. Patterson of St. Andrew was indignant that Barbadian taxpayers, and not the land speculators themselves, were expected to pay for water and sanitation services in the areas that had been cut up and sold. Patterson likened the activities of British World War I profiteers to those of Barbadian land speculators "who within the last twenty-five years have been engaged in the business of sucking the blood out of people who have to get somewhere to live."[42]

Under the influence of Panama money, black residential areas expanded and sprawled through the urban areas even more than they had in the past. As rural blacks invaded the city with enough remitted cash to make down payments for house plots, the urban streets and lanes that had formerly been either deserted or white residential areas now became lined with chattel houses from the countryside. And, as far as white observers were concerned, every black household was composed not only of parents, grandparents, and innumerable children, but also chickens, pigs, goats, and even cattle. These country people, and their animals, moreover, all seemed to awaken well before dawn with a clamor that proved annoying to residents of the previously sedate white neighborhoods. At the January 1917 meeting of the Civic Circle (a public-spirited group of women of the Bridgetown area) the unsightly state of the tenantry housing in the Tweedside Road area of Carrington Village was a subject of concerned discussion. One means of eliminating these repugnant spectacles, of course, was to prevent white owners from selling land to black Barbadians. Lady Carter, the wife of the former governor, mused that it might be advisable for the group to "agitate for a law . . . to remedy this evil."[43]

Prices for small plots varied from one part of the island to another, the highest prices being found in the urban area. In 1917 land in the outlying parishes sold for as little as £20 per acre but in

St. Michael parish, it sold for up to £100 per acre. Inflation had pushed prices up even further by 1920 so that land in St. John parish was reported to have been sold for as much as £200 per acre.[44] Wide price disparities seem to have existed throughout the island as sellers generally charged buyers as much as they thought they could ask. Panama money had played an important role in raising land prices, bidding up the prices of Barbadian land and creating its own inflationary spiral.

Land availability, in part created by the sudden presence of so much money, had caused its own migration momentum, stimulating yet more travel abroad to earn yet more money. After a returnee from Panama had built a house for his wife or mother, he might have enough cash left over to make a substantial down payment on a piece of land. The need for more money to pay off the incurred debt then often sent him away again, perhaps to Cuba or even to the United States. From those destinations, then, he remitted money to pay off a debt incurred originally with a down payment of money earned in Panama. It therefore seems futile, and even misleading, to attempt to delineate with accuracy the land and houses of Barbados that were purchased with Panama money as opposed to those purchased with money from another source. More important is that Panama money stimulated the demographic rural-to-urban shifts and the erection of new houses on newly purchased land plots in Barbados, setting further trends in motion in the first decades of the century. In describing the evolution of recent small-scale settlements in Barbados, Henry Lofty testified before the 1929 Sugar Commission that it really had begun when "people sent back money from Panama with which to buy land and put houses on them; and since then, other persons have bought places of two or three acres here and there."[45]

As an owner of a piece of land, regardless of its size, a black Barbadian had achieved tangible success usually far greater than that known by his or her father or grandfather. He or she also had earned a measure of independence from the plantocracy because the plot of land acted as a safety net. An elderly informant from St. Peter parish recalled how his father had gone to Panama and returned with a large steamer trunk. Then his father worked again on a local estate until he had enough total savings to buy a small plot of land, to which the family moved in 1925: "We could then tell the plantation to go to hell." Throughout Barbados and the Commonwealth Caribbean in general, working-class peoples have expressed (not always in such direct terms) similar sentiments about controlling land. Within the region, especially in Barbados, where black working peoples have been denied land for centuries, ownership of land, however small the plot, also has had much more than functional or economic significance. Throughout the islands there is "a deeply felt attachment to the land that transcends the realm of economics."[46] Sidney Mintz and Richard Price suggest that Afro-Caribbean "use of land as a means of defining both time and descent" may have an even more fundamental West African origin.[47]

In a more particularistic sense, the liquid quality of money, including Panama money, probably inspired black Barbadians to invest much of it in a fixed asset like land. The accumulation of cash gave a black Barbadian the capital necessary to be more flexible than ever before. But, as Mary Douglas has pointed out in an imaginative follow-through on the water metaphor for money, the "capacity that money has for flowing freely in all directions can be a great nuisance."[48] In order to keep their money from flowing to friends, kinsmen, and others, returnees from Panama had only a limited set of investment alternatives. Banking the money, an alternative chosen by hundreds of blacks possessing cash from Panama, still meant encountering and entrusting white bureaucrats and officials with one's savings. Investing the money in land, although it meant paying extraordinarily large sums, probably was considered by many a safer hedge against having their money "flow" away.

Although the collective term *peasantry* was usually used to depict the smallholders of Barbados early in the century, the proliferation of parceled plots of land and the establishment of individual houses on them did not represent a return to or a yearning by black Barbadians for more agrarian, traditional, subsistence, or rustic modes of livelihood. According to C.C. Skeete, who conducted a survey of small-scale holdings in Barbados in 1929, there were many "peasant proprietors" on the island but few "peasant farmers." In many cases, the possessors of small plots of land had avocations unrelated to agriculture.

These incongruous conditions, according to Skeete, were most marked in St. Michael parish, where much of the land was in the hands of small holders yet "a considerable portion of this land is entirely neglected and lying waste."[49] And, of course, the partitioning of small plots of land in the Bridgetown area, at Bank Hall or Carrington Village or any of the similar black residential areas, represented, on the surface, a proliferation of smallholders and would be included that way in islandwide land tenure surveys. But it would be entirely inappropriate to label newly arrived black urban dwellers "peasants," regardless of the barnyard noises that now reverberated throughout the Bridgetown area early every morning.

When small-scale landholders, many of whom had recently purchased their small bits of acreage with Panama money, did cultivate their land, they now usually chose to grow sugar cane. Land purchased by blacks for agrarian purposes in the rural parishes no longer served only as subsistence insurance against ecological catastrophe but represented more and more a potential source of cash. Using their land as collateral, small-scale cane farmers could borrow small amounts of money to finance sugar cane cultivation, which, in turn, yielded the high money returns from World War I prices. By 1916, the food deficit situation on Barbados was becoming troublesome. The main problems lay in the lack of interest by the local black labor force (the traditional producers of provision crops) in growing potatoes, corn, or any crop other than sugar cane, even on their rented tenantry plots.[50] In some rural areas, black smallholders—who grew sugar cane on their own land—were then obliged, ironically, to work on nearby estates in order to become eligible to receive the potatoes that the plantations now were legally mandated to produce by the Vegetable Produce Act.[51]

The growth of a small-scale, rural, landed class in Barbados during an area of modernization marked by a fully monetized economy, fading paternalism, and an emphasis on cash-paying jobs seems, at first sight, odd and inconsistent. It was, however, not land possession per se but the use of the land—in this case the cultivation of sugar cane—that was more important in understanding the motivations of black Barbadians at the time. Woodville Marshall has provided other keys to understanding these issues by pointing out that, on closer inspection, the small land plots that were sold almost invariably were in the hilly, dry, infertile parts of the island. Throughout the St. George Valley, for example, little land was sold to blacks save on the sloping "rabland" escarpments. And much of the drought-prone St. Philip and Christchurch littoral was sold out—not the moister interior zones. Also, according to Marshall, "it became obvious to some planters occupying estates near Bridgetown or on the shallow black soils . . . that it was far more profitable to convert their estates into residential areas."[52] Such a land divestiture strategy proved profitable for the planters in at least two ways. First, it caused them to be the ultimate recipients of a good deal of the Panama money in return for what was, in many cases, only marginal property. Second, it established a nearby, seasonally available workforce living independently of the estates, people to whom the estates owned none of the social and economic obligations of earlier days.

Changing conditions in Barbados meant that, for black workers, land ownership was all the more important. After the exodus to Panama, the inflation-creating scramble for small plots of Barbadian land had become even more intense than in times past, partly because those without land could no longer depend on planter generosity in a changing social atmosphere. The located laborer statutes binding landless workers to particular sugar cane plantations were still in effect, and, if anything, the eviction stipulations of these laws were carried out with even greater exactitude than before. Sugar cane planters often now could rely on nearby small landholders to work seasonally for cash and access to the estate's potato patch. And with higher sugar prices, estates coveted the provision grounds that they legally were obligated to provide for tenantry dwellers. Without the personal security that often had characterized the paternalistic plantation of the past, those rural black Barbadian men, women, and their children with little money and no land in the second decade of the twentieth century were, in several fundamental ways, even worse off than before.

Despite the profiteering by urban land speculators and also by individual planters, the release of thousands of tiny land plots to black Barbadians gave them a personal stake in local agriculture and a security they had never known. In more than one case, Panama money bought a piece of land which, in turn, yielded sugar cane profits that allowed a black Barbadian to become a petty entrepreneur or to buy even more land. As for the future, a small landowner had a modern independence; and the possession of land provided partial safety from the plantation excesses that had been so much a part of the Barbadian past. An octogenarian of St. George parish, while tending his own small garden plot, explained to me in 1982 what he thought was the significance of owning his own property: "You can't call yourself independent, waiting on another man's money."

Diet and Disease

In his research dealing with the subsistence ecology of the Miskito Indians of eastern Nicaragua, Bernard Nietschmann has elucidated the interrelated changes that accompany the alteration of local subsistence systems by external, cash-oriented, market demands. Local social relationships change, the local exploitation of cash-yielding resources is intensified, precarious dependency replaces self-sufficiency. Nietschmann places the differences between sharing and selling foodstuffs at the core of the changes he has described: "To sell a subsistence resource is a social contradiction. If a family produces food, they are obligated to share; if they purchase food, they are under no social obligation; if they sell what should be shared, they bring into conflict the opposing rules in the two economc systems."[53]

Analogous changes occurred among members of the black working class of Barbados early in the twentieth century, changes created by Panama money. By the century's second decade the need for black Barbadians to increase their "money income . . . to meet their subsistence requirements became magnified."[54] The pursuit of money, furthermore, detracted from family food production. Sharing no longer was expected or necessary. And the varied effects of these changes on the relationships among black individuals and families of rural areas was obvious, at least to those old Barbadians who witnessed them or recall what their parents had said. An old man born in 1897 in St. Andrew parish summarized these events for me in words only slightly different from the testimonies of at least a dozen other elderly Barbadians: "In those old days, people gave food to each other. If you had, you would give. Then they started to sell food. Now everybody looks out for himself. There was more love in their hearts back then."

Among the observations of the black West Indian labor force by American overseers in the earliest years of the canal construction was the oft-repeated suggestion "that they were not getting proper food in sufficient and regular amounts to give them strength for continuous work."[55] In the later years, the Americans provided mess halls at various locations in the Canal Zone. Nutritious, low-cost meals provided therein improved black workers' diets as well as their working efficiency. But the idea of spending one's wages—or at least a substantial part of one's wages—for subsistence had not been immediately accepted by the first Barbadian immigrants to Panama. Most of their food back home in Barbados had come from the garden plots. So, as far as the first Barbadian arrivals in Panama were concerned, food was not a commodity to be purchased with cash but, rather, it should be shared, much as mangoes and breadfruit are shared in some villages of the Windward Islands in the late twentieth century. Among the earliest Barbadian arrivals in the Canal Zone, this customary reluctance to buy food was combined with an insatiable appetite for money. The combination of scrimping on subsistence and also saving money had caused "Prince" from Barbados to work himself to death and had motivated the typical black Barbadian worker: "Money is his object. He saves it by living on cheap fare. Sardines and biscuits are resorted to. The doctors warn him that he is reducing his system by poor feeding to such a low point that, deprived of stamina, he must of necessity go under if fever or other illness attacks him."[56]

In the following decade, however, Barbadian canal workers had accepted the notion of paying for food and had sent the money home which itself had reoriented the Barbadian landscape so that it too might produce more cash. Throughout Barbados by 1917 smallholders were planting cane, and the near-disappearance of provisions in some areas led to lament as well as assertions that the tending of subsistence crops was a lost art on the island. Whereas in years past, neighbors had shared vegetables back and forth, small-scale landowners now were reluctant to plant yams, potatoes, or other food crops because the rate of garden pilferage was so high.[57]

The records for foodstuffs imported into Barbados between 1901 and 1920 support, in a general way, the observation that during these two decades sugar cane progressively dominated the acreage of the Barbadian countryside.[58] The published food import data, unfortunately, were not always recorded in comparable units. And any interpretation of these figures would have to take into account the changing conditions in the traditional North American food supplying areas (especially during World War I) as well as the declining population of Barbados during the years in question. In any case, in 1905 Barbados imported 39,000 barrels of wheat and rye flour from the United States and Canada. In 1910 the island imported 41,000 barrels, and in 1913, 57,000 barrels; these data suggest a growing dependency on external foodstuffs.

As black Barbadians were planting a higher percentage of their owned and rented land plots in sugar cane, they began to turn more to imported rice as a dietary staple. Rice sold for a penny per pint at both the markets and at small shops throughout the countryside. In 1901, Barbados imported 5.8 million pounds of rice, mostly from India. Imported rice increased to 8 million pounds by 1910 and climbed to over 13 million imported pounds during both 1915 and 1916, even though the local population was declining during these same years. The source for rice also was changing. In 1917, when Barbados imported 11.6 million pounds of rice, 9 million came from British Guiana. The British colony on the coast of South America was conveniently located for Barbadians during the war because of the possible disruptions of extra-Caribbean trade networks by hostile forces. In March 1918 the Barbados House of Assembly guaranteed ten dollars for each 180-pound bag of milled rice from British Guiana for 4,000 bags per month. The passage of this measure was described as "extremely urgent" because the rice from British Guiana "may turn out to be our principal resource for the supply of the wants of the community."[59]

But dependence even upon sister colonies for food in times of crisis and rampant price inflation could be dangerous. The Vegetable Produce Act, which remained in effect for the duration of the war, called for every Barbadian planter or manager controlling more than three acres to arrange to have planted "sweet potatoes, yams, eddoes, corn, cassava, peas, beans, and all plants . . . for human consumption" not to exceed 10 percent of their land. During the assembly debates preceding the act, individual planters moaned about having to forgo cane cultivation, although the seriousness of the local food deficit carried the day. The act affected not only plantation owners, but it also made clear that the easy-going days of tolerating petty larceny of foodstuffs in the countryside were over. Under section ten, any male caught stealing or aiding in the theft of vegetables in the Barbadian countryside was subject to flogging "in addition to undergoing any other punishment which may be awarded."[60]

With more money coming to black Barbadians, more local land in sugar cane, and therefore a greater amount of food imported and purchased with cash, parish medical officers began to notice new and different nutrition problems among the local populace. As early as 1910, the medical officer of St. John parish deplored the growing propensity of local peoples to buy imported foods in country shops. The people would be much better off, healthier, and more energetic if they were to eat "the good and wholesome vegetables . . . grown in this island instead of this shop good rubbish" according to Dr. W.B. Clarke.[61]

The nutrition problems associated with imported foods were not imaginary. In 1916 Barbados suffered what was considered, at first, an outbreak of yellow fever. In December, Dr. Juan Guiteras, a member of the International Health Board of the Rockefeller Institute of New York and a veteran of the recent campaign against yellow fever in Cuba, arrived in Barbados. Guiteras traveled throughout the island for more than a week, inspecting possible cases of yellow fever. He eventually pronounced the disease not yellow fever at all but probably febrile jaundice. One of the probable causes, according to Guiteras, was malnutrition, for which rising prices of foodstuffs were partly responsible.[62]

Pellagra, a disease caused by a shortage of the B vitamin niacin and an ailment with many symptoms but best known for scaly and rough skin, was rampant among the black populace of St. Lucy parish in 1907. Dr. Hallam Massiah, the parish medical officer, attributed it to poverty and the lack of meat in the local diet. Specifically, Massiah associated pellagra with "the eating habitually of maize . . . which is often lumpy, sour, and manifestly unfit for human consumption." Locally produced corn was all right, but corn imported in bags and spoiled by fermentation was responsible for pellagra, a disease which eventually could lead to death.[63]

Pellagra was not recognized as a vitamin deficiency ailment until quite late in medical history.[64] Almost certainly pellagra earlier had afflicted Barbadian slaves, whose diet traditionally had been supplemented by corn imported from America. Furthermore, after emancipation, pellagra probably had been confused with eczema or malaria. The apparent relationship between pellagra and drought in Barbados suggests further that the disease probably had attacked black Barbadians for decades. A high incidence of pellagra was reported throughout the island during the drought periods of 1912 and 1914, when prolonged aridity desiccated the beans and peas in black workers' provision plots.[65]

By the second decade of the twentieth century, pellagra among poor black Barbadians was being identified less with local climatic conditions than it was with the human decision to produce fewer local foodstuffs in favor of more sugar cane. Not surprisingly, the rates of pellagra were higher among the urban and suburban poor of St. Michael parish than in any other areas of the island. In the Bridgetown area, where crowded and unsanitary living conditions and a high rate of garden thievery all precluded widespread cultivation of vegetables, the urban poor relied heavily upon "imported and highly milled foods such as flour, rice, and perhaps corn-meal" for subsistence. Because of the dietary reliance on imported cereals in the urban area, the St. Michael almshouse now always had more inmates suffering from pellagra than anywhere else on the island.[66]

Diet was not the cause of all diseases, however. As St. Michael parish and adjoining areas of Christchurch became more crowded in the second decade of the century, the tenantries in and around Bridgetown were even less sanitary than before. Underlying causes aside, the planters and colonial officials were right to point out that, as more black families from the countryside jammed into the urban tenantries, the filth and squalor

The Social and Economic Changes 201

there accelerated. More and more chattel houses packed into confined areas, for example, disrupted existing drainage. At Jackmans tenantry, northeast of Bridgetown but still in St. Michael parish, the recent placement of houses near roads in 1916 deflected water from roadside standpipes so as to create "a quagmire alongside the road," inhibiting pedestrian locomotion through the village and hindering the travel of passers-by, problems existing elsewhere in the parish for the same reasons.[67]

The accumulation and stagnation of fresh water around the limestone groundsels of chattel houses, however, were minor aggravations when compared with those associated with human sewage disposal in the Bridgetown tenantries. Soils in many of the black residential zones had become, literally, saturated with cesspits. In theory, residents of these areas now were assigned nearby jetties to which they were supposed to journey each night to dump the family fecal matter into the ocean. More often than not, however, the family members disposed of their waste material by informally "going out" (finding an open drain, a cane field, or nearby gully in which to empty their kerosene tins and pails).[68] It hardly needs emphasis that, with the grounds and yards of urban and suburban tenantries absorbing ever-greater amounts of human waste, the cultivation of foodstuffs in these areas posed serious health hazards. The annual health report for Barbados in 1917 observed that in the Bridgetown area "when such products as lettuce, cucumber, radish, etc., which are commonly eaten uncooked, are grown under such conditions, it is wonderful that intestinal diseases are not even more prevalent than they are."[69]

Changing conditions in the Barbadian countryside, moreover, meant that rural areas no longer offered bucolic relief from the stench and squalor of urban tenantries. Early in 1916, the medical officer of St. Andrew parish remarked upon an "urgent matter" in his area. In several instances he had documented "foul drainage escaping from estate yards and polluting adjacent streams." Although the precise character of the discharge was unspecified, there seemed little doubt that the increase in rural pollution was related to the introduction of large factories into the Barbadian countryside. Eventually, the changes they brought about would alter irrevocably the quality of life for everyone in rural parishes, especially in the grinding season: "If each such factory is permitted to continue the present procedure . . . residence in the surounding districts—and so in the island generally—will become well-nigh intolerable for several months in each year."[70]

Although the influx of Panama money had improved living conditions for thousands of black Barbadian families, the incidence of pellagra was increasing in Bridgetown and the traditional diseases of both rural and urban tenantries continued to infect countless individuals. There still was no compulsory isolation required or any other official action prescribed by law to help prevent the spread of typhoid in the autumn of 1917. Unusually heavy September rains had blocked a tunnel leading from a spring near Plum Tree Gully in the northern part of the island. Apparently the surface water, badly contaminated with typhoid germs, gained access to the spring itself. More than 150 cases of typhoid, mainly in St. Lucy, St. Peter, an St. James parishes, resulted from the contamination. Black workers at Spring Hall estate in St. Lucy, drinking from a polluted spring that came out in the estate yard, were hit especially hard.[71]

Isolation requirements and other official measures were not taken against typhoid in Barbados until 1921, in the wake of a catastrophic epidemic of the disease. A total of 3,070 cases of typhoid were reported, the overwhelming majority as discussed in chapter 3, among the black population. A combination of drought, plummeting prices for sugar, and continued high prices for food were physical and social variables creating "low water supplies and low food supplies," all of which helped the epidemic along.[72] Under these conditions, the infant mortality rate soared. Of each 1,000 live births in 1921, 401 Barbadian babies died before their first birthday; the highest rate was 459 in St. Michael parish, the lowest (287) in St. Andrew. The exceptionally high overall death rate of more than 43 per 1,000 Barbadians in 1921 was attributed to a "wide-spread epidemic of enteric fever . . . a large number of deaths from pellagra, and the high infantile mortality."[73]

The local social and economic changes that had been inspired by world events and infusions of Panama money had not found their counterpart in the inert Barbadian health care system, still characterized by the same placid indifference as in the late nineteenth century. Dr. Gooding described the familiar ordeal involved for any black resident of St. Michael parish seeking official medical care as late as 1916: "Applicants for dispensary tickets in this parish first have to go to the inspector at the parochial buildings, and then take their ticket to the medical officer at the almshouse. This entails a double walk before they can be examined and, in case of serious illness, must add to their suffering."74

As more medical experts from abroad visited Barbados and as human knowledge of communicable diseases increased in general, the shocking backwardness exhibited by the dearth of local health measures on the island regressed from lamentable to intolerable. As in years past, local actions taken to improve health conditions and increase life expectancies of members of the working class had to be instigated by the Colonial Office. A Public Health Commission was convened in Barbados in September 1925, a conference called by the secretary of state for the colonies acting upon the criticisms of Barbados's inadequate health standards by the British Colonial Advisory Medical and Sanitary Committee.75 The commission could very well have adopted as an agenda a report published by Dr. John Hutson, the public health inspector of Barbados, during the previous year. In the *Official Gazette* of April 24, 1924, Hutson—in an apparent attempt at morbid humor—presented a report entitled "Ten Years of Sanitary Progress." Hutson listed forty-one different official recommendations for the improvement of public health on Barbados that had been made to various local officials since 1913. The recommendations ranged from the specific control of disease vectors and sanitary conditions (e.g., control of the local commercial milk supply, control of flies and rats, canalization of the Constitution River to reduce water stagnation in Bridgetown) to specific recommendations suggesting administrative improvements of the existing public health system (e.g., improved administration of the Vaccination Act, training and certification of parish sanitary inspectors, improved sanitary control over tenantries). For the overwhelming majority of these recommendations Hutson then listed little or no action; indeed, "No action taken" was the most common entry in his enumeration. Hutson concluded his report with disappointment but determination to keep recommending a modern, enlightened health care system for Barbados, reiterating the misgivings that he had stated originally in 1915 "that only epidemics seem to be able to wake up the authorities to the deficits of the system."[76]

The tragedies of continuously high infant mortality rates and the inadequate health standards in Barbados, both of which persisted into the 1920s, were reasons enough for the mass indignation, worker unrest, and incipient political activism that was beginning to stir. But the health and sanitation deficiencies of the island took on special political meaning because of the medical background of Charles Duncan O'Neale.[77] O'Neale, a black Barbadian whose picture now appears on the ten dollar currency note of Barbados, founded the Democratic League and also the Workingmen's Association on the island during the 1920s and generally is credited with orchestrating and articulating much of the frustration and resentment of Barbados's black working class at the time. O'Neale had attended Harrison College in Bridgetown and at the turn of the century had proceeded to Edinburgh University to study medicine. During nearly a quarter of a century in the United Kingdom, O'Neale had not only worked in medicine in the Edinburgh and Newcastle areas, but he also had witnessed first hand a good deal of working-class activism, strikes, and unrest. He had also become an enthusiastic exponent of Fabian socialism in Britain before returning home to Barbados in 1924.

As a committed socialist, O'Neale recognized the plight of the black Barbadian working class as analogous to the plight of the working class in the United Kingdom. As a trained medical specialist, O'Neale had seen little or no improvement in the miserable, unsanitary conditions he had left more than two decades earlier. Therefore, much of O'Neale's oratory to assembled black audiences in Barbados in the 1920s dealt precisely with health and sanitation issues: the sociopolitical apathy on the parts of colonial officials—not black ignorance—was to blame for these conditions, according to O'Neale. On many evenings during the 1920s, Charles Duncan O'Neale could be found at the speaker's podium at the meeting hall of the Workingmen's Association on Passage Road in Bridgetown "as usual . . . on the War Path" enumerating to black audiences the starving black children of the colony, their improper hospital treatment, lack of tenantry sanitation, malnourishment, and the exceptionally high black Barbadian death rates.[78]

Change in the Friendly Societies

The Barbadian friendly society movement, its mutual-aid objectives rendered ineffectual by the meager cash wages of the bounty sugar depression, was resuscitated by Panama money. The five or ten dollars received every six months from a husband, son, or father in Panama often was largely dissipated by the twelve cents paid each week to the local friendly society treasurer in return for the insurance of sick benefits and death benefits. Recent laws now required the officers of each friendly society to deposit funds collected from the membership into the society's account at the national savings bank. But the ultmate government banking control over local friendly society funds did not reduce the attractiveness to black Barbadians of being able to deposit their small amounts of money with trusted local treasurers in familiar surroundings.

This cumulative grass-roots investment strategy had a dramatic impact throughout the island (table 13). Long-standing friendly societies, whose funds had been nearly depleted, suddenly surged with new life and vigor. Old societies, stricken from the rolls in 1902 by Governor Hodgson's decree, reappeared. New societies were established, often by returnees who had themselves formed their own informal friendly societies in Panama during their work sojourns there. Back in Barbados, each year of the era of Panama money saw new friendly societies formed—fifty-eight (the most of any year) in 1907 and fifty-one in 1908. Had dozens of newly founded Barbadian friendly societies not failed (through small size, inexperience or dishonesty of the treasurers, or emigration of its officers or members), the growth of the colony's friendly society movement in the first twenty years of the twentieth century would have been even more remarkable.

By 1908 the total membership in Barbadian friendly societies had more than trebled from its 1904 membership (table 13). It is, moreover, likely that by 1908 almost every black family on the island was represented on the friendly society roles. This pros-

Table 13. Barbadian Friendly Societies, 1901–1920

Year	No. of Friendly Societies	Total No. of Members	Total No. of Dependents
1901	101	—	—
1902	98	—	—
1903	96	—	—
1904	92	13,933	—
1905	124	—	—
1906	156	25,564	—
1907	213	—	—
1908	233	43,416	—
1909	253	48,178	—
1910	268	45,493	—
1911	280	47,951	—
1912	278	46,668	126,157
1913	280	42,850	110,458
1914	285	42,458	114,895
1915	281	42,681	115,355
1916	278	43,678	121,161
1917	276	44,149	118,694
1918	269	42,234	116,259
1919	264	45,164	121,956
1920	260	46,201	121,783

Note: Dashes mean that data are unavailable.
Source: Data from Barbados, *Blue Books*, 1901–1921.

pect is at least suggested by the islandwide data gathered by the registrar of friendly societies and included in table 13. In 1912 the annual colonial *Blue Books* began to publish "numbers of dependents" as well as the total membership; it never was clear from these data if the numbers of the members were included along with dependents for statistical purposes. If not, Barbadian friendly society coverage included *more* people altogether than the 156,312 counted in the 1921 census. This possibility is more likely than it seems at first glance because so many Barbadians resided temporarily abroad. These data, on the other hand, could be misleading because of a widespread tendency for a single individual at the time to join two or even three friendly societies.

Friendly society membership was still usually based on one's residential location, especially in rural areas where individual familiarity with a society's officers and treasurer declined rapidly with distance. Most Barbadian friendly societies remained reasonably small and manageable; in 1914, of the 285 registered friendly societies, 44 had memberships of less than 50, 127 had memberships of less than 100, and 207 friendly societies had fewer than 200 members. The greatest number of friendly societies were found, not surprisingly, in St. Michael parish, where the offices of 102 were registered; the smallest number were in St. Andrew and St. Thomas, each of which had 7 friendly societies within its boundaries.[79]

The annual *Blue Books* maintained no cumulative investment data summing the money carried in the accounts of all of the friendly societies together, but for certain years in the first decades of the century they did publish individual society balances as they stood at the first of the year. However, for reasons explained shortly, the sums on January 1 of a given year were only fractions of the total amount collected by a friendly society during the rest of the year. The individual account ledgers for many of the friendly societies in the Panama money era are available in the Barbados National Bank volumes at the Barbados Archives. Perusing these old account ledgers reveals that it was not uncommon for individual friendly societies to maintain a balance of £100, and sometimes much more, between 1905 and 1920. Altogether, Barbadian friendly societies collected many thousands of pounds each year.

Unlike black expenditures of Panama money for food, clothing, lumber, or land, and unlike the establishment and maintenance of individual savings accounts, the investment of small sums of money in local friendly societies did not represent an immediate flow of cash into the hands of white merchants, land speculators, or bankers. Instead, friendly society money represented temporarily pooled savings. And black friendly society officials—individuals who often were officers in two or even more friendly societies—were authorized to withdraw a society's funds from the bank with the approval of the membership. In other words, the sudden black control of more cash than ever before represented an obvious threat to white officials, especially because of the temporary control of large sums of the money by relatively few friendly society officers. What if an islandwide friendly society movement were to coalesce black savings into even fewer hands? The implications of such a prospect required little imagination. Widespread and growing financial strength among black Barbadians, heretofore distributed as small sums in individuals' hands, could, within a seemingly innocuous institution like a friendly society, rapidly be focused toward a takeover of traditionally white resources. Even the land itself might be purchased with pooled friendly society money. The 1905 Friendly Societies Act passed by the Barbados legislature included a crucial proviso in order to prevent the unthinkable: "Nothing . . . shall authorize a benevolent Society to hold land exceeding one acre in extent."[80]

But at the same time that white Barbadian legislators were considering legal constraints to prevent the investment of friendly society savings in large blocks of land, individual black Barbadians were preoccupied with husbanding their precious nest eggs of money for more mundane purposes. And the community friendly society, heretofore providing mutual aid on the local level, thereby found itself transformed by Panama money into a kind of local savings bank. Remitted wages from the Canal Zone had not only swelled the number, membership, and total savings of Barbadian friendly societies; they also had changed the very nature of the societies themselves. Suddenly, members were much more interested in end-of-year "bonuses" to be paid out by friendly societies rather than their providing health insurance. In early 1908 the registrar of friendly societies for Barbados commented unfavorably on the new role of local friendly societies: "It occurs to me that a very large number of the Friendly Societies . . . are being worked more with the object of . . . a Bonus than on the primary idea of relieving the sick and distressed and burying the dead, which ought to be their proper basis."[81]

The Barbadian friendly society actually had become more of a "dividing society" or "share-out club," with its provision of sick benefits greatly diminished. The cash bonuses or payments (essentially, an accumulation of what a member had paid into the society during the year minus fees and deductions for society officials' payments) were paid out to the membership in mid-December. The surviving account ledgers demonstrate that, during the years of the influx of Panama money, Barbadian friendly societies paid out the great majority of their accumulated funds every year about two weeks before Christmas. Sometime between December 10 and 13 the society's account always showed a massive withdrawal—of at least one-half and often three-quarters and even more—of its funds.

The payment of the Christmas bonus from the local friendly society took on a festive air within each rural area of Barbados. Society members had deposited remittances, done without, and waited for months to receive as little as five dollars from the society's treasurer. But with even this relatively small amount of cash, a man or woman could buy a ham for Christmas, some paint for the weather-beaten chattel house, or long-promised toys and clothing for the children. Again the terms *craze* and *frenzy* came into common usage. This time they were used to describe the attitudes of black Barbadians as they anticipated, collected, and spent their Christmas savings each December. The anxiety produced among Barbadians, when compared with all other British West Indians, by the Christmas bonus from the friendly society during the early twentieth century has been described as "literally spectacular." On occasion, bonus-seeking crowds of would-be recipients of cash were said actually to besiege friendly society offices, breaking down the doors and climbing through the windows.[82]

The preoccupation with cash bonuses meant eschewing sick benefits, if at all possible, because a member receiving sick payments for himself or a dependent automatically became ineligible for the end-of-year bonus payment. In a number of cases, black families began to commit the old and enfeebled to parish almshouses rather than applying for society sick benefits. Then, when the elderly died, family members would retrieve their corpses from the almshouses, collect the death benefits from the local friendly societies, and provide proper burials. The several parish vestry officers complained bitterly. Members of friendly societies, according to vestrymen, should provide health care for their kinsmen rather than burden the parish taxpayers with such expenses. As early as 1909, St. Thomas and Christchurch parishes instituted rules against admitting the dependents of friendly society members to almshouses, although the enforcement of such regulations were, of course, most difficult to carry out. In November 1910 the St. Philip parish vestry passed a regulation "that the bodies of inmates dying in the almshouse should only be given up to relatives on the payment by the latter of sixpence a day for upkeep during residence in the almshouse." St. Philip vestry officials claimed that families of the deceased really were more interested in receiving friendly society death benefits than they were in providing appropriate interments for their parents and grandparents.[83]

In discussing with me the changing Barbadian friendly societies of the early twentieth century, an old man of St. Thomas parish combined and analyzed what he remembered and what he had been told by his mother: "After Panama, friendly societies was just money. There was no harmonizin' in it anymore." Indeed, almost everyone had noticed that, as the friendly societies had become explicitly economic institutions, their traditional moralistic, religious-oriented functions had all but disappeared. Funeral processions became rare, meetings went unattended, social activities no longer were important:

> The Barbadian Friendly Societies are . . . primarily share-out clubs. . . . There is . . . little evidence that popular interest in the Friendly Society extends beyond the claiming of Bonus and burial money, and the necessary . . . paying [of] dues; it is not a group with any vigorous social life. It appears that in times past such activities counted for rather more.[84]

And as the community-level friendly societies became more

like banking institutions than mutual-help societies, the relationships between members and treasurers were altered. The community-level appeal of the local friendly society—as a comfortable investment alternative to dealing with outsiders, mainly whites—had faded during the era of Panama money. For example, the local friendly society's treasurer—whose elusive whereabouts, fondness for new clothes, and questionable integrity had been the subjects of lighthearted jokes within the tenantry for years—now sometimes was viewed with the same suspicion earlier reserved for white Barbadians and colonial officials.

At the turn of the century, friendly societies had provided, through small amounts of cash and reciprocal moral support, insurance for destitute Barbadian blacks. The presence and familiarity of the friendly societies enabled them to receive tens of thousands of pounds of remitted Panama money. These substantial sums, however, and the changing Barbadian attitudes, turning away from paternalism and interdependence toward an individualism based on money transactions, transformed the local friendly society. Unlike village credit societies that exist in some less-developed areas of the world and which have served as bridges between unmonetized economies and later commercial systems, the Barbadian friendly society was not a temporal link between a subsistence system and the cash economy which followed. Nevertheless, the societies played crucial roles in mobilizing, pooling, and saving—all within a familiar environment—Panama money in the early twentieth century and thereby helped to shape the attitudes and values that motivated black Barbadians into the 1920s and 1930s. Like rotating credit societies elsewhere during a period of flux, the Barbadian friendly society had the "ability to organize traditional relationships in such a way that they are slowly but steadily transformed into non-traditional ones, as an institution whose functional significance is primarily to facilitate social and cultural change."[85]

Black Barbadians also continued to mobilize and save varying sums of cash by resorting to the same meeting turns they had used at the beginning of the century. Indeed, old informants who recall the era of Panama money remark that, after Panama, meeting turns became even more popular, just as they are today in Barbados in the late twentieth century.

Friendly societies also played important roles in the savings habits of black, working-class Barbadians well past the Panama era. In 1946, for example, a total of 161 friendly societies in Barbados had 97,639 dues-paying members who contributed £130,217 during the year, £93,913 of which was distributed in Christmas bonuses.[86] But in recent decades the friendly societies of Barbados have declined in importance owing to competition from provident funds and competing insurance programs. Thousands of older Barbadians in the late twentieth century continue as nominal members in friendly societies although their village-level administration—formerly the societies' strength—is considered now by many a mark of amateurish managerial weakness. More important, the scale of the friendly society has remained essentially unchanged and, by modern standards, it is entirely too limited. Sick benefits and death benefits now are much too small, and they are unable to keep pace with price inflation for medical care. Few young Barbadians even consider joining friendly societies in the 1980s. The Barbadian friendly society, a vital institution that served as both agent and product of the social changes among black, working-class Barbadians early in the twentieth century, may not survive into the twenty-first.

"Lawless Habits Which Have Become Prevalent"

As confrontation and impersonality replaced paternalism in the second decade of the twentieth century, and as more vigorous law enforcement replaced mutual accommodation, what was viewed as criminal behavior increased among black Barbadians. Criminal acts and lawlessness were not always cases of the impoverished satisfying desperate needs and thereby becoming "criminal" simply in the eyes of the white beholders. Small bands of wrongdoers—criminals by anyone's definition—did thrive in Bridgetown. For example, Joe Allman and George Henry (alias "Trinidad George") were the leaders of a city gang of robbers and swindlers who in 1915 preyed mainly on fellow blacks.[87] And the ruffians and incendiaries who returned from the Canal Zone hardly set laudable examples for the young men and boys of black Barbadian society. But as black workers in general pressed harder and harder to solidify and expand the material improvements they had realized during the era of Panama money, many white planters pushed just as hard in the other direction. Rigidity between naturally antagonistic classes had thereby replaced compromise, and law enforcement became an increasingly acceptable solution to problems that in earlier days would have called for conciliation or perhaps would not have occurred at all. For example, on December 23, 1919, Governor O'Brien presided over a secret meeting of select legislators, planters, and merchants in the chambers of the Legislative Council to discuss the rumor that an organized stike for higher wages among Barbadian blacks had been scheduled for January 2, 1920. One response was that any such strike action automatically would be supported and strengthened by the wharfside "idlers" in Bridgetown. A suggested preventive measure against such a strike was the immediate and wholesale arrest of black men who congregated around the dock with no visible work to perform.[88] It is not surprising that rates of "lawlessness" and "criminality" rose in such an atmosphere.

An increasingly monetized economy was helping to shape changing attitudes about what was and what was not criminal activity in Barbados. For instance, planters now routinely prosecuted vegetable thieves rather than looking the other way. It was certainly not as if Panama money had rendered malnutrition obsolete and potato raids unnecessary. Heartbreaking cases of near-starving black children remained easy to find and constituted ample justification for rural vegetable stealing. But in the last few years vegetables had become cash crops, a fact exemplified by the stringent punishments against vegetable theft specified by the Vegetable Produce Act of World War I. If a planter suffered the loss of his potatoes, he was now losing money. In late April of 1919, planter Stanley Robinson ranted during the meeting of the Barbados Agricultural Society that the clerk of the commissioners of the Vegetable Produce Act had set a planter-to-huckster price of ten cents for fifteen pounds of potatoes when the actual market price was ten cents for seven pounds. Hucksters' potential profits were unfair according to

Robinson. He was speaking in the same forum where fifteen years earlier the planters had acknowledged high rates of rural crop thievery and had agreed with a shrug that there was little action being taken against it. But times had been different then. In those earlier days, potatoes had been, as often as not, given away by planters and shared in the spirit of reciprocity among rural blacks.[89]

By all accounts, and despite ever-harsher legal stipulations against it, rural food crop pilferage increased in Barbados during the century's second decade. Agricultural reports and legislative records in these years commonly included complaints about increases in potato raids and in thefts of small livestock. The victims were not only planters but also small-scale landowners and even tenantry dwellers. Annoying at the individual level, food crop theft—if left unchecked and allowed to increase—could pose a serious islandwide nutrition problem because the combination of escalating cane prices and war uncertainties made the preservation of locally produced food all the more important. In June of 1917 a rash of potato raids in St. Lucy and the Speightstown area of St. Peter parish led to rewards of twenty-five pounds being offered for information leading to the conviction of any individual "where three or more persons are concerned in making a raid on a field of provisions."[90]

The character of some of the potato raids themselves had taken an ugly, unprecedented turn. Whereas in earlier days a spontaneous gathering of foodstuffs had been tacitly recognized as a desperate act by hungry people, large-scale uprooting of potatoes—because of their monetary value—had now become common in the countryside. There were even instances of armed thievery. At 1:00 A.M. on May 13, 1921, fourteen men stole "200 holes of potatoes" at Porter's estate, just up the hill from Holetown in St. James parish. During the raid, the thieves fired four revolver shots and wounded one of the estate watchmen, Alonza Beckles. In the conversations following the Porter's incident, planters complained that violent robbery was now commonplace as armed gangs had been involved in similar robberies elsewhere on the island.[91]

The Barbadians suffering the most from the legal responses to armed thievery of food crops were the desperately poor who, as in earlier days, stole for themselves or their children. They were usually subjected to the same harsh penalties as those who stole for money. Assemblyman H.W. Reece of St. Lucy warned fellow legislators of the distinctions between armed bandits who stole "provisions for marketing . . . [and] others [who] do so for the mere purpose of appeasing hunger." In particular, Reece considered it unfair that a provision thief who had stolen to satisfy hunger should be flogged after being caught in the legal net cast to ensnare members of rural, provision-stealing gangs.[92]

Although the changing nature of rural potato raids marked a significant departure from earlier times, Barbadian colonial authorities reserved their greatest concern for the "lawless habits which have become prevalent among the roughs of Bridgetown." The high population density of the urban area meant that any general protest or riot by black Barbadians would spread most easily from there, and police officials maintained close surveillance over the restive habits of potential troublemakers—especially those in groups—throughout the urban tenantries. In January 1919, Governor O'Brien informed the Barbadian assembly that the question of lawlessness in Bridgetown was receiving his most serious attention. In particular, O'Brien had noted a very recent spate of incidents, including resisting lawful arrest, and throwing stones at police and, in one instance, a police constable's receiving a bullet wound in the line of duty.[93] In March, a scuffle between police and some of the residents of the Golden Square area nearly erupted into a full-scale urban riot. A police constable arrested a boy for stealing coal, a routine incident that this time was accompanied by a quickly assembled mob who threw missiles at the police. One constable called for reinforcements from the central police station in Bridgetown. When the additional policemen got to Golden Square they assembled into two lines and were preparing to do battle with the crowd of protestors when they were called away personally by the inspector general of police.[94]

The growing antagonism between the police and black Barbadian urban dwellers was inevitable, given the changing attitudes in these years. Nevertheless, officials and planters continued to cling to happy thoughts of earlier days when a more quiescent urban population had been handled much more easily. Operating under the delusion that urban restiveness would disappear if only a few rotten apples were removed from the barrel, officials attempted to identify members of certain groups as troublemakers. "Young roughs" (people in their late teens and early twenties) and "idlers" were two categories singled out for special attention as menaces to law and order.

The vague category of "idler" was hardened into law with the passage of the Habitual Idlers' Bill by the assembly on March 4, 1919. Subsequent arrests under the law's provisions were as much self-fulfilling prophecies as they were the legal entrapments of habitual criminals. After prolonged discussion, the bill was passed with the object of arresting "loafers" who slouched in doorways and rum shops around Bridgetown, as well as in rural parishes, and whose natural tendencies, in the eyes of officials, were to steal and create disorder. The bill's opponents argued, rather sensibly, that individuals following certain occupations—such as dockyard laborers and porters—worked sporadically because of the nature of their jobs. Assembly members, however, were swayed by arguments that rampant idleness on the one hand and lawlessness on the other were so closely interrelated that to legislate against one certainly would deter the other.[95]

Acts of violence and confrontation with police had heretofore been mainly spontaneous events, such as the mass rock-throwing incident at Golden Square that had attracted a crowd instantaneously. But as the century's second decade drew to a close, frustration and resentment by black Barbadians in general was becoming increasingly widespread. Strikes for better wages at rural estates and also among urban blacks, significantly were beginning to attract mutual notice and hints of mutual support. General work stoppages and general strikes were not unknown in the pan-Caribbean region; labor organizers had been active, for example, in the Canal Zone. Barbadian planters and officials monitored closely the activities of the island's working class, especially those involving individuals with the capabilities or inclinations to convert the growing potential for mass violence or general strikes into actuality.

In this potentially inflammatory atmosphere, there was good reason for local officials to fear the return of the World War I veterans. A total of 902 Barbadians—20 white officers and the remainder black enlisted personnel—had served with the British West Indies Regiment in France and the eastern Mediterranean, and 63 had died.[96] Colonial administrators throughout the British empire knew that troops from the colonies presented a special problem when they returned home. Men who had served in combat for the British cause—as many Barbadians had—were unlikely to revert to their former subservient economic roles without complaint upon return. More specifically, these men had been trained in the deployment and uses of firearms. Governor O'Brien and others feared that if the returning veterans became disgruntled and gained access to the arms and ammunitition stored at the St. Ann's Fort magazine, a full-blown revolution might occur in Barbados.[97]

Fear of possible insurrection by returning soldiers was based not upon a vague possibility but on actual intelligence reports relayed to all British Caribbean governors by the Colonial Office early in 1919. These reports described the formation of the revolutionary "Caribbean League" by black sergeants of the West Indies Regiment stationed in Sicily late in 1918. Several battalions of the regiment recently had engaged the Turks in Palestine and had fought bravely alongside Australians and New Zealanders; but now the West Indian units had been relegated to the roles of labor battalions in Italy.[98] Black noncommissioned officers, disgusted over this demeaning duty and, more important, the active racial prejudice they had endured while serving the Crown, held what they had thought was a secret meeting on December 19 or 20, 1918, at the Tenth British West Indies Sergeants Mess in Cimeno, Italy. One sergeant of the Third Battalion made a speech to the effect that upon their return to the Caribbean "the black man should have freedom and govern himself in the West Indies and that force must be used, and if necessary bloodshed to attain that object." His remarks were roundly applauded. Most of the league's organizers were Jamaicans, although a good deal of support also came from the Ninth Battalion, where there always had been discipline problems, "most of the men coming from Panama."[99]

Governor O'Brien of Barbados was notified in January 1919 of the league's formation and advised by the Colonial Office to take special precautions against an uprising when the soldiers would return to Barbados for demobilization in March. O'Brien already had laid contingency plans to cope with civil disturbances. The Colonial Office had mandated that such plans be formulated for all British colonies following riots in Ceylon in 1915. O'Brien himself had had crowd-control experience as acting commissioner of the Transvaal Town Police during a strike in the South African Witwatersand in 1907. His solution to control urban riots was devastatingly straightforward: fire on the mob to protect lives and property.[100]

But O'Brien knew he would be outnumbered greatly if rebellious former soldiers enlisted the support of other black Barbadians. The British garrison's withdrawal from the island in 1906 had left only a skeleton militia and a contingent of police to control possible disorder. In the event of disturbances, a volunteer force might be assembled as it had been in the 1876 riots, but it could hardly be relied upon. On February 21, 1919, O'Brien telegraphed the secretary of state for the colonies to report that local forces were inadequate to handle possible disturbances accompanying demobilization. He also included in his message confirmations of potential trouble in Barbados, including remarks about a noticeable "sullenness" among members of the black working class and of threatening letters being sent to certain planters.[101]

Other British West Indian governors reported similar weaknesses in their local defense postures. The Colonial Office responded by arranging for the dispatch of two destroyers, the HMS *Cumberland* and the HMS *Cornwall*, to visit Barbados, Trinidad, and the Windwards during the month of March 1919, when contingents of soldiers—who might ignite potentially explosive atmospheres in each place—returned home. British bluejackets, moreover, were standing by on each ship, ready to go ashore to quell local disturbances. Had the bluejackets ever been needed on Barbados, Governor O'Brien had planned for them to take their initial positions at the St. Ann's Fort magazine, the Government House stables, and the central police station. As it turned out, however, no riotous conditions occurred when the soldiers came back and were mustered out, although the contingency plans were ample evidence that the local government expected trouble of the worst kind.

The absence of large-scale rioting on their arrival home was no guarantee that former soldiers of the British West Indies regiment would not eventually make trouble for Barbadian authorities. Colonial officials around the Caribbean were reminded of just that possibility on July 22, 1919, when four thousand blacks—some of them demobilized soldiers—rioted and looted in Belize, British Honduras.[102] Back in Barbados, Governor O'Brien had just recently, in fact, noted sullenness and unfriendliness "among the coloured people, particularly [the] returned soldier class."[103] The recent drought that had destroyed ground provisions and the high cost of everything were two contributing factors to the angry feelings of the returned soldiers in particular and of the black Barbadians in general. On July 30, O'Brien addressed a small gathering of planters and outlined the gravity of the situation around the West Indies. The governor urged the planters to be as generous as possible in increasing workers' wages, a sugestion he would make again in the coming months to little or no avail.

The planters did respond favorably to one of O'Brien's suggestions during the meeing, that for "emigration on an extended scale" for returned World War I veterans at Barbadian expense. In November 1919 the assembly authorized funds for bicycles, house repair, tools, and driver training for returned soldiers. More significantly, the legislators paid for the emigration of 152 war veterans, 133 to Cuba.[104] While conserving their own plantation wages, the planter-dominated assembly doubtless considered the exportation of potential troublemakers a worthwhile investment of government money.

A dockworkers' strike in Port of Spain, Trinidad, in early December 1919 and a related riot in Tobago created a stir in Barbados, especially since emigrant Barbadians were very active in the Trinidad Workingmen's Association, which had coordinated the strike.[105] But despite a general feeling of discontent and the indulgence in "reckless talk" by the more militant black Barbadians, the postdemobilization crisis of Barbados never precipitated a massive riot. Some local officials possibly interpreted these events in old-fashioned ways, deluding themselves that black Barbadians were somehow incapable of large-scale violence. This interpretation, however, would have been wrong. The inevitable simply had been postponed.

New Religious, Social, and Political Directions

High rates of crime in 1920, both actual and perceived, were mere symptoms of momentous change that had taken place among the black working class of Barbados since the turn of the century. The external and internal demographic changes alone were of stunning size and amplitude, and the decennial census data were simply caricatures of the effects that these changes must have had on families and individuals. Many of the young and able-bodied had traveled abroad permanently or had returned home only to leave again. Thousands of black families had left rural tenantries and settled near Bridgetown. Others had moved to different rural parishes. The sudden presence of large-scale sugar cane factories and the related reduction of windmills had, moreover, begun to alter the size and the character of the labor market. In addition there were all of the changes that Panama money had created.

In response to broad-based and unsettling change, black Barbadians found themselves involved in new social groupings, substituting, in a very general sense, class and ideological interests for those that had formerly been based primarily on common residential location. The lessened importance of traditional, tenantry-based ceremonial obligations in friendly societies had been only one such example. But social change did not mean blindly adopting the new and always discarding the old. Change, rootlessness, and social disorientation could be relieved and modified partly by maintaining familiar elements of traditional institutions. New social organizations and even the new political oganizations that were becoming inceasingly important during the 1920s retained some traditional features. Although the Panama Canal experience had ushered in a period of social change and disconinuity, black Barbadians insisted on maintaining some of the old ways of doing things so they could cope more readily with the new.

The sights and sounds of the urban tenantries in and around Bridgetown were a case in point. Rural-to-urban movement, such as that occurring in Barbados in the first two decades of the century, was a demographic dimension of change or modernization, the usual interpretation for such movement everywhere. But new arrivals to the Bridgetown area had brought with them elements of the countryside. Though colonial officials dichotomized the island's population into "urban" (St. Michael parish and the western end of Christchurch) and the rest "rural," black Barbadians did not conceptualize the differences that sharply. The Bridgetown area, to be sure, was different from the country. It offered a greater variety of jobs and social opportunities. But rural blacks had brought their chattel houses with them, providing their own familiar reference points in a new setting. Also, recently arrived blacks often insisted on planting vegetables or even rootcrops, as they had at home, in suburban tenantries (although thievery rates in town always were much higher). And no one had to remind the residents of nearby white residential areas that urban blacks were maintaining a semirural existence when the chickens and cows started vocalizing each day before dawn.

Fundamental changes had nevertheless occurred. Personal relationships between individual planters and workers were sharply reduced. Large sugar-grinding factories encouraged the formation of an undifferentiated laboring class whose activities were becoming standardized. Groupings which promised a feeling of togetherness, mutual identity, and class consciousness were more attractive than ever before. Even subtle changes in clothing reflected the new feeling and spirit among the black working peoples. Male estate workers "increasingly donned hats and caps in place of the old picturesque headkerchiefs."[106] Doubtless the changes in Barbadian headwear was a carryover from Panama days, although common clothing characteristics—especially the prevalence of caps—had been a visual group symbol of proletarian identity decades earlier in Europe.

Thousands of black Barbadians turned to the revivalist churches as lifeboats of stability and group identity in a sea of social change. Missionaries and preachers of these small, new churches were usually from the United States, some of them by way of

Panama. Throughout the Bridgetown area especially, but in rural Barbadian parishes too, "the results of the religious upheaval were momentus."[107] The attractions of the fundamentalist churches to poor, landless black Barbadians caught up in pivotal social changes were not unlike the attractions they have provided to similar groups in many different settings:

> The revivalist churches are the churches of the detribalized, the de-cultured, and the disinherited. They fill many needs for lower-class people who, one way or another, have lost their stake in "the old ways." The revivalist churches provide an important source of recreation, and this should not be disparaged. They provide group membership, with all the psychological satisfactions such membership can give.[108]

In numerical growth of adherents, the fundamentalist churches of Barbados had realized their most sizable increases between the 1891 and 1911 censuses. In 1891, members of "Other Denominations" numbered only 1,560, according to census takers; the number had grown to 17,344 by 1911, the largest congregations being "Christian Missionaries and Christians" (8,705), "Plymouth Brethren" (3,073), "Brethren" (2,643), and "Protestants" (1,775). Between 1911 and 1921, as the population of Barbados fell by more than 15,000, the Anglicans and the middle-class Wesleyans and Moravians all suffered substantial losses. The fundamentalist "Other Denominations," on the other hand, still counted more than 17,000 members in 1921, a figure that, for all practical purposes, represented an increase in strength in light of the overall population loss in Barbados during the decade.[109]

Increasingly, fundamentalist church sermons were providing not only escape and identity but also taking on quasi-political tones. Although most black Barbadians were better off than in the pre-Panama era, they had improved just enough to see how little they had in comparison with whites. More and more black congregations were challenged by their own preachers to contemplate the basis for black-white inequities. Colonial authorities were aware of the inherent dangers. In particular, they worried about instigators and agitators from abroad coming to Barbados in religious disguise. For example, Barbadian authorities were well aware of the reputation for creating trouble of "Bishop Jack," a preacher of the "Episcopal Orthodox Church" of St. Vincent.

The Social and Economic Changes 223

When Bishop Jack came to Barbados in October 1925 there was nothing local authorities could do to prevent him from opening a branch of his church in Bridgetown. But Barbadian police and other government officials monitored his activities closely, just as they did other individuals with reputations for political agitation.[110]

The Barbadian landship movement, voluntary neighborhood associations composed exclusively of members of the island's black working class, also was coming to the fore.[111] Individual landship units drew their memberships ("crews") from particular residential districts and were organizations modeled upon the various ranks within the military hierarchy found upon British naval vessls. The "ship" itself was usually a small wooden house upon which local carpenters had affixed wooden masts. On meeting ("dock") nights, the uniformed male officers and enlisted personnel of the particular ship were augmented by the presence of the female nurse members ("stars") and young male cadets ("blues"). On board "ship," failure to observe strict military discipline and ritual could lead to a court-martial and even dismissal from the organization.

The most important decade of the landship movement of Barbados, as far as membership and group enthusiasm was concerned, was the 1920s. During that decade and the next, landships from neighboring parishes competed with one another in dress, marching, and ritual display, with pride and distinction the sole prizes. Particular ships were named the *Iron Duke*, *Indefatigable*, or *Calcutta*, but they really represented the black working peoples of particular districts of St. John, St. Philip, St. Michael, or the other island parishes. During its heyday, the landship movement was comprised of more than sixty "ships" scattered throughout Barbados; the island's landship enrollment in the 1920s has been estimated as 3,000 male and 800 female, although the movement had a far wider effect.[112] In the decades after Panama, everyone agreed that the Barbadian landship was "a powerful social factor in the life of those whom we designate the masses."[113]

Landship origins were hazy. Most agreed that the idea of the landship—which had no readily observable counterpart elsewhere in the Caribbean—was brought home by a Barbadian seaman during the 1870s after his years in the British Isles. Thereafter, landship organizations appeared in the several Barbadian parishes and achieved their most contagious appeal in the years immediately following the Panama exodus. Some observers felt that the drumming accompanying landship parades and also the drumming at a landship's meeting night signified an African inheritance. Indeed, there is at least one West African instance of organizations with fundamental similarities to the Barbadian landships. Michael Banton reports that the Kru of Sierra Leone have, in the past, fitted some of their houses with masts in the pattern of British warships. The houses are the meeting places for men's friendly societies in Freetown whose members consider themselves divided into different "ships."[114]

On meeting nights, Barbadian landship members turned out in starched uniforms, just as they did on Sunday mornings when the landship unit marched to church accompanied by drumbeats. A landship procession through a black residential district was certain to attract onlookers, especially the children who followed the uniformed parade through the streets. If young people desired to join a "ship," they were required to swear loyalty to the Crown, the British flag, and the Bible. The group's meetings demanded a good deal of time; members of the *Rosetta* ship society on Bay Street in Bridgetown, for example, met from 7:00 to 9:30 P.M. every Monday, Wednesday, and Friday.[115]

On the surface, the landship movement appeared laughable to some observers; it was simply another reminder of black preoccupation with clothing, music, and display, and a naive attempt by black Barbadians to achieve British levels of wealth and respect by emulating military dress and mannerisms. Indeed, the uniforms and ribbons were important elements of self-respect. But the enforced discipline and the rigid hierarchy of a community's landship unit also approximated a more modern, urbanized Barbados, different from the paternal past and the life in rural tenantries of the nineteenth century. In other words, the landship's real social significance may have been in its insistence on punctuality, discipline, and the adherence to specific rules of conduct, thereby smoothing the transition for black working-class Barbadians from the social universe of the nineteenth century into that of the twentieth. The significance of somewhat similar urban voluntary associations in West Africa is that they provide social links between an earlier, traditional way of life and an urban future.[116] The comparison is tenuous because Barbados was by no means a traditional, non-Western society, in the West African sense, in the early twentieth century. At the same time, the Barbadian landship, not unlike voluntary associations in West Africa, represented a means by which new social standards were taught in familiar settings among peers. In this regard it represented an adaptational association bridging the future and the past.

Landships always assumed the important mutual-aid functions that friendly societies had provided in earlier days. Members paid dues at regular intervals, often weekly. Usually officers paid more than enlisted personnel. The dues afforded partial protection "against the expenses of sickness, unemployment, and death. Thus the habit of thrift was encouraged."[117] The entire landship unit also was expected to turn out for funeral processions on the occasion of a member's death, thereby assuming the duties and obligations of the traditional Barbadian friendly society and reinforcing an old Barbadian, and even older West African, burial tradition.

By all reports, the Barbadian landship of the 1920s was an apolitical social grouping. Members of each unit were preoccupied with internal order, and neither written reports nor interviewees indicated that political indoctrination played any part whatever in landship meetings. Nevertheless, the Barbadian landship had an obvious capacity for organizing large numbers of black Barbadians, regardless of residence, and was able to effect a coalescence of members of black Barbadian working peoples that never had been accomplished before. The landship tradition itself reinforced working-class identity. Competition between and among ships from neighboring parishes, moreover, underlined the importance of class in an extra-village sense. In 1933, nearly all of the Barbadian landships were organized into the "fleet" of the Barbados Landship Association.[118] Although the fleet itself—with a flourishing admiralty in full command—was without political aims, its very existence suggested a class identity and organizational capability with far-reaching political possibilities.

The Barbadian landship is still alive late in the twentieth century, although barely. Its membership is a tiny fraction of what it was in the third and fourth decades of the century, and its importance in the daily lives of black Barbadians now is almost nil. Clyde Gollop, the national Barbados Landship Patron, laments that, despite recent attempts at resuscitation, the custom is dying out. In 1982, there were only seven Barbadian ships remaining "afloat."[119] The landship units still perform at official functions. One small landship group marched at the Barbadian Independence Day celebration in 1981, its members in full naval regalia. As the marching unit passed in review, it was greeted with self-conscious hoots and catcalls from the assembled crowd, a suggestion that the old-fashioned landship tradition remains much closer to many black Barbadians of the late twentieth century than they would care to admit.

Exclusively black, working-class organizations reinforced a group consciousness. Middle-class Barbadians, whether by reason of occupation or color, looked down on landship activities as clearly indicative of lower-class behavior. "You could go to prison and still be a member of a landship," exclaimed an older businessman in Bridgetown. But the Barbadian middle classes were not without their own class-based clubs and organizations. These were the fraternal lodges that had existed since shortly after emancipation for nonwhite Barbadians but which, like the landship movement, had become much more important in the early twentieth century. I discussed early lodge membership with an old man from Christchurch parish who formerly had belonged to the Corinthian Lodge of Mechanics, a fraternal group that met fortnightly at the Mechanics' meeting hall on Roebuck Street in Bridgetown. Was membership open to anyone? "No, not everyone could join. They looked at the kind of work you were doing. You had to invite people who lived a decent life."

In 1920 several black middle-class Barbadian lodges—Foresters, Gardeners, Good Templars, Mechanics, Oddfellows, and others—flourished, sustained by memberships of the upwardly mobile, or those who wished to be considered and accepted as middle class. Not all lodges were registered, and nothing approximating a census or even an estimate of the number of members had been attempted. Probably Barbadian lodge membership included 2,000–3,000.[120] Members were predominantly male, although female auxiliaries, such as the St. Michael's Gem court of a local branch of the Ancient Order of Foresters, were not unknown on the island.[121]

Barbadian lodges traced their lineage to Britain where social orders such as the Foresters and Mechanics had themselves evolved from early friendly societies. Unlike those in landships, middle-class Barbadian lodge members were thereby able to buttress their aspirations of upward mobility by claiming membeship in institutions derived originally from Britain and a white, British tradition. But the Barbadian lodge movement also was stimulated by sources from the United States and the Caribbean, not the least from Panama. Emigrants to the Canal Zone often had become lodge members there and then brought their fraternal interests back home with them. Old informants suggest that a group called the Loyal Sons of Concord had come directly to Barbados from Panama. The Mechanics and Solomon's Temple lodges also had been influenced by returnees from Panama. Simply being involved in one or more voluntary associations during an era of group membership was as important as adhering to a particular lodge or order; and a good "lodge man" was willing to extend himself to give what help he could to others. An old woman of St. Lucy parish recalls that her father had been an officer in the Order of Ancient Free Gardeners while in Panama. After his return he lived too far from Bridgetown to attend lodge meetings regularly, so he devoted his civic efforts to acting as secretary of the Golden Rose Friendly Society at Checker Hall, St. Lucy.

Lodge meeting halls were in urban places—Oistins, Speightstown, and overwhelmingly in Bridgetown. As an old lodge member told me, "Meetings were held in town, that's where the money and the intellect were." Meetings were marked by good fellowship, a prime attraction of the lodges according to elderly informants. Mutual expectations of exemplary behavior, both inside the meeting hall and outside, reinforced the good conduct of individual lodge members. Barbadian lodges, like landships, also provided mutual-aid benefits for the sick and burial expenses. Much the same happened in the English countryside in the early nineteenth century. At that time, the traditional mutual-support functions of English friendly societies often were assumed by local branches of the Oddfellows and Foresters, as lodges supplanted friendly societies as the main voluntary mutual-help units among the common people of England.[122]

Barbadian lodges emphasized ritual, learning, and teaching. A man capable of memorizing lengthy ceremonial passages from the Bible or from lodge manuals thereby acquired prestige in the eyes of fellow lodge members. Learning, intellect, formal education—the hallmarks of middle-class identity—were prized by lodge members. And from all indications, Barbadian lodge ceremonies were taken more seriously than those of their English counterparts, and the Barbadian initiation ceremonies were considered "elaborate and formidable." Altogether, the ceremony, secrets, and ritual were enough to cause the Barbadian lodges "to be held in great esteem by the ordinary people."[123]

Lodges, like landships, were apolitical social groupings; but the popularity and the success of these voluntary associations reinforced class identities among black and brown Barbadians in the post-Panama years with inevitable political consequences. While maintaining traditional mutual-benefit functions, the lodges and landships now spanned interests and identities among residents of both rural parishes and the Bridgetown area. The rural-urban gap was also bridged by individuals who maintained contacts with friends and kinsmen at home and abroad, often through mutual interests in organizations. Furthermore, members of the same lodge or landship unit might meet together on another night of the week as members of the Workingmen's Association and then again at church on Sunday. The question as to whether landships and lodges served as nuclei for an eventual political thrust among black Barbadians is answered by the realization that all of these associations were interrelated in a wider social movement involving multistranded ties among friends and families. The successes of working-class politics, as Eric Wolf points out, are not confined to the workplace alone, but "they are the outcome of many links that extend into the larger society."[124]

As the second decade of the twentieth century came to a close, political institutions were emerging in Barbados that would serve to organize and articulate black working-class interests and frustrations. The important actions by a handful of politically oriented individuals were as courageous as they were politically crucial because Barbados government officials were repressive, not accommodating, toward those promoting radical or even progressive political ideas. I interviewed an old man who migrated to Barbados from British Guiana in 1920 and who later became a Barbadian labor leader. He described the Barbadians at the time as having "such a terrible fear of their government that they couldn't even think about trade unions." Nevertheless, in 1919, the *Barbados Herald*, a weekly newspaper with biting, acerbic, working-class views, was begun by Clement Inniss. The *Herald* was strengthened and sustained by the efforts of Clennell Wickham, a black Barbadian veteran of the British West Indies Regiment in World War I. In October 1924, Charles Duncan O'Neale formed the Democratic League, a political party with a frankly socialist agenda. By early 1927, O'Neale also had formed the Workingmen's Association, an alliance based in Bridgetown but which held meetings elsewhere and thereby attracted adherents from rural parishes too. The Workingmen's Association had broadly economic aims. It was a cooperative group that attempted to coalesce black economic strength—expressed in sums of money—for the benefit of all black workers and their families.

Indigenous black political institutions of Barbados were influenced by similar groupings in neighboring colonies; and the Trinidad Workingmen's Association and the British Guiana Labour Union (the latter formed in 1919) both had former Barbadians among their leaders and organizers. Black Barbadian political aspirations also were affected by the teaching of Marcus Garvey, the presence in Barbados of copies of his weekly newspaper, *Negro World*, and the formation of Garvey's Universal Negro Improvement Association (UNIA). By 1920, a UNIA branch existed in Barbados, and on August 1, 1920, a UNIA concert at the Olympic Theatre in Bridgetown attracted a crowd of nearly eight hundred. The organization's presence in the British Caribbean alarmed officials of the Colonial Office in London who saw in its appeal the potential for fomenting riot and revolution throughout the region. Governor O'Brien of Barbados, however, discounted these fears, at least as far as Barbados was concerned. Despite heated rhetoric about white repression and "bloodsucking capitalists" at local UNIA gatherings, the meetings seemed focused more toward collecting money contributions for Garveyite aims. Besides, in 1920, O'Brien felt assured that the Barbadian police force remained allied with the island's government against the kinds of real trouble that could be instigated by the "rowdy classes."[125]

The Panama Canal Zone also was a source of political inspiration. Barbadians residing there influenced directly black Barbadian political directions back home in the 1920s. Marcus Garvey himself had worked in the Canal Zone in 1911, an experience that helped to crystallize his feelings of indignation and humiliation about the treatment of black peoples throughout the hemisphere.[126] The continuous labor union organization activities and workers' militance among the black "silver employees" in the Canal zone beginning in 1915 were marked by several abortive strikes.[127] These activities and many more were followed closely back in Barbados; Barbadians in Panama, New York, and elsewhere sent home letters, pamphlets, and publications, all reinforcing class and political identities. Returned veterans from Panama, like the veterans of World War I, were among the most vociferous political spokesmen among black Barbadians in the 1920s. When individuals like George Abraham Bell, a Barbadian who had been a shopkeeper in Panama, spoke out against repression back home a decade later, his remarks were taken seriously by assembled black crowds owing partly to the local respect he had earned by working successfully abroad.

Governor O'Brien monitored closely the activities of political groups like the UNIA and the Barbados Workingmen's Association through the police department. A uniformed police corporal attended scheduled meetings of these groups and took written notes of the proceedings, including the chronology of events and what was said and by whom. Significantly, the meetings always were marked by hymns and prayers. And Workingmen's Association meetings in 1927 were terminated with the recital of the doxology. As in other local voluntary associations, black Barbadian political organizations of the 1920s had thus incorporated traditional religious elements into their formal gatherings. The hymns and prayers doubtless increased the appeal of the political

The Social and Economic Changes 231

groupings to members of the black working class of the island and reinforced multiple class, religious, and political identities of Barbadian blacks, connections evidently misunderstood by Governor O'Brien. When he wrote to the secretary of state for the colonies about the innocuous character of the UNIA meetings in Barbados in 1920, he stressed that the prayers and the singing of the national anthem at the meetings "discounts the work of agitators in a considerable degree."[128] Almost certainly O'Brien had interpreted the religious elements in political meetings in exactly the wrong way. The deep religious feelings and emotions of black Barbadians were aroused by the elements of liturgy, and the political preachings that inevitably followed were therefore all the more effective.

Political groupings in Barbados also increased their appeal by assuming the traditional sick benefit and burial functions; the Workingmen's Association sick benefit dues usually were four cents a week in the 1920s. In the same vein, and in keeping with Garveyite ideas, black Barbadian political leaders exhorted their followers to patronize only black shops rather than white stores, to help their peers of the working class prosper rather than to enrich white Barbadians and thereby subsidize those who had always repressed them.

The political militance that animated black Barbados in the 1920s and into the following decade could not have occurred in 1900. At the turn of the century, the majority of black Barbadians were locked into a rural, quasi-feudal socioeconomic system, their collective livelihoods complementing those of members of the white plantocracy. The infusion of millions of dollars of Panama money and the associated economic dislocations on Barbados in the next twenty years had created rapid, unprecedented change that had heightened economic competition among antagonistic classes. Paternal reciprocity in 1920 was dying, if not dead, in Barbados. Everyone, black and white, now competed for similar ends but from vastly different starting points. Black politicians demanded both an end to institutionalized inequalities on the island and a beginning to equal access to jobs and money.

Money now was at the heart of interclass competition and bitterness. Individual whites had so much of it, and most black individuals still had relatively little. Barbadian blacks no longer could count access to subsistence plots, mutual reciprocity, and expected kindnesses from white planters as assets. Everything now had a monetary price. Black Barbadians of the 1920s exhorted one another at political gatherings to improve themselves materially. They each could get ahead, all agreed, if they had land, good jobs, and compulsory education for their children. All of these things and more were possible only if blacks could obtain more money. Moses Small, a spokesman for the Workingmen's Association, addressed a gathering at the group's meeting hall on Passage Road in Bridgetown on the evening of December 8, 1927. Small condemned the cynicism of the institutionalized, white-oriented, Anglican church on the island, whose clergy preached every Sunday of the benefits of storing up treasures in heaven. For nearly three centuries black Barbadians had stored quite enough heavenly treasures, and it was about time for them to start banking some here on earth. Moses Small sneered at the hypocritical religious arguments that money was at the root of all evil. "[D]on't stand for any more [of] that rot," proclaimed Small, "[D]on't let them fool you, money is a blessed thing."[129]

CHAPTER 7

Epilogue: The 1937 Riots and Beyond

The political, social, and economic changes in the second and third decades of the twentieth century put the black Barbadian working class on a collision course with the island's white powerholders. The collision itself did not occur, however, until the Bridgetown riots of July 1937. While the actual riots were short-lived, they forcibly brought the plight of the island's black working peoples into the open. Public hearings following the riots spelled out long-standing inequities in painful detail, and solutions to these problems inevitably were expressed at the hearings in terms of money.

This book has dealt specifically with the changes occurring during only the first two decades of the twentieth century in Barbados—the era of Panama money. In this final chapter, I suggest, without positing a linear cause-and-effect relationship, that these migration-induced changes contributed in no small way to the climactic events of 1937, events that represented a watershed, dividing two eras of Barbadian social history. First I briefly describe how many Barbadians extended their migrations to the Greater Antilles and the United States in the 1920s. Then I continue with a description of the depression decade and the Bridgetown riots. Most important in this final chapter is the hypothesis that the riots were, in part, an expression of the incompatibility between black Barbadians' rising expectations—hopes financed originally with Panama money—and the anachronistic system of white planter control.

Although Barbadians had been traveling back and forth to neighboring West Indian colonies since emancipation, the Panama Canal established a precedent for Barbadian migration on a truly massive scale as an alternative to working for minuscule and seasonally fluctuating wages at home. At the individual and the family level, migration and return, once successful, was worth trying again, even if the destination was different. And Panama money, of course, often had financed only part of a house or had represented only a down payment for an acre of land and thereby had created its own migration momentum, necessitating further emigration to earn money to bring or send back to Barbados.

By 1920, the Greater Antilles, not the traditional destinations of Trinidad and British Guiana, had become for Barbadian blacks the most attractive external sources of wage labor within the Caribbean. Barbadians in Panama had found that relatively high American wages were ample compensation for serving gruff Yankee supervisors, conditions they rightfully expected at the giant American sugar estates in Cuba and Santo Domingo. Many Barbadians had traveled directly to Cuba from Colón when the Panama Canal was finished. Others went on to the Greater Antilles after returning to Barbados. Still more began to migrate from Barbados seasonally via the "slave ships"—sailing schooners carrying workers north at the first of the year and back home in July after the sugar cane harvest—all without the formalities of passports or other documents. White Barbadian officials were not certain how these informal movements were accomplished. Apparently, ship captains provided the passage north on credit, and then they received payment either from estate officials at their destinations or from the workers when they were paid.[1]

Seasonal migration from Barbados to work on the sugar cane plantations of Cuba and Hispaniola also involved legal shipments of laborers as well, arrangements facilitated by written contracts witnessed by local emigration agents. Emigrating legally precluded the possibility of being stranded away from home with no chance for repatriation. For example, in the late summer of 1921, the sailing schooner *Gladys B. Smith,* carrying 202 Barbadians home from Cuba, ran aground in a storm off Santo Domingo. An agent for an American sugar cane plantation originally had chartered the vessel through a Barbadian emigration agent. Under the circumstances, the Barbados House of Assembly had little choice but to provide funds for the laborers' relief abroad and eventual passage home.[2]

Probably more important than American estates in the Greater

Antilles to black Barbadians in 1920 was the United States itself as an emigration destination. Earlier, the poor whites and Barbadians of mixed ancestry had been the ones most likely to emigrate to North America, their passages aided by a combination of legislative grants and church donations at the turn of the century.[3] But during the last years of the Panama exodus, dark-skinned, working-class Barbadians were going "to the United States in large numbers and to Canada to a lesser extent." In general, the "great majority of these emigrants are black and coloured people of both sexes who find employment there in menial offices." In the United States, black Barbadians worked as domestics, waiters, and casual laborers, mainly in the New York area. Similarly, immigrant Barbadians of mixed blood also often took these kinds of jobs in New York, positions they normally would have shunned in Barbados. One reason was that they were paid much better for such work in North America.[4]

Not all Barbadians who emigrated to the United States stayed there, but almost certainly the majority who did sent money home to relatives. The postal remittance data from the period provided a rough measure of the ascendancy of the United States as an emigration destination for Barbadians as the Panama Canal was winding down. In 1916, for the first time in a decade, postal remittances to Barbados from the United States (£22,500) were greater than from the Canal Zone (£17,500).[5] Four years later, in 1920, postal remittances to Barbadians from United States sources totaled £57,200, those from the Canal Zone only £9,200.[6]

By the 1920s, certain smallholder areas of Barbados were beginning to be associated closely with United States money, just as Panama money had bought up other settlements a decade earlier. Beginning in 1924, Athelstan Watson began to sell one-and two-acre land plots to black Barbadians. By 1929, Watson had sold roughly 1,600 acres, most of the land in the arid coast of Christchurch from South Point north to Pilgrim Place. Watson commented that "the land was purchased with money remitted . . . by persons in America" to relatives staying behind. The new, stone-foundation houses appearing on the land eventually were to be used by Barbadians residing temporarily in the United States "as they hope some day to return and live here."[7] Nor was Christchurch the only parish where United States money was buying up small land plots. The same thing was happening to some extent in every Barbadian parish. The best-known places outside Christchurch were Deacons Road just north of Bridgetown and at Salters and Haggatt Hall estates, both located near the St. George-St. Michael parish boundary.[8]

The mass exodus to Panama, continued in spirit by the movements to the Greater Antilles and the United States, had established emigration from Barbados not simply as a livelihood strategy of last resort but as a routine alternative to working at home. Local planters by 1920 found themselves competing directly with external employers for local laborers whose own family members now, rather than just hoping, expected them to seek work outside the island. Migration to the United States was especially prevalent among members of specialized groups of the Barbados workforce. The exodus of specially trained personnel created actual labor shortages in some instances, something altogether new for Barbados. Of the forty-seven Barbadian men in 1923 who failed to re-enroll in the local police force at the expiration of their terms of service, thirty-six were known to have emigrated to the United States. The emigrants all had been attracted there by reports of high wages, either through letters from friends and relatives or from hearing stories from those who had returned temporarily.[9]

Some of the old-time Barbadian planters/assemblymen, never known for innovative or enlightened views, attempted to keep Barbadian workers at home by spreading rumors of the horrible prospects awaiting those who ventured abroad. It was reminiscent of the old Putumayo rubber days, when Barbadian planters had publicized atrocities committed against Barbadian migrants. Stanley Robinson of St. George parish rendered a gruesome account in the House of Assembly in 1918 of a young Barbadian boy who had been taken to St. Lucia and sacrificed by an obeah man who took the youth's "vitals" out of his body. Three years later, Robinson—in an attempt to relieve the assembly of paying for the repatriation of the shipwrecked workers on the *Gladys B. Smith*—deplored the system of "blackbirding," whereby Cuban sugar factories engaged Barbadian blacks to come and work only to have "some of those emigrants return here starving and practically naked."[10]

But black Barbadians had become too familiar with external destinations, often through personal experience, to take such anachronistic scare tactics seriously. Moreover, migration now had become ingrained in the local populace. Assemblyman H.W. Reece of St. Lucy responded to Robinson's "blackbirding" rumor by supporting the Barbadian government's eventual repatriation of the shipwrecked emigrants with an eloquent statement about how much Barbadian emigration, Barbadian freedom, and Barbadian livelihood had become intertwined by the early 1920s:

> Barbadians are free. . . . A man had only to come here and say that there would be a ship leaving for Cuba on such a day, and people who were engaged in regular work threw down their tools, whether it was a drill or a saw or anything else, and went off. . . . If there had been any attempt to prevent them going there would have been a riot, because everybody would have said that people in this country were trying to prevent labourers going to Cuba where they could better themselves merely to keep them to work on the local plantations. You cannot have everything. They are free people. . . . you cannot blame the Government; you cannot blame the people themselves. Such is the nature of these people that if tomorrow there was an opportunity for work opening up in the middle of South America they would go: they are adventurers. They say if the North Pole is reached again you will find a Barbadian there. Nobody is to be blamed, we must look the thing in the face. . . . If it costs five or six hundred pounds to assist them we must be prepared to vote the amount. It is a portion of our hurricane bill, just like the repair of the wharf walls. This ship was caught by the same hurricane which passed in this direction a few weeks ago.[11]

Migration as livelihood, however, depended not only on being free to leave one's point of origin but also on successfully locating a destination. This point became all too obvious to potential Barbadian emigrants to the United States in 1924. On July 1 of that year the U.S. immigrant quota law limited immigrants from the entire British West Indies to 200 per year. During 1923, some 2,000 were said to have left Barbados for the United States, although reliable records were not kept at either origin or destination. In any case, the closing of the most important emigration outlet for Barbadians could create only hardship. Spokesmen for the Barbados Workingmen's Association suggested that intergovernmental conspiracy might really be the reason why "the big man closed the door of America against us." Why, asked George Abraham Bell, could 245,000 persons from other places be admitted each year to the United States and only 5 from Barbados? "Somebody is misleading us," concluded Bell.[12]

Thrown back on their own resources by emigration quota decisions made abroad and therefore well beyond their control to influence, black Barbadians labored at home under slumping world sugar prices that were similarly beyond their control. From the 1920 high of fifty-eight shillings per hundred pounds, the raw sugar price on the London market had fallen precipitously to eighteen shillings in 1921. Then, after creeping back to nearly twenty-six in 1923, the price plunged again, this time much lower. The price paid for Barbadian raw sugar dropped to nine shillings per hundredweight in 1929. It dropped still further to less then five shillings in 1934 and stayed that low for the next three years.[13]

With most emigration possibilities closing down, dramatically so as the Caribbean region entered the depression decade, Barbadian planters felt no need to raise estate workers' wages. Male plantation workers on Barbados still were receiving roughly one shilling per day. Incredibly, in the mid-1930s in Barbados "the average wage of the agricultural labourer had not changed materially since 1838" despite the ravages of inflation which had raised food prices—especially early in the twentieth century.[14] Small landholders were somewhat better off, and some of them switched back from cane to vegetables in light of lowered sugar prices. But agricultural reorientation, always easier to prescribe than to accomplish, involved several possible pitfalls. The inertia engendered by having cane already planted on one's small plot created hesitation; a smallholder might root out his growing cane plants in favor of potatoes, only to have unpredictably volatile sugar prices prove him wrong in six months' time. Larceny of foodstuffs, becoming ever more prevalent in the Barbadian countryside, was another drawback. But most important was that small landholders now had become cash-crop farmers, preferring the prestige and the amenities that money could buy. So when the 1929 Sugar Commission investigated the effects of low sugar prices on Barbados, its members learned that sugar cane was preferred by the island's smallholders. If for no other reason, it was the black Barbadians' only source of cash credit, "the only crop on which one can borrow a cent."[15]

As internal conditions worsened for the working class of Barbados and for those throughout the British Caribbean in the depression years, despair inevitably led to violence. An estate workers' dispute over cash bonuses and wage levels on St. Kitts flared into riot and bloodshed in January 1935. A mob of plantation workers marched through the southern part of the small island, turning livestock loose and beating an estate manager. Local police eventually quelled the St. Kitts riot, which lasted into the following day, but not before they had shot three rioters dead and wounded eight others.[16]

The St. Kitts riot detonated an uneven chain reaction of riots and disturbances that "raced through the Caribbean like fire on a windy day."[17] From 1935 to 1938, labor unrest, fueled by economic depression, led to confrontations between black working classes and white bosses all through the British West Indian colonies. Workers throughout the region—sugar cane workers on St. Kitts, coal carriers on St. Lucia, oil field laborers on Trinidad—invariably wanted more money. As on Barbados, extraisland migration destinations had all but disappeared for the black, working-class men of the region who had learned out of necessity routinely to supplement meager wages at home through migration and return. Incipient political movements on every island, moreover, had appeared in the 1920s and 1930s in response to labor unrest. These labor parties and unions then helped to coordinate and articulate grievances, as on Barbados, as well as to disseminate news of events on neighboring islands, thereby providing a pan-Caribbean thrust to what had earlier been local concerns.

The Bridgetown riot, which spilled over briefly into rural areas of Barbados, began on July 27, 1937. Barbadian officials reacted with professed surprise, even shock. The last time real violence had erupted on the island had been during the Confederation Riots six decades earlier. The fabled adaptability and willingness of the typical, peace-loving, Barbadian laborer had carried the island safely through the ravages of the bounty depression at the turn of the century and also through the period of demobilization of the soldiers at the end of the war. Given this background, the

1937 riots had occurred "practically without warning and like lightning out of a clear sky, a storm . . . leaving in its wake a trail of devastation and death."[18]

In retrospect—and with the decidedly advantageous perspective of a half-century's hindsight—it seems incredible, not that the disturbances occurred, but that they had not taken place much earlier. All of the constituent elements for violent action by black Barbadians had been in place at least a decade earlier: depressed wages, inflationary food prices, the lack of alternative emigration outlets, even the presence of groups like the Workingmen's Association that were beginning to speak for and orchestrate working-class grievances. But riot is not the natural predilection of any people, least of all of Barbadians. It was oppression, misery, and hardship that had created a kind of "madness" among Barbadian working peoples according to George M. Ellis, a seventy-one-year-old witness to the riots: "Hardship will make a snake climb a tree, and oppression will drive a wise man mad. The people would never have attempted to pull down Bridgetown if they weren't mad."[19]

The particular circumstances igniting the riots concerned the deportation of thirty-three-year-old Clement Payne, a Trinidadian labor organizer who claimed Barbadian birth. Payne's fiery oratory around the Bridgetown area focused on black, working-class despair and was spiced with anticapitalist rhetoric. His speechmaking, moreover, had won him a considerable following, especially among younger Barbadian blacks. The Barbadian police, in collaboration with their counterparts in Trinidad, sent Payne back to Trinidad after a well-attended court hearing and after Payne had led an estimated five thousand "idle and curious" Bridgetown blacks to demand an audience with the governor of Barbados. Payne's hasty deportation on the evening of July 26, 1937, was accompanied by a clash between blacks and police in Golden Square, the smashing of cars parked near the Empire Theatre, and the breaking of street lamps on River Road and Jemmott's Lane.

The next morning a mob assembled, armed themselves with sticks and bottles, and invaded the Bridgetown business district.[20] The crowd's indignation had been aroused by the rumor that the police had killed a black infant. One angry group of men headed for the railway station, with looting and destruction in mind. The larger group, however, surged onto Broad Street, smashing storefront windows, pushing automobiles into the sea, and beating a policeman within an inch of his life.

After breaking nearly all the shop windows along Broad Street, the mob arrived at the Barbados Mutual Building where the white employees of the Cable and Wireless office cowered behind heavy wooden shutters listening to hostile shouts outside from men exhorting one another to kill "the blasted sons of white bitches."[21] The crowd attempted to burn the building down, although they were routed by a squad of armed police firing blanks from their rifles.

By noon, detachments of police—armed with rifles and fixed bayonets and also smarting from the verbal abuse and physical bruises from stones and bricks the night before—were pursuing disorganized groups of rioters through the downtown area. The police fired blanks in order to disperse the crowds, volleys that were reportedly answered with at least some revolver shots. At some point in the confusion, the police began using live rounds and thereby killed several of the rioters. The killing quickly dispersed the mobs, and for the rest of the day an ominous silence—almost as frightening as the discordant shouts and threats from the angry crowd—hung over Bridgetown.

News of the Bridgetown riot spread like wildfire through the urban and suburban tenantries of St. Michael parish. Lawless behavior, moveover, spilled out into the countryside, where small bands of hungry people invaded potato fields, raids more common in impoverished St. Lucy parish than anywhere else. Some of the rural blacks stoned passing automobiles, and white planter families—frightened for their lives—armed themselves. Seasonally heavy rainshowers eventually dampened the activities of both urban and rural rioters as well as the island itself. By July 30 all was quiet but fearful. The overall toll of the riots had been 14 dead, 47 injured, and more than 500 arrested or imprisoned.

Today, late in the twentieth century, most Barbadians see the 1937 riots as a political and cultural watershed because they opened the eyes of the plantocracy to the frustrations and thwarted aspirations of members of the black working class. More immediately, they signaled the lengths to which some black Barbadians were willing to go in order to achieve a measure of decency for themselves and their families. The political and economic gains for black Barbadians derived from the 1937 riots are therefore often said to underpin historically the considerable achievements Barbadians have made since. The political sophistication, exemplary public facilities, and the relative prosperity many Barbadians enjoy today often are attributed ultimately to the courage their grandfathers displayed a half century ago in standing up to the plantocracy. And throughout the Barbadian countryside, old persons still point out that black political fortunes rose in the 1930s in the person of Grantley Adams, a black lawyer whose visibility and leadership eventually carried him to the island's prime ministership at Barbados's independence in 1966. The same elderly Barbadians explain that, on the other hand, white power and political fortunes began to fade in the 1930s because Adams was instrumental in overturning the located laborer statutes that were the legal embodiments of white planter oppression going back to slavery.[22]

The remarkably comprehensive, detailed, and candid public hearings in Barbados that followed the 1937 riots suggested that many of the reasons for working-class despair could be traced, at least indirectly, to the social and economic changes that had taken place during the era of Panama money. A month of public hearings and the testimony of dozens of witnesses in 1937 from every color and social class on the island revealed that malnutrition, price inflation, declining paternalism, fewer external migration destinations, and related changes since the turn of the century all had contributed to the current crisis. White oppression of black laborers and located laborer laws, to be sure, formed the broad, centuries-old framework of the plight of black workers. But, more immediately, the 1937 flashpoint had been reached by a conflict between old and new. The white plantocracy of Barbados had attempted to maintain control over their black laborers in the 1930s as they had during the nineteenth century by keeping them tied to particular estates and by doling out tiny wages. But times had changed. A quasi-feudal system of labor control and the impersonal, monetized economy that the Barbadian emigrants had brought home from Panama were incompatible. And it had taken the desperation of the depression decade, combined with rising black expectations that had been awakened with Panama money, to bring the inherent conflicts between old and new to a head.

Few witnesses at the post-riot hearings confined their observations to present conditions. Instead, the majority took a longer view, pointing out that the subtleties of social and economic transformation in Barbados that had led to the riots could be understood only by considering the changes since the turn of the century. Hampden A. Cuke, an accountant familiar with the records of several Barbadian sugar estates, described changes since 1900 and their effects on the labor force:

> Forty or forty-five years ago there were some 340 windmills in this island, and about 100 small steam plants. . . . In those days there was a large number of mill carpenters and carts were used extensively for freighting the canes to the mill and the sugar to town. . . . You also had wheelwrights and blacksmiths, and the same people who worked in tilling the land also worked in the boiling-house. They were paid in the land by task and in the reaping by production. What has happened is that those 340 windmills have . . . dwindled to 30, and the 100 steam plants have dwindled to about 40, and in their places have sprung up about 36 factories. . . . What you have got now is that the same people who till the soil are not exclusively employed in the factory.[23]

But it was at the level of the individual field laborer where these islandwide data were translated into hunger and hopelessness. Caught between decreased local subsistence acreage on the one hand and increased prices for imported foodstuffs on the other, many black estate workers and their families suffered in the 1930s as much or more than they had during the bounty depression. Biscuits—produced by local bakeries with imported flour—and either water or lime juice now was the staple diet of black workers rather than the vegetables that in earlier years had been cultivated in tenantry gardens. Several respondents at the 1937 hearings thought that Barbadian field workers actually had deteriorated in physique since 1900, partly because of subsistence shortfalls over the past decades. And it was common knowledge that hungry field workers routinely supplemented their caloric intake by chewing canes while they worked in the fields. This point had been raised eight years earlier in Barbados during the Sugar Commission hearings. A member of the Workingmen's Association offered that cane cutters had to chew cane on the job. His interviewer retorted that sugar was a nutritious food. "Yes, Sir," came the reply. "It is a very good food when it is supplemented by something else."[24]

During the 1937 postriot hearings, Grantley Adams emphasized the double bind of a lack of local subsistence acreage and price inflation on the Barbadian working peoples. He suggested that sugar cane estates, as in World War I, be urged to grow more vegetables and that lumber merchants reduce their prices. Other witnesses echoed Adams's assertions that malnutrition, inflation, and low wages all worked together against black Barbadians—urban and rural dwellers alike—and that the combined effects of this interrelationship had worsened over the past decade. Even small landholders were not immune; the low wages and depressed sugar prices had forced a number of landed blacks into debt, a condition that threatened possible foreclosures and a wiping out of the most substantial material gains black Barbadians had been able to achieve with Panama money.[25]

Local conditions in Barbados had, however, always been difficult for black laboring classes. The profiteering by local merchants and planters—who bore the brunt of the accusations during the 1937 postriot hearings—was no worse than it always had been, although it never had been exposed so clearly to the light of public scrutiny. Price inflation for food and low prices for sugar, moreover, were less calculations of local businessmen than they were reflections of external economies. But local buffers had become less effective in modifying the impersonal amplitude of world economic cycles. Everyone on Barbados now was tied to a cash economy for survival, and the related problems of money and impoverishment were reiterated time and again during the hearings.

Worst of all, emigration outlets were few and far between in the 1930s. In times past, black Barbadians had been able to travel away during depressions, extending themselves beyond the island for cash and at the same time reducing the number of mouths to feed back home. Now migration was much more important than ever before for black Barbadians; with low wages and reduced subsistence acreage at home, they simply had to travel elsewhere. But in these desperate times, external emigration destinations had been reduced, not increased. A few still were able to travel, such as Arnold C. Griffith, a master carpenter from St. Lucy parish, who migrated back and forth to British Guiana to make ends meet, spending six months at home followed by six months in the South American colony. But relatively few Barbadians possessed Griffith's carpentry skills. And for the many unskillled laborers, traditional migration outlets were nearly nonexistent. The Panama Canal was completed. The United States had shut its doors. Cuba and the Dominican Republic had virtually closed its ports to seasonal migrants from the British Islands. H.A. Vaughan, a black lawyer and a recently elected member of the Barbadian House of Assembly, pointed out during the hearings that Barbadians traditionally had coped with their open economy by traveling away and then remitting wages to those back home. Those remittances, according to Vaughan, now were no longer coming home from abroad in any volume, another point echoed several times by other witnesses during the 1937 hearings.[26]

Those hearings reviewed and analyzed the riots of 1937 which had been precipitated in part by socioeconomic change. And out of the hearings emerged the kernel of an agenda for eventual political change in Barbados. Voting qualifications were lowered in 1944. Universal suffrage came in 1951. Barbados achieved full internal self-government in 1958. Independence came in 1966, four years after the formal dissolution of the West Indies Federation. Barbadian working peoples finally had achieved a measure of self-direction for the first time in their history. Accompanying their political advances, Barbadians also achieved unprecedented prosperity. Much of their economic success, moreover, could be attributed to the resourcefulness of the Barbadians themselves. And this resourcefulness has been manifested no more clearly than by the Barbadian willingness to engage in what is now a custom of long-standing: migration and return.

The precedent established by the massive exodus to Panama inspired thousands of Barbadians to travel away again after the depression decade, and subsequent decades have seen further emigration to North America and the United Kingdom. In the

1940s hundreds of Barbadians went to Trinidad and British Guiana to work on United States armed forces bases; others labored in oil refineries in the Netherlands Antilles. In the next decade, Barbadians joined tens of thousands of English-speaking West Indians in emigrating to England; perhaps thirty thousand Barbadians traveled to the United Kingdom prior to the enactment of the Commonwealth Immigrants Act, which in 1962 curtailed the exodus abruptly.[27] After that, Barbadians rediscovered Canada and the United States as migration destinations. Thousands of Barbadians have emigrated to the United States since 1965, when it abolished the national origins system in its immigration laws. Today, in the mid-1980s, it is difficult to find any Barbadians without friends or kinsmen who reside in North America. And despite the recent emigrations to metropolitan countries, Barbadians continue to emigrate permanently and temporarily—as they always have—to neighboring West Indian states where they serve as teachers, policemen, and civil servants.

The tenacity and resourcefulness that generations of Barbadians have displayed in migrating away and coming home again are, in turn, reflected in the island's contemporary modernization and prosperity. Thousands of Barbadians continue to rely on cash and gifts from family members who reside abroad. And few Barbadian professionals have not been elsewhere for education and training. Late in the twentieth century, Barbadians enjoy sanitary, piped water and electricity for virtually all of the dwellings on the island; new housing developments—often financed by those working abroad—add to Bridgetown's sprawl; and local politicians are fond of telling visitors that fully half of the local families have direct access to some kind of family-owned automotive transportation.

Yet Barbados has not been completely transformed by modernization or indelibly stamped by external ideas wholeheartedly or indiscriminately adopted from elsewhere. Throughout the island, including in the Bridgetown area, sights and sounds often are similar to what they must have been like at the time of the Panama exodus when rural tenantry dwellers were moving to town. While thousands of cars honk and smoke their way into Bridgetown during the morning rush hour, thousands of black

Barbadians in the lanes and sidestreets of the city itself continue to retain elements of earlier life-styles. Chattel houses—now elaborated with concrete foundations—are still the norm in many sections of Bridgetown. Neighbors interact socially and continue to depend upon one another in a variety of ways. Goats and sheep browse through tiny house gardens. Market women sell sweets from their trays to uniformed schoolchildren in the early morning hours and then again when school is over in the afternoon.

There is nothing romantic, however, about the continuing precariousness of Barbados's open economy. The island still is monopolized by sugar cane, although negotiations between labor unions and management, now mediated annually by the Barbados government, become more protracted each year. And, as any sugar exporter knows, even protected world sugar markets remain notoriously volatile. During the 1970s, the Barbadian economy shifted noticeably as the local hotel industry boomed, and tourism recently has become the most important sector of the Barbadian economy. But tourism on a massive scale carries with it the germ of potentially dangerous social and economic problems as other Caribbean countries have learned in recent decades. Dependence upon a fickle tourist market that, for the foreseeable future will be centered in Europe and especially North America, reinforces the Barbadian dependence upon external decision-making that has been the island's fate for three and one-half centuries.

Today, in the mid-1980s, the era of Panama money is the furthest point back in living memory on Barbados. Very few of those who traveled to work in Panama are left to talk about it, and soon even the children born there or who remember their parents' stories will be gone too.

Nor is the direct tangible evidence of the Panama era on Barbados easy to find and double-check. Land purchased with Panama money has been assigned to heirs or sold to others.[28] Although old Barbadians still point out houses and property that were supposedly purchased with remittances from the Canal Zone, their conviction about the authenticity of their remembrances seems embellished with more than a hint of nostalgia.

Although accurate and direct memories of the Canal Zone soon will no longer exist, Barbadians in years to come will still recall Panama through images of great-grandfathers, and they will pass on stories of fact and fancy concerning the exodus to their children and grandchildren. Though the stories doubtless will continue to be animated by colorful images associated with straw hats, the rigors of sleeping in sodden hammocks, or a bag of coins brought home, many Barbadians also may remind their children of the significant islandwide changes that the exodus helped to bring about. The courage, perseverance, and faithfulness to family and friends of the thousands of black men and women from Barbados who journeyed to the Canal Zone produced a pivotal socioeconomic momentum in the early twentieth century, doubtless improving conditions for later generations. In short, what began as a journey for higher wages elsewhere turned out to be much more.

Arthur Bullard, the American who, eight decades ago, observed sailing day for Colón at the Bridgetown wharf, prophesied that subsequent generations of Barbadians would be proud of what their ancestors had accomplished. Almost certainly Bullard predicted these feelings of pride and importance in the context of aiding the geopolitical ascendance of the United States rather than in the eventual internal changes the Panama experience would create for Barbados itself. As Bullard watched tearful mothers' farewells to proud young men, he described the scene as if it were a necessary, if poignant, element in a grandiose American project. Most Barbadians today will forgive Bullard for not realizing that he was actually watching the agents, rather than the pawns, of momentous social and economic change. At sunset, as the Panama-bound steamer sailed west, Bullard observed the men huddled on deck. His off-hand prediction was more accurate than he ever could have dreamed: "Although they are not interested in anything but their dollar a day, I warrant that their children's children will boast that their grandfathers worked on this job."[29]

Notes

Chapter 1

1. McCullough, *The Path between the Seas*, 11–12.
2. Sibert and Stevens, *The Construction of the Panama Canal*, 110.
3. Photographs of the Panama Canal construction era fill six bound volumes located in the Still Pictures Division of the National Archives in Washington. Other photographs, which I have not consulted, exist in Panama. For a recent pictorial history of the canal construction see Keller, *The Building of the Panama Canal*.
4. See the correspondence between Stevens and labor recruiters in file 2-E-1, General Correspondence, ICC, 1905–14, Record Group 185 (Panama Canal) in the Suitland, Maryland, annex of the National Archives.
5. At the time of the construction itself, literally dozens of journal and magazine articles appeared, many entitled something like "Our Workers on the Canal." More recent scholarly studies include Conniff, *Black Labor on a White Canal*; Davis, "West Indian Workers on the Panama Canal"; Lewis, *The West Indian in Panama*; Newton, "Recruiting West Indian Labourers for the Panama Canal," and *The Silver Men*, both based upon her thesis "British West Indian Emigration"; and Westerman, *Los Inmigrantes Antillanos en Panama*.
6. Patterson, "Migration in Caribbean Societies"; Richardson, *Caribbean Migrants*; Thomas-Hope, "The Establishment of a Migration Tradition."
7. Roberts, "Emigration from the Island of Barbados."
8. Migration in Barbados since emancipation has played a fundamental role similar to food marketing in Jamaica, which evolved during slavery and has since become a vehicle for local improvement and change. See Mintz, *Caribbean Transformations*, chs. 7 and 8.
9. Among many others, see Amin, *Modern Migrations in Western Africa*; Burawoy, "The Functions and Reproduction of Migrant Labour," for interesting comments on the "renewal" and "maintenance" of mobile workforces; Nikolinakos, "Notes towards a General Theory of Migration," which includes an apparently original coining of "sub-proletarian" to designate migrant workers; Portes, "Migration and Underdevelopment"; Sassen-Koob, "The Internationalization of the Labor Force." For recent arguments in favor of a structural approach toward Caribbean migration, see Rubenstein, "Remittances and Rural Underdevelopment in the English-Speaking Caribbean," and Watson, "Theoretical and Methodological Problems"; for a response to structuralist arguments see Richardson, "The Impact of Panama Money in Barbados."
10. Wood, "Equilibrium and Historical-Structural Perspectives on Migration," 299.
11. For exceptions see Painter, *Exodusters*; Redford, *Labour Migration in*

England, 1800–1850; Rhoades, "Foreign Labor and German Industrial Capitalism, 1871–1978."

12. My principal complaint about "theory" that attempts to embrace human migration in its totality is that it tries to deal with all human movement, a ubiquitous human trait that defies theorizing or model-building. The inevitable result in such an attempt is the continuous lament that we need more data, concepts, etc., and that we have not really progressed much further than did Ravenstein in the late nineteenth century. See, for example, Lewis, *Human Migration,* 4.

13. Carnegie, "If You Lose the Dog, Grab the Cat," 28.

14. Wolf, *Europe and the People without History,* x.

15. "The West Indian Negro," *Barbados Agricultural Reporter,* July 16, 1901, from H. Lewis Neville in *Chambers Journal.*

16. One must keep in mind that a scholarly objective among some so-called "scientists" early in the twentieth century was to verify, scientifically, the racial inferiority of non-European peoples. See Gould, *The Mismeasure of Man.*

Chapter 2

1. Vernon and Carroll, *Soil and Land-Use,* 4.

2. Froude, *The English in the West Indies.*

3. *Correspondence Relating to the Hurricane on 10th–12th September, 1898.*

4. "Agricultural Report and Packet Summary," *Barbados Agricultural Reporter,* July 20, 1901.

5. Interrelationships between drought and human activities on Barbados are discussed at length in Starkey, *The Economic Geography of Barbados.*

6. Barbados is said to have been named for the abundance of "bearded" fig trees on the island. See Innes, "The Pre-Sugar Era," for descriptions of early natural vegetation and its removal. For the clearing itself of the vegetation in the seventeenth century, see Bridenbaugh, *No Peace beyond the Line.*

7. "Report of the Forestry Committee," *Official Gazette,* Oct. 16, 1899, pp. 3025–29 (hereafter, *OG*).

8. *Report of the West India Royal Commission* (1897), General Conclusions, 29. For the testimony of the clergymen Oehler, Payne, and Sealy see appendix C, vol. 2, pt. 3, "Barbados," 267–69. The commission held hearings in Bridgetown, Feb. 17–22, 1897.

9. Dunn, *Sugar and Slaves,* 26.

10. For a stimulating cross-cultural discussion of the disillusionment of former slaves working under coercive labor systems after emancipation, see Cooper, *From Slaves to Squatters,* ch. 1. For the Commonwealth Caribbean, see Hall, "The Flight from the Estates Reconsidered."

11. Beckles *The Barbados Disturbances (1937),* 102. The quotation is from

the testimony of F.A. Small, former president of the Workingmen's Association.

12. Deerr, *The History of Sugar*, I, 166–68; Dash, "The Windmills and Copper Walls of Barbados."

13. McLellan, *Some Phases of Barbados Life*, 30–31.

14. Campbell, "Barbados Vestries, 1627–1700."

15. In 1900 in Barbados, commercial bank notes, British coins, and coins from elsewhere circulated side by side. Until 1949, government accounts were required by law to be kept in pounds, shillings, and pence, although most private accounts were kept in dollars. See Greaves, "Money and Currency in Barbados," 164–69.

16. Sugar and sugar by-products were by far the most important staples exported from Barbados. A central cotton factory was opened in Bridgetown in 1903, but cotton accounted only for 1,600 acres on the entire island and was unpopular among planters because of its costs and susceptibility to pests and disease. See *Agricultural News* (1903): 339, and (1904): 37, 369. An incipient banana trade from Barbados to Britain failed in the first decade of the twentieth century. Cold-storage compartments on ships destined for London already were full of Trinidadian bananas on arrival in Bridgetown, and Barbadian bananas were thus stored outside and rotted before reaching their destination. See *Barbados (Illustrated)*, 24–25.

17. The complete enumeration of imports may be found in any of the early Barbados *Blue Books* which were published each year.

18. In 1911–12 total government revenue was £222,000, of which £119,000 were from import duties. See the *Blue Book*, 1911–12, C1.

19. *Report of the West India Royal Commission* (1897), 30. In assessing Commonwealth Caribbean taxation policies, the commission suggested that mutual self-interest between local government taxation schemes and black West Indians' general welfare (expressed in terms of purchasing power) would produce advantages for all. On the other hand, the high population and small subsistence acreage of Barbados assured that at least a threshold of imported food items would be purchased (and thereby taxed) under any conditions, which meant that the guaranteed revenue threshold therefore bore little relationship to workers' welfare.

20. See Harlow, *A History of Barbados*, chs. 2–4, for a discussion of the early colonial government.

21. W.K. Marshall, "The Termination of Apprenticeship," 5.

22. Levy, *Emancipation, Sugar, and Federalism*, ch. 7.

23. "Executive councils" played similar roles elsewhere in the Commonwealth Caribbean at the time. See Will, *Constitutional Change in the British West Indies*, 277.

24. A hierarchy of power and prestige based on land and wealth in which Barbadian assembly members would automatically outrank "lower" officials (vestrymen, low-ranking militia officers, etc.) was established in the seventeenth century. See Dunn, *Sugar and Slaves*, 98–99.

25. Report by Francis Perkins to C.R.M. O'Brien, Aug. 31, 1919, "Labour Troubles and Unrest in the West Indies," File GH 3/5/1, LT/S/1, Barbados Department of Archives, Black Rock, St. Michael (hereafter, BDA).

26. Wickham, *Pen and Ink Sketches*, 17.

27. Bullard, *Panama*, 21–22.

28. The term *located laborer* is still used throughout Barbados to sum up the social and demographic character of the island in the early twentieth century, but there never was a specific act with "located laborer" in the title.

29. "An Act to consolidate and amend the Acts of this Island relating to Master and Servant," *Laws of Barbados* (Barbados: Advocate Printing Works, 1912), I, 677.

30. *Report of the West India Royal Commission* (1897), app. C, vol. II, pt. 3, "Barbados," 218.

31. "An Act for the Suppression and Punishment of Vagrancy," *Laws of Barbados* (Barbados: Advocate Printing Works, 1912), II, 265–66.

32. "Police Court News," *Barbados Standard*, July 12, 1910.

33. Hobsbawm, *Industry and Empire*, 88.

34. Schomburgk, *The History of Barbados*, 130.

35. John Hutson, "The Half-Yearly Report of the Poor Law Inspector," *OG*, Oct. 25, 1909, p. 1822. The 10 percent estimate did not refer to the same 10 percent every year, so it is likely that a considerably higher number appealed for poor relief over a longer period of time.

36. "Half-Yearly Reports of the Poor Law Inspector, for the Half-Year Ending June 30th, 1902," *OG*, Nov. 20, 1902, pp. 2105–32; "July-December, 1902," ibid., Apr. 21, 1903, pp. 981–1015; and "Jan.-June, 1903," ibid., Nov. 26, 1903, pp. 1825–69.

37. Cordle, *Overheard*, 24. Cordle was the black son of an army schoolmaster.

38. See remarks by H.G. Yearwood of St. Joseph parish, Mar. 3, 1908, *Debates in the Barbados House of Assembly, 1907–8*, (Bridgetown: Government of Barbados, 1908), 112 (hereafter, *Debates HA*).

39. Campbell, *Commercial Hall*, 65.

40. *Barbados Agricultural Gazette and Planters' Journal* 8 (Nov. 1902), 249.

41. Letter from "Citizen" about "Our Vaccinist Governor" in the *Barbados Agricultural Reporter*, May 22, 1902. The intensity of the antivaccination campaign in 1902 seems all the more absurd when one realizes that the importance of smallpox inoculation had come to public attention in Barbados as early as 1805. See Higman, *Slave Populations*, 278.

42. "Half-Yearly Report of the Poor Law Inspector," *OG*, Oct. 11, 1909; Oct. 25, 1909; Nov. 8, 1909; and Oct. 1, 1914.

43. "Committee . . . West Indian Sanitary Convention 1904," *OG*, June 13, 1910, p. 1154.

44. *Debates HA*, Feb. 26, 1907, pp. 127–30.

45. *Agricultural News* 1 (1902): 163; for a brief discussion of the bounty depression, see Beachey, *The British West Indies Sugar Industry*, 47–48.

46. *Report of the West India Royal Commission* (1897), app. C, vol. I, p. 78.
47. Cordle, *Overheard*, 13.
48. Hobsbawm, *Industry and Empire*, 198; Wolf, *Europe and the People*, 311–13.
49. Hobsbawn, *Industry and Empire*, 162–63; Deerr, *The History of Sugar*, II, 506–7.
50. *Barbados Agricultural Gazette and Planters' Journal* 7 (Nov. 1901): 180.
51. P.P. 1905/LI/63, "Annual Report for Barbados," 1903–4.
52. Beachey, *The British West Indies Sugar Industry*, 173–74; P.P. 1908/LXVIII/181, "Annual Report for Barbados," 1906–7.
53. Minutes of the Barbados General Agricultural Society, 1902–9, BDA.
54. Amery, *The Life of Joseph Chamberlain*, IV, 241–42.
55. *Correspondence Relating to the Hurricane on 10th–12th September, 1898*, 91–92, 109.
56. Amery, *The Life of Joseph Chamberlain*, IV, 249.
57. "Agricultural Report and Packet Summary," *Barbados Agricultural Reporter*, Apr. 26, 1902.
58. Beachey, *The British West Indies Sugar Industry*, 171. The Barbadian economy was further depressed by the withdrawal of British troops in late 1906 and the near abandonment of the garrison. In 1903–4 the imperial government had expended over £73,000 to maintain the soldiers (P.P. 1905/LI/63, "Annual Report for Barbados," 1903–4).
59. "Agricultural Report," *Barbados Agricultural Reporter*, July 21, 1906.
60. Hutson, "Sugar Manufacture circa 1900."
61. Beachey, *The British West Indies Sugar Industry*, 34–35.
62. *Report of the West India Royal Commission* (1897), app. C, vol. II, pt. 3, "Barbados," 194.
63. Ibid., 157.
64. Ibid., app. C, vol. I, p. 101, and vol. II, pt. 3, "Barbados," 170–71, 197, 231.
65. *Debates HA*, Mar. 7, 1911, p. 76.
66. *Debates in the Legislative Council of Barbados, 1910–11* (Bridgetown: Government of Barbados, 1911), May 23, 1911, pp. 30–31 (hereafter, *Debates LC*); P.P. 1905/LI/64–65, "Annual Report for Barbados," 1903–4.
67. "Agricultural Report," *Barbados Agricultural Reporter*, Sep. 7, 1905, p. 3.
68. Bovell, "Notes on Rotation and Catch Crops."
69. *West Indian Bulletin* (1900?), 154.
70. Reece and Carrington, *Report on the Elementary Education*; Gordon, *A Century of West Indian Education*, 121–22.
71. "Are the Masses Responsible?" *Barbados Agricultural Reporter*, Oct. 26, 1905, p. 3.
72. For a useful typology and discussion of "color" and "class" in the Caribbean, see Lowenthal, *West Indian Societies*, ch. 3.
73. Mintz, *Caribbean Transformations*, 316.
74. Bernard, *Wayside Sketches*, 3.
75. Hobsbawm, *Industry and Empire*, 97–98.

76. Bullard, *Panama*, 21–22.
77. *Agricultural News* 2 (1903): 46.
78. Beckles, *The Barbados Disturbances*, 89. This asymmetry in black-white perceptions of one another is Caribbean-wide; see Mintz and Price, *An Anthropological Approach*, 14.
79. Mintz, *Caribbean Transformations*, 115.
80. Dash, "The Windmills and Copper Walls of Barbados," 60.
81. *Report of the West India Royal Commission of 1897*, app. C, vol. I, p. 101.
82. McLellan, *Some Phases of Barbados Life*, 54.
83. Craton, *Testing the Chains*, 254; Handler, *The Unappropriated People*, 190–91.
84. McLellan, *Some Phases of Barbados Life*, 47.
85. Bernard, *Wayside Sketches*, 89.
86. Sheppard, *The "Redlegs" of Barbados*.
87. Bernard, *Wayside Sketches*, 8.
88. Lofty, *Report on the Census of Barbados, 1911–1921*, 36.
89. Personal interview with Keith Hunte, at Cave Hill, Barbados, June 10, 1982. For early background see Campbell, *The Church in Barbados*.
90. McLellan, *Some Phases of Barbados Life*, 57.
91. Handler, *The Unappropriated People*, 16–17.
92. See Bernard, *Wayside Sketches*, which provides distinctions among the "Broad Street Girl," "Swan Street Girl," and "Tudor Street Girl," 23–28.
93. *The West Indies Illustrated*, 343.

Chapter 3

1. Mintz, "The Folk-Urban Continuum." Under extremely repressive conditions where "conditions of production" are controlled directly by "an exploiting class," the term *feudal* may even be appropriate. See Ennew, Hirst, and Tribe, "Peasantry as an Economic Category," 309.
2. Mintz, "Slavery and the Rise of Peasantries," 230.
3. Shanin, "Defining Peasants," 43.
4. Bundy, *The Rise and Fall of the South African Peasantry*, 9. Post, " 'Peasantization' and Rural Political Movements in Western Africa," 228.
5. Wolf, *Peasants*, 4–6.
6. *Report of the West India Royal Commission*, app. C, vol. II, pt. 3, "Barbados," 166.
7. W.K. Marshall, T. Marshall, and Gibbs, "The Establishment of a Peasantry in Barbados," 86.
8. *Report of the West India Royal Commission*, app. C, vol. II, pt. 3, "Barbados," 193.
9. Mintz, "The Rural Proletariat," 304–7.
10. Smith, "The Nuclear Family."

11. "Report of Commission on Poor Relief," *OG*, Jan. 15, 1878.
12. "Still-Born Infant Thrown into a Well," *Barbados Agricultural Reporter*, May 22, 1902. I am indebted to Ronnie Hughes for his interpretation of this newspaper article.
13. "The Half-Yearly Report of the Poor Law Inspector, January-June 1903," *OG*, Nov. 26, 1903, p. 1834.
14. Mintz, *Caribbean Transformations*, 231–32.
15. McLellan, *Some Phases of Barbados Life*, 59.
16. Boyce, *Report on the Census of Barbados, 1911*, table L, 31.
17. Bolden, "The Barbadian Chattel House."
18. Williams to Joseph Chamberlain, Nov. 25, 1898, *Correspondence Relating to the Hurricane*, 73–74.
19. Treves, *The Cradle of the Deep*, 12.
20. *Debates LC*, Mar. 29, 1910, p. 28.
21. *Report of the West India Royal Commission*, app. C, vol. II, pt. 3, "Barbados," 182.
22. "Fires," *Barbados Agricultural Reporter*, Feb. 23, 1911, p. 3.
23. McLellan, *Some Phases of Barbados Life*, 61.
24. *Debates HA*, Mar. 12, 1912, p. 36.
25. Mintz, "The Employment of Capital," 272–73.
26. Cordle, *Overheard*, 48.
27. D'Albuquerque, "Notes on the Present and Future Lines of Manurial Experiments," 180.
28. *Agricultural News* 1 (Apr.-Dec. 1902): 40.
29. Ibid., 7.
30. Dirks, "Resource Fluctuations and Competitive Transformations," 160–66.
31. Cordle, *Overheard*, 16.
32. Nietschmann, *Between Land and Water*.
33. *Agricultural News* 2 (1903): 54.
34. Warren Alleyne, "The Bowmanston Potato Riot," *Nation*, Dec. 21, 1981.
35. *Debates HA*, Nov. 13, 1917, p. 90.
36. Minutes of the Barbados General Agricultural Society, Dec. 10, 1904, BDA.
37. Scott, *The Moral Economy of the Peasant*, 191.
38. Material about Barbadian bush teas are from interviews with old people and from two very useful articles in the *Journal of the Barbados Museum and Historical Society*: Bayley, "The Bush-teas of Barbados;" and Gooding, "Facts and Beliefs about Barbadian Plants," the latter appearing as a series under the same title.
39. In the mid-twentieth century only "six to seven hundred" flowering species of plants remained from the "thousands" before European settlement (Bayley, "The Bush-teas of Barbados," 103).
40. Gooding, "Facts and Beliefs about Barbadian Plants" (1942), 126.
41. The use of bush teas by Afro-American slaves in the southern

United States was widespread and possibly represented a psychological defense against slavery. See Genovese, *Roll, Jordan, Roll*, 224–29.

42. Cordle, *Overheard*, 36.
43. "Report of Commission on Poor Relief," *OG*, Jan. 15, 1878.
44. *Report of the West India Royal Commission*, app. C, vol. II, pt. 3, "Barbados," 158.
45. Greaves, "Money and Currency in Barbados" (1952–53), 64–65.
46. See Handler, "Small-scale Sugar Cane Farming," 279–80, on the interrelationships between land and cash in the mind of the small landholder in Barbados.
47. Money's "special purpose" character in mediating some transactions but not all usually is applied to non-Western economies (Schneider, *Economic Man*, 158–59).
48. Greaves, "Money and Currency in Barbados" (1952–53), 61.
49. Bernard, *Wayside Sketches*, 2.
50. *Barbados Agricultural Gazette and Planters' Journal* 6, no. 7 (July 1900): 180.
51. *Debates HA*, July 24, 1900, p. 93.
52. Greaves, "Money and Currency in Barbados" (1952–53), 63.
53. Tallis, *About Barbados*, 55.
54. "The Half-Yearly Report of the Poor Law Inspector, January-June 1899," *OG*, Oct. 23, 1899, p. 3113.
55. "The Half-Yearly Report of the Poor Law Inspector, January-June 1903," *OG*, Nov. 26, 1903, p. 1835.
56. "The Half-Yearly Report of the Poor Law Inspector, July-December 1908," *OG*, Nov. 8, 1909, p. 1901.
57. "The Half-Yearly Report of the Poor Law Inspector, July-December 1904," *OG*, May 15, 1905, pp. 808–9.
58. "The Half-Yearly Report of the Poor Law Inspector, January-June 1901," *OG*, Nov. 28, 1901, pp. 1981–82.
59. "Vaccination a Danger," *Barbados Agricultural Reporter*, Apr. 12, 1902.
60. *Barbados Agricultural Gazette and Planters' Journal* 8, no. 10 (Oct. 1902).
61. "The Half-Yearly Report of the Poor Law Inspector, January-June 1910," *OG*, Nov. 2, 1914, p. 1810.
62. "The Half-Yearly Report of the Poor Law Inspector, July-December 1897," *OG*, May 12, 1898, pp. 842–43.
63. Hutson, "The Half-Yearly Report of the Poor Law Inspector, January-June 1907," suppl. to *OG*, Nov. 10, 1908, pp. 37–38.
64. Kiple and King, *Another Dimension to the Black Diaspora*, 145–46.
65. Hutson, *Annual Report of the Public Health Inspector* (1921), 6–7.
66. C.E. Gooding, "The Fourth Annual Report of the Acting Public Health Inspector," *OG*, Aug. 16, 1917, pp. 1570–78.
67. *The West Indies Illustrated*, 321.
68. *Weekly Illustrated Paper*, Feb. 2, 1907.

69. "The Half-Yearly Report of the Poor Law Inspector, July-December 1897," *OG*, May 12, 1898, p. 845.
70. Hobsbawm, *Industry and Empire*, 159–60.
71. Hutson, "The Half-Yearly Report of the Poor Law Inspector, July-December 1907," *OG*, Oct. 11, 1909, p. 1719.
72. "The Half-Yearly Report of the Poor Law Inspector, January-June 1912," 25, BDA; "The Half-Yearly Report of the Poor Law Inspector, January-June, 1913," 14, BDA.
73. "The Half-Yearly Report of the Poor Law Inspector, July-December, 1913," 1, BDA.
74. "Poor Relief in St. George," *Barbados Agricultural Reporter*, May 18, 1905.
75. Genovese, *Roll, Jordan, Roll*, 495–96.
76. For descriptive historical accounts of various parts of Bridgetown from earliest times, see Alleyne, *Historic Bridgetown*.
77. *OG*, July 21, 1890.
78. McLellan, *Some Phases of Barbados Life*, 75.
79. *Barbados Agricultural Reporter*, July 25, 1910.
80. "The Roebuck Smallpox Case," *Barbados Agricultural Reporter*, Aug. 1, 1902.
81. A good summary discussion of the chaotic growth of the Bridgetown tenantries at the turn of the century is in the *Debates HA*, July 3, 1906, pp. 293–94.
82. "Plan of Part of Bank Hall Plantation" (dated 10 May 1895), Plan B 1/7, BDA.
83. To my knowledge, no single cadastral survey for St. Michael parish exists for the early twentieth century. The plantations or land blocks named here come from "British Union Oil Company Records," no. Z8/1/10, BDA; Sinckler, *The Barbados Handbook*, 83; and a personal interview with Mr. Frank Gibbons at Black Rock, St. Michael, Barbados, on June 10, 1982.
84. *Debates HA*, July 3, 1906, p. 294.
85. "Report of Commission on Poor Relief," *OG*, Jan. 15 and 19, 1878.
86. Hutson, "The Bridgetown Dry Dock," 106–7.
87. *Report of the West India Royal Commission*, app. C, vol. II, pt. 3, "Barbados," 221.
88. Beckles, *The Barbados Disturbances*, 256–57.
89. Verrill, *Isles of Spice and Palm*, 148–49.
90. *Report of the West India Royal Commission*, app. C, vol. II, pt. 3, "Barbados," 221.
91. *Report on Census of Barbados (1881–'91)*, 69.
92. See Mintz, *Caribbean Transformations*, 220–22, for similar marketing strategies in Jamaica.
93. McLellan, *Some Phases of Barbados Life*, 75.
94. Ibid., 65.
95. Cordle, *Overheard*, 26.

96. *Report of the West India Royal Commission*, app. C, vol. II, pt. 3, "Barbados," 219.

97. Cordle, *Overheard*, 16.

98. *Proceedings of West Indian Sugar Commission*, 42. Whether or not Barbados really has a "village" tradition would, in a manner similar to peasant-proletariat controversies, doubtless reveal different points of view. See W.K. Marshall, T. Marshall, and Gibbs "The Establishment of a Peasantry." Also, for a discussion of early slave "villages" see Handler and Lange, *Plantation Slavery in Barbados*, 29–42.

99. Mintz and Price, *An Anthropological Approach*, 12.

100. Meetings are still common throughout Barbados, and similar groupings exist among many impoverished peoples. See Barrow, "Meetings"; Torres, "Meetings"; Kurtz, "The Rotating Credit Association."

101. Torres, "Meetings," 10.

102. "Report of Commission on Poor Relief," *OG*, Mar. 16, 1878.

103. Ardener, "The Comparative Study of Rotating Credit Associations."

104. A most valuable summary is Wells, *Friendly Societies in the West Indies*. A very similar report that contains more specific information about Barbados is in typescript form and available at the Office of the Registrar of Friendly Societies at the Garrison Savanna in Bridgetown: A.F. Wells, "The Friendly Societies of Barbados."

105. J. Gittens Knight, "Report of Friendly Societies for the Half-Year, January-June 1901," *OG*, Oct. 3, 1901, p. 4.

106. Beckles, *The Barbados Disturbances*, app. H.

107. Hobsbawm, *Industry and Empire*, 88.

108. Personal interview with Keith Hunte, at Cave Hill, Barbados, June 10, 1982.

109. Handler and Lange, *Plantation Slavery in Barbados*, ch. 6, "The Mortuary Patterns of Plantation Slaves."

110. Lynch, *The Barbados Book*, 227.

111. Wells and Wells, *Friendly Societies in the West Indies*, 18.

112. Knight, "Report of Registrar of Friendly Societies," *OG*, July 24, 1902, p. 1421.

113. "The Friendly Societies and the Government," *Barbados Agricultural Reporter*, Jan. 21, 1902.

114. "Friendly Societies," *Barbados Agricultural Reporter*, June 26, 1901.

115. C.O. 884/1/iv/app. 3.

116. *Weekly Illustrated Paper*, Dec. 9, 1905.

117. *Debates LC*, Nov. 13, 1906, p. 19.

118. P.P. 1905/LI/63.

119. "The Manners of the Masses," *Barbados Agricultural Reporter*, Feb. 14, 1901.

120. Treves, *The Cradle of the Deep*, 34.

121. *Report of the West India Royal Commission*, app. C, vol. I, p. 79; for the Lawrance testimony see app. C, vol. II, pt. 3, "Barbados," 205.

Notes to Pages 95-108

122. Similar points have been made elsewhere in different contexts. See Genovese, *Roll, Jordan, Roll,* 90–91, 658, on acquiescence, and Scott, *Moral Economy of the Peasant,* 225–40, on "Nonrevolt."
123. *Report of the West India Royal Commission,* app. C, vol. II, pt. 3, "Barbados," 222.
124. Genovese, *Roll, Jordan, Roll,* 237.
125. *Report of the West India Royal Commission,* app. C, vol. II, pt. 3, "Barbados," 174.
126. Vaughan, "Some Social and Political Tendencies," 60.
127. *Report of the West India Royal Commission,* app. C, vol. I, p. 79.
128. "Agriculture and Agricultural Labourers," *Barbados Agricultural Reporter,* Feb. 12, 1901.
129. McLellan, *Some Phases of Barbados Life,* 61.
130. "Agricultural Report and Packet Summary," *Barbados Agricultural Reporter,* Feb. 16, 1901.
131. *Debates LC,* Mar. 3, 1908, p. 45.
132. *Debates HA,* Feb. 2, 1904, p. 219, and Nov. 21, 1911, p. 330.
133. McLellan, *Some Phases of Barbados Life,* 60.
134. *Report of the West India Royal Commission,* app. C, vol. II, pt. 3, "Barbados," 173.
135. P.P. 1842/XIII/137, "Report from the Select Committee on West India Colonies."
136. Roberts, "Emigration from the Island of Barbados," 256.
137. P.P. 1875/LI/63, Rawson W. Rawson to Lord Carnarvon.
138. Johnson, "Barbadian Immigrants in Trinidad," 8.
139. Roberts, "Emigration from Barbados," 247–48.
140. Rodney, "Barbadian Immigration into British Guiana, 1863–1924."
141. P.P. 1865/XXXVII/35, James Walker to Hon. Edward Cardwell.
142. *Report of the West India Royal Commission,* app. C, vol. II, pt. 3, "Barbados," 173.
143. Rodney, *A History of the Guyanese Working People,* 187.
144. Brereton, *Race Relations in Colonial Trinidad,* 112–14.
145. Johnson, "Barbadian Immigrants in Trinidad," 19.
146. "Report of Commission on Poor Relief," *OG,* Mar. 16, 1878.
147. Schomburgk, *The History of Barbados,* 75–76.
148. "Report of Commission on Poor Relief," *OG,* Mar. 16, 1878.

Chapter 4

1. *Debates LC,* July 16, 1907, pp. 85–87.
2. "Despatch from the Acting British Consul of Loanda," *OG,* Dec. 12, 1892, p. 1482.
3. *Debates HA,* June 14, 1904, p. 4.
4. *OG,* Sept. 18, 1890, and Apr. 23, 1906, p. 572; "Bishop of Guiana on Surinam as a Field of Labour," *Barbados Agricultural Reporter,* May 5, 1906.

5. *Barbados Agricultural Reporter,* May 3 and 6, and June 11, 1901.
6. "Warning to Intending Emigrants to Pará," *OG,* Oct. 21, 1897.
7. Greenfield, "Barbadians in the Brazilian Amazon," and his "Barbadians and Barbadian House Forms."
8. "Emigration to Brazil and Its Perils," *Barbados Agricultural Reporter* June 3, 1910.
9. George R. Shanton to J.C.S. Blackburn (May 2, 1908), and George W. Goethals to George R. Shanton, Dec. 3, 1908, file 2-E-3, General Correspondence, ICC.
10. *Barbados Agricultural Reporter,* June 18, 1910, and Sept. 28, 1911.
11. "Emigration to Peru," *Barbados Advocate,* Apr. 9, 1906.
12. Collier, *The River That God Forgot,* 62–63, 166; B.L. Reid, *The Lives of Roger Casement,* 119–20, 126; *Debates HA,* Apr. 25, 1911, 163–64.
13. *Weekly Illustrated Paper,* Feb. 4, 1905.
14. Personal communication from Michael Conniff, Aug. 30, 1983.
15. R.E. Wood to John Stevens, Oct. 22, 1906, and ICC memorandum, Oct. 24, 1906, file 2-E-1, General Correspondence, ICC.
16. "Chief Engineer" to Karner (Dec. 22, 1904), file 2-E-1, General Correspondence, ICC.
17. "The Late Mr. S.E. Brewster," *Barbados Advocate,* Sept. 3, 1913.
18. "Emigrants for the Isthmus," *Barbados Advocate,* Jan. 23, 1905.
19. A sliding scale of expenses, based on number of laborers transported, eventually was arranged between Karner and the steamship company's local representative. Capt. W.H. Owen to Karner, Jan. 9, 1906, file 2-E-1, pt. 1, General Correspondence, ICC.
20. Bullard, *Panama,* 27.
21. S.W. Settoon to Jackson Smith, Feb. 10, 1906, file 2-E-1, General Correspondence, ICC.
22. Settoon to R.E. Wood, Aug. 6, 1907, C. Brun, Legation of Denmark, to Elihu Root, Mar. 5, 1908, and Settoon to Smith, Mar. 28, 1908, file 2-E-1, General Correspondence, ICC.
23. *Barbados Advocate,* Oct. 27, 1904, Nov. 14, 17, 1905.
24. Newton, "Aspects of British West Indian Emigration," 19–20; Roberts, "Emigration from the Island of Barbados," 265.
25. Newspaper reports of Mar. 3, 1906, and Dec. 24, 1906, in *Barbados Agricultural Reporter.*
26. "The Panama Canal Commission's Barbados Recruiting Arrangements," *Weekly Illustrated Paper,* Aug. 21, 1909.
27. Personal interview with Mr. Howard Skinner, at Black Bess Estate, St. Peter, Barbados, Mar. 23, 1982. His brother was Beresford Skinner, who has since died but whose name appears on the surviving "emigrants' register."
28. Bullard, *Panama,* 27–29. Michael Conniff, however, reports medical rejection rates in Barbados as only 25%, based on CZ Records 2-E-2, Barbados, 24 May 1906. The rejections, according to Conniff, were mainly because of venereal disease, hernia, and generally poor condition.
29. I am indebted to Fitzgerald Burnham of Bridgetown who signed

his service contract with the ICC on July 27, 1907, and who allowed me to photocopy the document seventy-five years later!

30. Karner to Smith, July 4, 1908, file 2-E-1, General Correspondence, ICC.
31. "Agricultural Report," *Barbados Agricultural Reporter,* May 2, 1908.
32. "The Exodus to Panama," *Barbados Advocate,* Apr. 9, 1906.
33. Bullard, *Panama,* 31.
34. "Labourers for Panama," *Barbados Advocate,* June 11, 1908.
35. *OG,* Aug. 16, 1909.
36. "Immigrants from Barbados," *Barbados Agricultural Reporter,* Aug. 12, 1909.
37. *OG,* Nov. 10, 1908.
38. *Annual Report of the Isthmian Canal Commission* (1914), 294. Not all sources agree on the exact numbers. A memo produced by R.E. Wood in the Canal Zone on Oct. 1, 1912 (file 2-E-1, pt. 5, General Correspondence, ICC), enumerated 3,095 (not 3,019) Barbadians leaving for contract work in 1905. Newton, "Aspects of British West Indian Emigration," 20, cites the *Canal Record* 8 (Oct. 28, 1914): 91, and reports 20,885 Barbadians sent to Panama as contract workers from 1904 through 1914.
39. Bishop, *The Panama Gateway,* 303.
40. "Police Court News," *Barbados Advocate,* Mar. 22, 1909.
41. Lofty, *Report on the Census of Barbados 1911–1921,* 9.
42. Boyce, *Report on the Census of Barbados 1911,* 4.
43. Newton, "Aspects of British West Indian Emigration," 20–22, estimates that a total of 60,000 Barbadians went to the canal from 1904 through 1914. I find this figure extraordinarily high.
44. *Weekly Illustrated Paper,* Aug. 3, 1907.
45. For a computer printout showing each of the 5,728 names arrayed by village and parish, see Richardson, "Barbadian Contract Laborers to the Panama Canal, 1906–7," at the Barbados Department of Archives. The printout is derived from the handwritten "Emigrants' Registers" (BDA).
46. *Plan of the City of Bridgetown; Bridgetown and Environs.*
47. Personal interview, June 8, 1982.
48. "Agricultural Report," *Barbados Agricultural Reporter,* Aug. 3, 1907.
49. *Barbados Agricultural Reporter,* Aug. 26, 1905, and Feb. 3, 1906.
50. *Weekly Illustrated Paper,* Feb. 9, 1907.
51. *Debates HA,* 1903–4, pp. 244–45, Aug. 15, 1905, pp. 36–38, May 15, 1906, pp. 223–26.
52. *Debates HA,* July 2, 1907, pp. 200–4; *Debates LC,* July 16, 1907, pp. 83–8.
53. *Weekly Illustrated Paper,* July 20, 1907.
54. Edgar Lowe to Wood, Aug. 7, 1907, file 2-E-1, General Correspondence, ICC.
55. Apparently the ship captain was referring to the Imperial Merchant Shipping Act. See *OG,* Sept. 16, 1907, p. 1476.
56. *OG,* Sept. 5, 1907, p. 1405.

57. Lewis, *Main Currents in Caribbean Thought*, 323.
58. *Barbados Agricultural Reporter*, Sept. 7, 1905, and July 10, 1907.
59. "Half-Yearly Report of the Poor Law Inspector, January-June, 1910," *OG*, Nov. 2, 1914, p. 1734.
60. Letter from J.W.B., *Weekly Illustrated Paper*, July 13, 1907.
61. Genovese, *Roll, Jordan, Roll*, 146–47.
62. See Scott, *Moral Economy of the Peasant*, 180–92, for more on individual rights in coercive social systems.
63. *Annual Report of the Governor of the Panama Canal* (1915), 238.

Chapter 5

1. Starkey, *Economic Geography of Barbados*, 132.
2. P.P. 1912–13/LVII/61, "Annual Report for Barbados," 1911–12.
3. *Debates HA*, Feb. 2, 1909, p. 96.
4. *Debates LC*, May 23, 1911, p. 31.
5. Personal interview, Mar. 23, 1982.
6. See the annual harbor master reports in the Barbados *Official Gazette* for these years.
7. "Death by Nationality" tables were maintained by the Sanitation Department in the *Annual Reports, Isthmian Canal Commission*, 1907–20.
8. Fred Barker, "Panama Society and the Canal Zone," *Barbados Advocate*, Aug. 12, 1913.
9. McCullough, *The Path between the Seas*, 501–2.
10. "Report on the Police Force of the Colony for 1909," *OG*, Feb. 17, 1910, p. 313.
11. *Debates HA*, Dec. 31, 1918, p. 112.
12. "Barbados Labourers on the Panama Canal," *Barbados Advocate*, Feb. 23, 1911.
13. George F. Enoch, "On the Canal Strip," *Barbados Advocate*, June 16, 1906.
14. McLellan, *Some Phases of Barbados Life*, 63.
15. "Return of Emigrants from Panama," *Barbados Advocate*, Nov. 14, 1905.
16. McLellan, *Some Phases of Barbados Life*, 78.
17. Walrond, *Tropic Death*, 42.
18. McLellan, *Some Phases of Barbados Life*, 79.
19. "The Police, Panama Men, and the Coronation Festivities," *Barbados Agricultural Reporter*, June 17, 1911.
20. "Report on the Police Force of the Colony for 1906," *OG*, Mar. 7, 1907, p. 327.
21. "Report on the Police Force of the Colony for 1916," *OG*, Apr. 23, 1917, p. 817.
22. C.E. Gooding, "The Fifth Annual Report of the Public Health Inspector, 1917," *OG*, June 13, 1918, p. 1049.
23. "Agricultural Report," *Barbados Agricultural Reporter*, Feb. 8, 1908.

24. "Report of Cane Fires Commission," *OG*, June 28, 1915, p. 1092.
25. See Richardson, *Caribbean Migrants*, 130, for a discussion of increased crime rates in St. Kitts and Nevis when men seasonally returned from the Dominican Republic early in the twentieth century.
26. T. Marshall, McGeary, and Thompson, *Folk Songs of Barbados*, 60.
27. *Debates HA*, Mar. 7, 1910, p. 450.
28. Hutson, "Public Health Inspector Report for 1913," *OG*, June 18, 1914, p. 30.
29. Walrond, *Tropic Death*, 49.
30. McLellan, *Some Phases of Barbados Life*, 63–64.
31. Frederic J. Haskin, "The Panama Canal—Paying Off," *Barbados Agricultural Reporter*, Sept. 3, 1908.
32. "Remittances from Panama," *OG*, Aug. 6, 1906.
33. "The Report on Trade Statistics," *Barbados Agricultural Reporter*, Nov. 18, 1911.
34. *OG*, Aug. 27, 1906, p. 1271.
35. Both Roberts, "Emigration from the Island of Barbados," 283–84, and Starkey, *Economic Geography of Barbados*, 129–30, also consider estimates of Panama money remitted to Barbados.
36. *Debates HA*, Mar. 15, 1910, p. 105.
37. "The Post-Office Money Order Department," *Weekly Illustrated Paper*, Sept. 15, 1906.
38. *Debates HA*, 30 Oct. 1900, p. 124.
39. *OG*, Sept. 28, 1903.
40. "Report on the Post Office for 1910," *OG*, Sept. 14, 1911, p. 1703.
41. McLellan, *Some Phases of Barbados Life*, 76.
42. Greaves, "Money and Currency in Barbados."
43. Barbados *Blue Book* of 1920–21, sect. 19, p. 1.
44. *Debates HA*, 1915–16, p. 409.
45. *OG*, Sept. 5, 1907, p. 1411–12.
46. *Debates HA*, June 16, 1914, p. 35.
47. *Debates LC*, Aug. 25, 1914, p. 34.
48. E. Goulburn Sinckler, "Report on the Barbados Government Savings Bank, 1919–20," suppl. to *OG*, Nov. 15, 1920, p. 2.
49. "That Panama Money," *Barbados Standard*, July 2, 1910.
50. McLellan, *Some Phases of Barbados Life*, 37.

Chapter 6

1. Boyce, *Report on the Census of Barbados 1911*, 5.
2. Lowenthal, "The Population of Barbados."
3. "Conserving Our Labour Supply," *Barbados Agricultural Reporter*, Nov. 17, 1910.
4. *Proceedings of West Indian Sugar Commission*, 54.
5. Boyce, *Report on the Census of Barbados 1911*, 5–6.
6. *Debates HA*, Mar. 7, 1911, p. 75.

7. Greenfield, "Stocks, Bonds, and Peasant Canes," 642–43.
8. Vaughan, "Some Social and Political Tendencies," 31.
9. "Conserving Our Labour Supply," *Barbados Agricultural Reporter*, Nov. 15, 1910.
10. Wolf, *Europe and the People without History*, 317.
11. Mintz, *Caribbean Transformations*, ch. 4. See also his foreword to Guerra y Sánchez, *Sugar and Society in the Caribbean*.
12. Beckford, *Persistent Poverty*, 102–10.
13. "Conserving Our Labour Supply," *Barbados Agricultural Reporter*, Nov. 15, 1910.
14. Deerr, *The History of Sugar*, I, 166–67; Leverick, *Leverick's Directory*.
15. "Agricultural Report," *Barbados Agricultural Reporter*, Sept. 30, 1911.
16. Leverick, *Leverick's Directory*.
17. *Debates HA*, Dec. 21, 1909, p. 28.
18. *Agricultural News* 15 (May 6, 1916): 156.
19. Beckles, *The Barbados Disturbances*, 57.
20. Deerr, *The History of Sugar*, II, 531.
21. Campbell, *Commercial Hall*, 45.
22. *Agricultural News* 15 (Nov. 4, 1916): 365.
23. *Agricultural News* 18 (Nov. 2, 1919): 357.
24. "The Half-Yearly Report of the Poor Law Inspector, July-December 1912," p. 25, BDA.
25. *Agricultural News* 8 (Apr. 17, 1909), 124, and ibid., 19 (Dec. 24, 1919): 5.
26. Handler, "Small-scale Sugar Cane Farming," 279–80.
27. Greaves, "Money and Currency in Barbados" (1952), 165.
28. Beckles, *The Barbados Disturbances*, app. E.
29. See the monthly reports in the *Agricultural News* 19 (1920).
30. Beckles, *The Barbados Disturbances*, 74.
31. Mintz, "The Rural Proletariat," 309.
32. *Proceedings of West Indian Sugar Commission*, 74–75.
33. *Debates HA*, July 29, 1913, pp. 179, 182–83.
34. Lowenthal, *West Indian Societies*, 60.
35. Sinckler, *The Barbados Handbook*, 95.
36. *Debates HA*, May 15, 1917, p. 347.
37. Skeete, *The Condition of Peasant Agriculture*, 1.
38. W.K. Marshall, T. Marshall, and Gibbs, "The Establishment of a Peasantry," 96.
39. "Map of Barbados Shewing Division into Oil-Mining Areas," (1917), Plan Roll 176/7D, BDA.
40. Reid, "The Growth of a Twentieth Century Fiction."
41. *Proceedings of West Indian Sugar Commission*, 47–50.
42. *Debates HA*, Apr. 10, 1928, pp. 368–69.
43. Records of the Civic Circle, Minutes Book, May 1916-May 1917, doc. Z12/1, BDA.

44. W.K. Marshall, T. Marshall, and Gibbs, "The Establishment of a Peasantry," 98; Mark, *The History of the Barbados Workers' Union*, 20–21.
45. *Proceedings of West Indian Sugar Commission*, 42.
46. Lowenthal, "Caribbean Views of Caribbean Land," 4.
47. Mintz and Price, *An Anthropological Approach*, 34.
48. Douglas, "Primitive Rationing," 139–40.
49. Skeete, *Condition of Peasant Agriculture*, 15, 25.
50. Minutes of the Barbados Agricultural Society, entry for May 13, 1916, BDA.
51. *Agricultural News* 17 (Aug. 10, 1918): 251.
52. W.K. Marshall, T. Marshall, and Gibbs, "The Establishment of a Peasantry," 100–1, includes a map showing "Villages in Barbados by 1930."
53. Nietschmann, "Ecological Change, Inflation, and Migration," 13.
54. Greenfield, "Stocks, Bonds, and Peasant Canes," 625.
55. Sibert and Stevens, *The Construction of the Panama Canal*, 113–14.
56. McLellan, *Some Phases of Barbados Life*, 63.
57. *Debates HA*, May 15, 1917, p. 347.
58. See the Barbados *Blue Books* for these data.
59. *Debates HA*, Mar. 26, 1918, p. 287.
60. *Agricultural News* 16 (June 11, 1917): 195.
61. "The Half-Yearly Report of the Poor Law Inspector, July-December, 1910," *OG*, Nov. 12, 1914, p. 1811.
62. Gooding, "The Fourth Annual Report of the Acting Public Health Inspector," *OG*, Aug. 16, 1917, p. 1578.
63. "The Half-Yearly Report of the Poor Law Inspector, January-June 1907," *OG*, Nov. 10, 1908, p. 52.
64. Kiple and King, *Another Dimension to the Black Diaspora*, 125.
65. *Agricultural News* 16 (Aug. 2, 1917): 245.
66. Gooding, "The Fifth Annual Report of the Public Health Inspector," *OG*, June 13, 1918, p. 1071.
67. *Debates HA*, Dec. 5, 1916, p. 140.
68. Hutson, "Public Health Inspector Report for 1913," *OG*, June 18, 1914, pp. 8–10.
69. C.E. Gooding, "The Fifth Annual Report of the Public Health Inspector," *OG*, June 13, 1918, p. 1055.
70. "The Half-Yearly Report of the Poor Law Inspector, January-June, 1916," *OG*, Dec. 7, 1916, pp. 2424–25.
71. Gooding, "The Fifth Annual Report of the Public Health Inspector," *OG*, June 13, 1918, p. 1052.
72. Starkey, *The Economic Geography of Barbados*, 134.
73. Hutson, "Annual Report of the Public Health Inspector, 1921," 2, BDA.
74. Gooding, "The Half-Yearly Report of the Acting Poor Law Inspector," *OG*, Aug. 30, 1917, p. 1673.
75. *The Report of the Public Health Commission, 1925–26*.

76. Hutson, "Ten Years of Sanitary Progress," *OG*, Apr. 24, 1924, p. 14.
77. Hoyos, *Builders of Barbados*, 107–16.
78. "Reports of Certain Meetings," entry for Jan. 13, 1928, file 4/37b, BDA.
79. "Report of the Registrar of Friendly Societies for the Half-Year January-June 1914," *OG*, Dec. 14, 1914, p. 1981.
80. "An Act to consolidate the Acts of this Island relating to Friendly Societies," *Laws of Barbados* (Barbados: Advocate Printing Works, 1912), III, 86–120, ref. 98.
81. "Report of the Registrar of Friendly Societies for the Half-Year January-June 1908," *OG*, Oct. 1, 1908, p. 1504.
82. Wells and Wells, *Friendly Societies in the West Indies*, 50.
83. "The Half-Yearly Report of the Poor Law Inspector, July-December, 1910," *OG*, Nov. 12, 1914, p. 1801.
84. Wells, "The Friendly Societies of Barbados," 6.
85. Geertz, "The Rotating Credit Association," 260–61.
86. Wells, "The Friendly Societies of Barbados," 10.
87. "Report on the Police Force of the Colony for 1915," *OG*, May 1, 1916, p. 851.
88. "Labour Troubles and Unrest in the West Indies," file GH 3/5/1, LT/S/1, BDA.
89. Minutes of the Barbados Agricultural Society, Apr. 26, 1919, BDA.
90. *Debates HA*, Nov. 13, 1917, p. 90.
91. *Debates HA*, July 19, 1921, pp. 380–82.
92. *Debates HA*, Apr. 27, 1920, p. 234.
93. *Debates HA*, Jan. 28, 1919, pp. 139, 143.
94. *Debates HA*, Mar. 18, 1919, p. 310.
95. *Debates HA*, Mar. 4, 1919, pp. 239–48.
96. Lofty, *Report on the Census of Barbados, 1911–1921*, 14.
97. "Labour Troubles and Unrest in the West Indies," file GH 3/5/1, LT/S/1, BDA.
98. Joseph, "The British West Indies Regiment, 1914–1918"; Elkins, "A Source of Black Nationalism."
99. "Labour Troubles," file GH 3/5/1, LT/S/1, BDA, entries for Dec. 27, 1918, and Jan. 14, 1919.
100. "Scheme of Organization against Civil Disturbances," file GH 3/4/4/LF/S/40 (i), BDA
101. "Labour Troubles," file GH 3/5/1, LT/S/1, BDA, entry for Feb. 21, 1919.
102. Elkins, "Marcus Garvey," 64–65.
103. "Labour Troubles," file GH 3/5/1, LT/S/1, BDA, entry for July 14, 1919.
104. *Debates HA*, Nov. 11, 1919, 27.
105. Elkins, "Black Power in the British West Indies."
106. Vaughan, "Some Social and Political Tendencies," 58.
107. Ibid., 60.
108. Mintz, *Worker in the Cane*, 258.

109. Boyce, *Report on the Census of Barbados, 1911*, 78–79; Lofty, *Report on the Census of Barbados, 1911–1921*, 36.
110. "Bishop Jack of Episcopal Orthodox Church," file GH 3/6/3, BDA.
111. Surprisingly little has been written about the Barbadian landship. See Bernard, *Wayside Sketches*, 17–20, and Lynch, *The Barbados Book*, 229–33.
112. Vaughan, "Some Social and Political Tendencies," 60.
113. Bernard, *Wayside Sketches*, 19.
114. Banton, *West African City*, 188–89.
115. "Breach of the Friendly Societies Act," *Barbados Agricultural Reporter*, Sept. 18, 1901.
116. Kenneth Little has written extensively on the development of urbanism and the related importance of voluntary associations in West Africa. See his *Urbanization as a Social Process* and his *West African Urbanization*.
117. Lynch, *The Barbados Book*, 230–31.
118. Bernard, *Wayside Sketches*, 17.
119. Personal interview, Bridgetown, July 6, 1982.
120. In the mid-1940s "probably not 1,000" members of secret lodge orders could be found in Barbados (Wells, "The Friendly Societies of Barbados," 22).
121. Sister Enid Harris, "Origin of A.O.F. in W.I.," *Ancient Order of Foresters, 1846–1971*, pamphlet A806, BDA.
122. Hobsbawn and Rudé, *Captain Swing*, 295.
123. Wells, "The Friendly Societies of Barbados," 22.
124. Wolf, *Europe and the People without History*, 360.
125. "Universal Negro Improvement Association, 1920," file GH 3/5//4, LT/S/7, BDA.
126. Cronon, *Black Moses*, 14–15.
127. Davis, "West Indian Workers on the Panama Canal," 115–22.
128. "Universal Negro Improvement Association, 1920," BDA, entry Aug. 10, 1920.
129. "Reports of Certain Meetings," file GH 4/37b, BDA, entry for Dec. 8, 1927.

Chapter 7

1. *Proceedings of West Indian Sugar Commission*, 40.
2. *Debates HA*, Sept. 27, 1921, pp. 497–501, and Nov. 15, 1921, p. 554.
3. "Victoria Emigration Society Minutes Book, 1897–1919," BDA.
4. "Emigration of West Indians to the United States," *Barbados Agricultural Reporter*, Oct. 23, 1911.
5. "Report on the Post Office, Barbados, for the Year 1916," *OG*, Apr. 19, 1917, p. 780.
6. Barbados *Blue Book* (1920–21), sec. 33, p. 3.
7. *Proceedings of West Indian Sugar Commission*, 47.

8. Skeete, *The Condition of Peasant Agriculture*, 26–27, 31, 36–38.
9. "Unrest in Police Force," file GH 3/6/2, Mis/G/22, BDA.
10. *Debates HA*, May 7, 1918, pp. 334–35, and Sept. 27, 1921, p. 499.
11. *Debates HA*, Sept. 27, 1921, pp. 499–500.
12. "Reports of Certain Meetings," file GH 4/37b, BDA, entry for Nov. 21, 1927.
13. Deerr, *The History of Sugar*, vol. 2, p. 531.
14. Beckles, *The Barbados Disturbances*, 10.
15. *Proceedings of West Indian Sugar Commission*, 71.
16. Richardson, *Caribbean Migrants*, 141–42.
17. Knight, *The Caribbean*, 179.
18. Beckles, *The Barbados Disturbances*, 1.
19. Ibid., 100.
20. For lengthier descriptions of the 1937 Bridgetown riots see Beckles, *The Barbados Disturbances*, and Mark, *The History of the Barbados Workers' Union*, 1–8.
21. Edward Stoute, "Flashback to 1937 Riots," *Barbados Advocate-News*, Sept. 20, 1981.
22. Hoyos, *Grantley Adams and the Social Revolution*.
23. Beckles, *The Barbados Disturbances*, 204–5.
24. *Proceedings of West Indian Sugar Commission*, 61.
25. Beckles, *The Barbados Disturbances*, 5, 7, 41.
26. Ibid., 10–13, 34, 45.
27. Segal, *Population Policies in the Caribbean*, 219.
28. Early in the 1940s a small group of individuals representing "The Barbadian Progressive Society" from Panama spent thousands of pounds from the society's treasury in purchasing five sugar estates along the west coast of Barbados in St. James and St. Peter parishes. Mismanagement and dissension among the individuals representing the society caused the eventual demise and selling off of the properties, according to both archival sources and interviewees (see "West Indian Court of Appeals, Barbados [Judgments, 1953]," pamphlet C521, BDA.
29. Bullard, *Panama*, 42–43.

Bibliography

Barbados government publications and newspapers are cited in the notes. Also cited in the notes are records and correspondence of the Isthmian Canal Commission from Record Group 185 (Panama Canal) at the Suitland, Maryland, annex of the U.S. National Archives.

Barbados government publications, including *Debates in the Barbados House of Assembly* (abbreviated in the notes as *Debates HA*), *Debates in the Legislative Council of Barbados* (abbreviated as *Debates LC*), the *Official Gazette* (abbreviated as *OG*), and some published and unpublished reports, are located at the Barbados Department of Archives at Black Rock, St. Michael. Also at the Barbados Department of Archives are early newspaper files of the *Barbados Agricultural Reporter*, the *Barbados Advocate*, and the *Barbados Standard*. Of these three, only the *Advocate* is still published, and a few volumes from the early twentieth century are available at the current newspaper office building in the Fontabelle district of Bridgetown. The Bridgetown Public Library also maintains newspaper files, including those of the *Weekly Illustrated Paper*, although all of these files were closed in 1981 because of deterioration and insect damage. The *Agricultural News*, cited in the notes, refers to reports from Barbados and neighboring islands that were published early in the twentieth century; these reports are available in bound volumes at the library maintained by the Barbados Department of Agriculture on the grounds of Harrison College in Bridgetown.

Abbreviations are used in the bibliography for three regional journals of the Caribbean that are cited often: *The Journal of the Barbados Museum and Historical Society (JBMHS); Journal of Caribbean History (JCH);* and *Social and Economic Studies (SES)*. The British Colonial Office and the British Sessional Papers, or "Parliamentary Papers," are conventionally abbreviated as C.O. and P.P., respectively, in the few cases where they are cited.

Alleyne, Warren. *Historic Bridgetown*. Barbados: Barbados National Trust, 1978.
Amery, Julian. *The Life of Joseph Chamberlain*. London: Macmillan, 1951.
Amin, Samir, ed. *Modern Migrations in Western Africa*. London: Oxford Univ. Press, 1974.
Annual Report of the Governor of the Panama Canal. Washington: Government Printing Office, 1915.

Annual Report of the Isthmian Canal Commission and the Panama Canal. Washington: Government Printing Office, 1907–14.

Ardener, Shirley. "The Comparative Study of Rotating Credit Associations." *Journal of the Royal Anthropological Institute* 94 (1964): 201–29.

Banton, Michael. *West African City: A Study of Tribal Life in Freetown.* London: Oxford Univ. Press, 1957.

Barbados (Illustrated): Historical, Descriptive, and Commercial. Barbados: Cave, Shepherd, 1911.

Barrow, Christine. "Meetings: A Group Savings Arrangement in Barbados." *African Studies Association of the West Indies*, bull. no. 8 (1976): 32–40.

Bayley, Iris. "The Bush-teas of Barbados." *JBMHS* 16 (1949): 103–12.

Beachey, R.W. *The British West Indies Sugar Industry in the Late 19th Century.* 2d ed. Westport, Conn.: Greenwood Press, 1978. (Original edition, 1957.)

Beckford, George L. *Persistent Poverty: Underdevelopment in Plantation Economies of the Third World.* New York: Oxford Univ. Press, 1972.

Beckles, W.A., comp. *The Barbados Disturbances (1937): Review—Reproduction of the Evidence and Report of the Commission.* Bridgetown: Advocate Co., 1937.

Bernard, George [Gordon Bell]. *Wayside Sketches: Pen-Pictures of Barbadian Life.* Barbados, 1934.

Bishop, Joseph Bucklin. *The Panama Gateway.* New York: Scribner's, 1913.

Bolden, Phinorice. "The Barbadian Chattel House." Honors thesis, Colgate Univ., 1982.

Bovell, J.R. "Notes on Rotation and Catch Crops." *West Indian Bulletin* 1 (1900?): 204–12.

Boyce, E.P., comp. *Report on the Census of Barbados, 1911.* Barbados: T.E. King, 1911.

Brereton, Bridget. *Race Relations in Colonial Trinidad, 1870–1900.* Cambridge: Cambridge Univ. Press, 1979.

Bridenbaugh, Carl, and Roberta Bridenbaugh. *No Peace beyond the Line: The English in the Caribbean, 1624–1690.* New York: Oxford Univ. Press, 1972.

Bridgetown and Environs. (A 1:5000 map.) London: British Ministry of Overseas Development, 1975.

Bullard, Arthur. *Panama, the Canal, the Country, and the People.* New York: Macmillan, 1914.

Bundy, Colin. *The Rise and Fall of the South African Peasantry.* London: Heinemann, 1979.

Burawoy, Michael. "The Functions and Reproduction of Migrant

Labour: Comparative Material from Southern Africa and the United States." *American Journal of Sociology* 81 (1976): 1050–87.
Campbell, P.F. "Barbados Vestries, 1627–1700." *JBMHS* 37 (1983): 35–56.
———. *The Church in Barbados in the Seventeenth Century.* Barbados: Barbados Museum and Historical Society, 1982.
———. *Commercial Hall.* Barbados: Advocate Commercial Printing, 1969.
Carnegie, Charles V. "If You Lose the Dog, Grab the Cat." *Natural History* 92 (Oct., 1983): 28, 30–34.
Collier, Richard. *The River That God Forgot: The Story of the Amazon Rubber Boom.* New York: Dutton, 1968.
Conniff, Michael. *Black Labor on a White Canal: Panama, 1904–1980.* Pittsburgh: Univ. of Pittsburgh Press, 1985.
Cooper, Frederick. *From Slaves to Squatters: Plantation Labor and Agriculture in Zanzibar and Coastal Kenya, 1890–1925.* New Haven: Yale Univ. Press, 1980.
Cordle, Edward A. *Overheard: Poems Originally Published in the Weekly Recorder.* Barbados: C.F. Cole, 1903.
Correspondence Relating to the Hurricane on 10th–12th September, 1898, and the Relief of Distress Caused Thereby. London: HMSO, 1899.
Craton, Michael. *Testing the Chains: Resistance to Slavery in the British West Indies.* Ithaca: Cornell Univ. Press, 1982.
Cronon, Edmund David. *Black Moses: The Story of Marcus Garvey and the Universal Negro Improvement Association.* Madison: Univ. of Wisconsin Press, 1964.
D'Albuquerque, J.P. "Notes on the Present and Future Lines of Manurial Experiments in Barbados." *West Indian Bulletin* 1 (1900?): 172–81.
Dash, J. Sydney. "The Windmills and Copper Walls of Barbados." *JBMHS* 31 (1965): 43–60.
Davis, Raymond A. "West Indian Workers on the Panama Canal: A Split Market Interpretation." Ph.D. diss., Stanford Univ., 1981.
Deerr, Noel. *The History of Sugar.* 2 vols. London: Chapman and Hall, 1949.
Dirks, Robert. "Resource Fluctuations and Competitive Transformations in West Indian Slave Societies." In Charles D. Laughlin, Jr., and Ivan A. Brady, eds., *Extinction and Survival in Human Populations,* 122–80. New York: Columbia Univ. Press, 1978.
Douglas, Mary. "Primitive Rationing." In Raymond Firth, ed., *Themes in Economic Anthropology,* 119–47. London: Tavistock, 1967.
Dunn, Richard S. *Sugar and Slaves: The Rise of the Planter Class in the*

English West Indies. New York: Norton, 1973. (Original edition, 1972.)
Elkins, W.F. "Black Power in the British West Indies: The Trinidad Longshoremen's Strike of 1919." *Science and Society* 33 (1969): 71–5.
———. "Marcus Garvey, the *Negro World*, and the British West Indies: 1919–1920." *Science and Society* 36 (1972): 63–77.
———. "A Source of Black Nationalism in the Caribbean: The Revolt of the British West Indies Regiment at Taranto, Italy." *Science and Society* 34 (1970): 99–103.
Ennew, Judith, Paul Hirst, and Keith Tribe. "Peasantry as an Economic Category." *Journal of Peasant Studies* 4 (1977): 295–322.
Froude, James Anthony. *The English in the West Indies*. New York: Scribner's, 1888.
Geertz, Clifford. "The Rotating Credit Association: A Middle Rung in Development." *Economic Development and Cultural Change* 10 (1962): 241–63.
Genovese, Eugene D. *Roll, Jordan, Roll: The World the Slaves Made*. New York: Random House, 1972.
Gooding, E.G.B. "Facts and Beliefs about Barbadian Plants." *JBMHS* 7–10 (1940–43).
Gordon, Shirley C. *A Century of West Indian Education*. London: Longman, 1963.
Gould, Stephen Jay. *The Mismeasure of Man*. New York: Norton, 1981.
Greaves, Ida. "Money and Currency in Barbados." *JBMHS* 19 (1952): 164–69, and 20 (1952–53): 3–18, 53–66.
Greenfield, Sidney M. "Barbadians and Barbadian House Forms in the Brazilian Amazon." *JBMHS* 36 (1981): 252–65.
———. "Barbadians in the Brazilian Amazon." *Luso-Brazilian Review* 20 (1983): 44–64a.
———. "Stocks, Bonds, and Peasant Canes in Barbados: Some Notes on the Use of Land in an Overdeveloped Economy." In G.K. Zollschan and Walter Hirsch, eds., *Explorations in Social Change*, 619–50. Boston: Houghton Mifflin, 1964.
Hall, Douglas. "The Flight from the Estates Reconsidered: The British West Indies, 1838–42." *JCH* 10–11 (1978): 7–24.
Handler, Jerome S. "Small-scale Sugar Cane Farming in Barbados." *Ethnology* 5 (1966): 264–83.
———. *The Unappropriated People: Freedmen in the Slave Society of Barbados*. Baltimore: Johns Hopkins Univ. Press, 1974.
Handler, Jerome S., and Frederick W. Lange. *Plantation Slavery in Barbados: An Archaeological and Historical Investigation*. Cambridge: Harvard Univ. Press, 1978.

Bibliography

Harlow, Vincent T. *A History of Barbados, 1625–1685.* New York: Negro Univs. Press, 1969. (Original edition, 1926.)
Higman, B.W. *Slave Populations of the British Caribbean, 1807–1834.* Baltimore: Johns Hopkins Univ. Press, 1984.
Hobsbawm, E.J. *Industry and Empire: From 1750 to the Present Day.* New York: Penguin Books, 1969.
Hobsbawm, Eric, and George Rudé. *Captain Swing: A Social History of the Great Agricultural Uprising of 1830.* New York: Norton, 1975.
Hoyos, F.A. *Builders of Barbados.* London: Macmillan, 1972.
―――. *Grantley Adams and the Social Revolution.* London: Macmillan, 1974.
Hutson, Frank C. "The Bridgetown Dry Dock." *JBMHS* 34 (1973): 106–7.
―――. "Sugar Manufacture circa 1900: The OpenTayche Method." *JBMHS* 34 (1974): 209–16.
Innes, Frank. "The Pre-Sugar Era of European Settlement in Barbados." *JCH* 1 (1970): 1–22.
Johnson, Howard. "Barbadian Immigrants in Trinidad, 1870–1897." *Caribbean Studies* 13 (1973): 5–30.
Joseph, C.L. "The British West Indies Regiment, 1914–1918." *JCH* 2 (1971): 94–124.
Keller, Ulrich. *The Building of the Panama Canal in Historic Photographs.* Mineola, N.Y.: Dover, 1983.
Kiple, Kenneth F., and Virginia Himmelsteib King. *Another Dimension to the Black Diaspora: Diet, Disease, and Racism.* Cambridge: Cambridge Univ. Press, 1981.
Knight, Franklin W. *The Caribbean: The Genesis of a Fragmented Nationalism.* New York: Oxford Univ. Press, 1978.
Kurtz, Donald V. "The Rotating Credit Association: An Adaptation to Poverty." *Human Organization* 32 (1973): 49–58.
Leverick, Perry Sinclair. *Leverick's Directory of Barbados, 1921.* Barbados, 1921.
Levy, Claude. *Emancipation, Sugar, and Federalism: Barbados and the West Indies, 1833–1876.* Gainesville: Univ. Presses of Florida, 1980.
Lewis, G.J. *Human Migration: A Geographical Perspective.* New York: St. Martin's Press, 1982.
Lewis, Gordon K. *Main Currents in Caribbean Thought: The Historical Evolution of Caribbean Society in Its Ideological Aspects.* Baltimore: Johns Hopkins Univ. Press, 1983.
Lewis, Lancelot S. *The West Indian in Panama: Black Labor in Panama, 1850–1914.* Washington: Univ. Press of America, 1980.
Little, Kenneth. *Urbanization as a Social Process: An Essay on Movement*

and *Change in Contemporary Africa*. London: Routledge and Kegan Paul, 1974.
———. *West African Urbanization: A Study of Voluntary Associations in Social Change*. Cambridge: Cambridge Univ. Press, 1965.
Lofty, Henry W., comp., *Report on the Census of Barbados, 1911–1921*. Barbados: Advocate Co., 1921.
Lowenthal, David. "Caribbean Views of Caribbean Land." *Canadian Geographer* 5 (1961): 1–9.
———. "The Population of Barbados." *SES* 6 (1957): 445–501.
———. *West Indian Societies*. New York: Oxford Univ. Press, 1972.
Lynch, Louis. *The Barbados Book*. London: Andre Deutsch, 1972.
McCullough, David. *The Path between the Seas: The Creation of the Panama Canal, 1870–1914*. New York: Simon and Schuster, 1977.
McLellan, George H.H. *Some Phases of Barbados Life: Tropical Scenes and Studies*. Demerara, British Guiana: Argosy, 1909.
Mark, Francis. *The History of the Barbados Workers' Union*. Barbados: Barbados Workers' Union, n.d.
Marshall, Trevor G., Peggy L. McGeary, and Grace J.I. Thompson. *Folk Songs of Barbados*. Barbados: Macmarson Associates, 1981.
Marshall, Woodville K. "The Termination of Apprenticeship in Barbados and the Windward Islands: An Essay in Colonial Administration and Politics." *JCH* 2 (1971): 1–45.
Marshall, Woodville K., Trevor Marshall, and Bentley Gibbs. "The Establishment of a Peasantry in Barbados, 1840–1920." In *Social Groups and Institutions in the History of the Caribbean*, 85–104. Proceedings of the Sixth Annual Conference of Caribbean Historians. Puerto Rico: Assn. of Caribbean Historians, 1975.
Mintz, Sidney W. *Caribbean Transformations*. Chicago: Aldine, 1974.
———. "The Employment of Capital by Market Women in Haiti." In Raymond Firth and B.S. Yamey, eds., *Capital, Saving, and Credit in Peasant Societies*, 256–86. London: George Allen and Unwin, 1964.
———. "The Folk-Urban Continuum and the Rural Proletarian Community." *American Journal of Sociology* 59 (1953): 136–43.
———. Foreword to Ramiro Guerra y Sánchez, *Sugar and Society in the Caribbean: An Economic History of Cuban Agriculture*, xi–xliv. New Haven: Yale Univ. Press, 1964.
———. "The Rural Proletariat and the Problem of Rural Proletarian Consciousness." *Journal of Peasant Studies* 1 (1974): 291–325.
———. "Slavery and the Rise of Peasantries." *Historical Reflections* 6 (1979): 213–42.
———. *Worker in the Cane: A Puerto Rican Life History*. New York: Norton, 1974. (Original edition, 1960.)

Mintz, Sidney W., and Richard Price. *An Anthropological Approach to the Afro-American Past: A Caribbean Perspective.* Philadelphia: Institute for the Study of Human Issues, 1976.
Newton, Velma. "Aspects of British West Indian Emigration to the Isthmus of Panama, 1850–1914." Paper presented at the Ninth Annual Conference of Caribbean Historians, Cave Hill, Barbados, April 3–7, 1977.
――――. "British West Indian Emigration to the Isthmus of Panama, 1850– 1914." Master's thesis, Univ. of the West Indies, Jamaica, 1973.
――――. "Recruiting West Indian Labourers for the Panama Canal and Railroad Construction Projects, 1850–1913." *JBMHS* 37 (1983): 9–19.
――――. *The Silver Men: West Indian Labour Migration to Panama, 1850–1914*, Mona, Jamaica: Institute of Social and Economic Research, 1984.
Nietschmann, Bernard. *Between Land and Water: The Subsistence Ecology of the Miskito Indians, Eastern Nicaragua.* New York: Seminar Press, 1973.
――――. "Ecological Change, Inflation, and Migration in the Far Western Caribbean." *Geographical Review* 69 (1979): 1–24.
Nikolinakos, Marios. "Notes towards a General Theory of Migration in Late Capitalism." *Race and Class* 17 (1975): 5–17.
Painter, Nell Irvin. *Exodusters: Black Migration to Kansas after Reconstruction.* New York: Knopf, 1976.
Patterson, Orlando. "Migration in Caribbean Societies: Socioeconomic and Symbolic Resource." In William H. McNeill and Ruth S. Adams, eds., *Human Migration: Patterns and Policies*, 106–45. Bloomington: Indiana Univ. Press, 1978.
Plan of the City of Bridgetown. Surveyed by James A.P. Bowhill (1926). Document located at Barbados Museum and Historical Society in Bridgetown.
Portes, Alejandro. "Migration and Underdevelopment." *Politics and Society* 8 (1978): 1–48.
Post, Ken. " 'Peasantization' and Rural Political Movements in Western Africa." *European Journal of Sociology* 13 (1972): 223–54.
Proceedings of West Indian Sugar Commission. Barbados: Advocate Co., 1929.
Redford, Arthur. *Labour Migration in England, 1800–1850.* Manchester: Manchester Univ. Press, 1964.
Reece, J.E., and J.A. Carrington. *Report on the Elementary Education for the Year 1899.* Barbados: Advocate Printing, 1899.

Reid, B.L. *The Lives of Roger Casement.* New Haven: Yale Univ. Press, 1976.
Reid, Molly A. "The Growth of a Twentieth Century Fiction: The Foreclosure Suit in Barbados." *SES* 22 (1973): 358–83.
The Report of the Public Health Commission, 1925–26. Barbados: Advocate Co., 1926.
Report of the West India Royal Commission. London: HMSO, 1897.
Report on Census of Barbados (1881–91). Bridgetown, 1891.
Rhoades, Robert E. "Foreign Labor and German Industrial Capitalism, 1871–1978: The Evolution of a Migratory System." *American Ethnologist* 5 (1978): 553–73.
Richardson, Bonham C. *Caribbean Migrants: Environment and Human Survival on St. Kitts and Nevis.* Knoxville: Univ. of Tennessee Press, 1983.
———. "The Impact of Panama Money in Barbados in the Early Twentieth Century." *Nieuwe West-Indische Gids* 59 (1985).
Richardson, Bonham C., and Linda B. Richardson. "Barbadian Contract Laborers to the Panama Canal, 1906–7." Barbados Department of Archives, 1982. Computer printout.
Roberts, G.W. "Emigration from the Island of Barbados." *SES* 4 (1955): 245–88.
Rodney, Walter. "Barbadian Immigration into British Guiana, 1863–1924." Paper presented at the Ninth Annual Conference of Caribbean Historians, Cave Hill, Barbados, Apr. 3–7, 1977.
———. *A History of the Guyanese Working People.* Baltimore: Johns Hopkins Univ. Press, 1981.
Rubenstein, Hymie. "Remittances and Rural Underdevelopment in the English- Speaking Caribbean." *Human Organization* 42 (1983): 295–306.
Sassen-Koob, Saskia. "The Internationalization of the Labor Force." *Studies in Comparative International Development* 15 (1980): 3–25.
Schneider, Harold K. *Economic Man: The Anthropology of Economics.* New York: Free Press, 1974.
Schomburgk, Robert H. *The History of Barbados.* New York: Augustus M. Kelley, 1971. (Original edition, 1848.)
Scott, James C. *The Moral Economy of the Peasant: Rebellion and Subsistence in Southeast Asia.* New Haven: Yale Univ. Press, 1976.
Segal, Aaron Lee. *Population Policies in the Caribbean.* Lexington, Mass.: Lexington Books, 1975.
Shanin, Teodor. "Defining Peasants: Conceptualizations and De-Conceptualizations Old and New in a Marxist Debate." *Peasant Studies* 8 (1979): 38–60.

Sheppard, Jill. *The "Redlegs" of Barbados: Their Origins and History.* Millwood, N.Y.: KTO Press, 1977.
Sibert, William L., and John F. Stevens. *The Construction of the Panama Canal.* New York: Appleton, 1915.
Sinckler, E. Goulburn. *The Barbados Handbook.* London: Duckworth, 1913.
Skeete, C.C. *The Condition of Peasant Agriculture in Barbados.* Barbados: Advocate Co., 1930.
Smith, Raymond T. "The Nuclear Family in Afro-American Kinship." *Journal of Comparative Family Studies* 1 (1970): 55–70.
Starkey, Otis P. *The Economic Geography of Barbados.* Westport, Conn.: Negro Univs. Press, 1971. (Original edition, 1939.)
Tallis, Rev. J.Y. *About Barbados.* London: C. Tallis, 1890.
Thomas-Hope, Elizabeth M. "The Establishment of a Migration Tradition: British West Indian Movements to the Hispanic Caribbean in the Century after Emancipation." In Colin G. Clarke, ed., *Caribbean Social Relations,* 66–81. Univ. of Liverpool: Centre for Latin American Studies, 1978.
Torres, Arlene. "Meetings: A Group Savings Arrangement in Barbados." Honors thesis, Colgate Univ., 1981.
Treves, Sir Frederick. *The Cradle of the Deep: An Account of a Voyage to the West Indies.* London: Smith, Elder, 1908.
Vaughan, H.A. "Some Social and Political Tendencies." *Silver Jubilee Magazine,* 1935, pp. 31–33, 57–61.
Vernon, K.C. and D.M. Carroll. *Soil and Land-use Surveys no. 18, Barbados.* St. Augustine, Trinidad: Imperial College of Tropical Agriculture, 1965.
Verrill, A. Hyatt. *Isles of Spice and Palm.* New York: Appleton, 1915.
Walrond, Eric. *Tropic Death.* New York: Collier Books, 1972. (Original edition, 1926).
Watson, Hilbourne A. "Theoretical and Methodological Problems in Commonwealth Caribbean Migration Research." *SES* 31 (1982): 165–205.
Wells, A.F. "The Friendly Societies of Barbados" (1948). Office of the Registrar of Friendly Societies, Bridgetown. Typescript.
Wells, A.F., and D. Wells. *Friendly Societies in the West Indies.* London: HMSO, 1953.
The West Indies Illustrated: Historical and Descriptive, Commercial and Industrial, Facts, Figures and Resources. London: Collingridge, 1909.
Wickham, Clennell. *Pen and Ink Sketches by a Gentleman with a Fountain*

Pen. Reprinted from the *Barbados Herald*, 1921. (Pamphlet located at BDA.)

Will, H.A. *Constitutional Change in the British West Indies, 1880–1903: With Special Reference to Jamaica, British Guiana, and Trinidad*. Oxford: Clarendon Press, 1970.

Wolf, Eric R. *Europe and the People without History*. Berkeley: Univ. of California Press, 1982.

———. *Peasants*. Englewood Cliffs, N.J.: Prentice-Hall, 1966.

Wood, Charles H. "Equilibrium and Historical-Structural Perspectives on Migration." *International Migration Review* 16 (1982): 298–319.

Index

Adams, Grantley, 242, 244
African origins: bush teas, 67; death ceremonies, 91; landships, 224; savings institutions, 89–90
Agricultural Aids Act of 1887, 39
Agricultural Department of the West Indies, 36
agriculture. *See* subsistence, sugar cane
almshouses. *See* poor relief, vestry system
American attitudes toward West Indian workers, 1–2, 147–50
Anglican Church: attitudes toward education, 43–44; funerals, 91; relationship with plantocracy, 19, 50, 232
Antigua, 130

bank currency, 163–164; *see also* Barbados Savings Bank
Bank Hall, 82, 190–91
Barbados Agricultural Society, 35, 43, 65–66, 213–14
Barbados Court of Chancery, 38, 131
Barbados General Board of Health, 27
Barbados Herald, 229
Barbados House of Assembly. *See* House of Assembly
Barbados Landship Association, 225–26
Barbados Legislative Council. *See* Legislative Council
Barbados Savings Bank, 70–72, 164–68
Barbados Sugar Industry Agricultural Bank, 40
Bastardy Act, 57
Belgian Congo, 107–8
Bell, George Abraham, 230, 238
bounty sugar depression, 32, 34–35, 188; and disease, 72–74; *see also* economic depression
Bovell, John R., 42
Boxill, Dr. N.L., 79

Boyce, Sir Rupert, 30
Brazil as a migration destination, 108–9, 130
Bree Commission Report of 1896, 43
Brewster, S.E., 111, 113, 115, 123
Bridgetown, 21, 81–87, 246–7; crime in, 215–6; riots in, 239–45; rural familiarity with, 86, 162–3
Britain. *See* United Kingdom
British Colonial Office, 22, 218
British Guiana: boilermen from, 178; compared to Barbados, 88; contract workers from, 130; migration to, 101–4, 246; potatoes sent to, 63, 66; rice from, 198; riots in, 93
British Royal Commission of 1897, 32–33, 36, 38; advocates central milling in Barbados, 40; attitudes toward migration, 7, 17, 100; testimony in Barbados, 16–17, 55–56, 68
Brussels Convention of 1902, 36–37
Bullard, Arthur, 120–21, 248
Bush Hall, 190–91
bush teas, 66–68

Canada, 21, 35
Canal Zone. *See* Panama Canal
cane fires. *See* fires
Caribbean League, 217
Carrington, George, 32, 94
Carrington Village, 81, 191, 194
Carter, Governor Gilbert T., 112
Casement, Roger, 110
census data. *See* population of Barbados
central milling of sugar cane, 39–41; as a condition of Imperial grant of 1902, 36; social implications, 174–80
Chamberlain, Joseph, 35–37
Chancery. *See* Barbados Court of Chancery
Chandler, W.K., 39, 93

279

chattel houses, 57–59, 170; in Bridgetown, 83, 191
children, 49, 57, 60, 91; as laborers, 43–44; responsibility for, 57; see also "third class gangs"
Christchurch parish, 20, 125–26, 235–36
Church Village, 81
climate of Barbados, 14–15
clothing of black Barbadians, 60
Colón. See Panama Canal
Colonial Office. See British Colonial Office
"colored" Barbadians, 45, 51–52
corn, imported, 21; and pellagra, 200
criminal activity, 65–66, 212–20; attributed to Panama returnees, 150–51
Crown Lands in Caribbean, 6, 16
Cuba, 176; as a migration destination, 146, 154, 219, 234, 236

Danish West Indies, 112, 114
deaths of Barbadians in Panama, 145–46
Democratic League, 204, 229
dependency theory, 31
diet, 55, 196–200
disease, 72–80, 200–5; laws pertaining to, 26–31; in Panama, 115, 145, 197; in Surinam, 108
Dominica, 93
Dominican Republic, 112, 234
Douglas, Mary, 193
drought, 15–16, 182; and disease, 73, 181

economic depression, 5–6, 31–36; related to emigration, 138
Ecuador as a migration destination, 108
education, 43–44, 187–88
Executive Committee, 22–23, 133–34

families, 56–57, 119–120; effects of migration on, 102–4, 147, 153–54
farming. See subsistence, sugar cane
fathers, 57, 153–54
finances of plantations, 38–41
fires in sugar cane fields, 97–98, 150–51
food: imported, 21, 63–64, 198–200; sharing, 64–65, 196–97; see also subsistence
France, 32
friendly societies, 90–93, 205–12, 225; in British Guiana, 102
Friendly Societies Act of 1905, 208
fundamentalist churches, 96–97, 221–23

funerals, 91, 209–10, 225, 231

Garvey, Marcus, 229–30
Gay, Douglas, 131–32
geology. See physical geography
Golden Square, 81, 215, 240
Gollop, Clyde, 226
Gooding, Dr. C.E., 76
Gooding, Dr. C.G., 100
Great Britain. See United Kingdom
Great Depression of 1873–96, 33–34
Greaves, Kenneth, 143
Greenfield, Sidney, 174
Grenada, 114, 130; yellow fever from, 30
Guyana. See British Guiana

Habitual Idlers' Bill, 216
Haiti, 93, 112
Handler, Jerome, 183
Hay, Governor James Shaw, 84
health conditions. See disease
Hodgson, Governor Frederick M., 35, 92, 108; takes action against smallpox, 28–30
House of Assembly, 18, 22–23, 49; disease legislation, 31; education petition, 187–88; friendly society act, 90; land speculation, 191; migration, 101, 133–34, 146–47; rice imports, 198
housing, 57–60; and remitted money, 168–69; see also chattel houses
hurricane of 1898, 15, 36–37, 58
Hutson, Dr. John, 29–30, 203–4

illegitimacy, 56–57, 79–80
Immigration of Paupers (Prevention) Act, 143, 158
Imperial grant of 1902, 36–37, 39–40
imported goods to Barbados, 21
infant mortality, 17, 77–80, 202
inflation of prices, 184–86, 191–92
Isthmian Canal Commission, 2, 7, 134, 139; recruits Barbadians, 111–15; keeps death records, 145

Jamaica, 6, 16, 88; dissident soldiers from, 217; possible labor source, 112; riots in, 93

Karner, William J., 111–15
kinship, 56–57, 64; see also families
Knaggs, S.W., 134

Index

land, 17, 39, 54–56, 72, 87; as house plots, 59–60; purchased with remittances, 188–96, 235–36
landlessness, 17–18, 88
Landlord and Tenant Act of 1897, 24–25
landship movement, 223–26
Lawrance, C.J., 55, 65
laws: circumvented in land sales, 189–90; and plantation working conditions, 24–26
Legislative Council, 22, 49; considers antiemigration laws, 133–34
letters. *See* postal service
livestock, 60–61, 191, 221; and changes in cane milling, 179–80
"located laborer" acts, 24, 195, 252
lodges and social classes, 226–28
Lofty, Henry, 124, 192
longshoremen, 84–85, 213
Lowenthal, David, 188
Lynch, J. Challenor, 106, 131, 133

Madeira–Mamoré railroad, 109, 130
mail. *See* postal service
malnutrition, 64, 66–67; and disease, 73, 76, 199–200
managers of plantations, 48–49
marriage among black Barbadians, 56–57
Marshall, Woodville, 194–95
Martinique, 112, 114, 131
Massiah, Dr. Hallam, 199–200
Master and Servant Act of 1891, 24
medical care, 27–31, 73–75, 202–5
medical examination for Panama Canal, 118
meeting turns, 88–90
Methodists, 51
middle class. *See* "colored" Barbadians
migration: a Barbadian right, 136–39; a Barbadian trait, 7–8, 107, 237; Barbados to Panama Canal, 3, 115–31; Caribbean, 6–8; creates social change, 3–4, 7–9, 176–77; decreases population, 170–72; folktales, 160; laws, 101, 133–34; nineteenth century, 100–4; and respect, 153, 230; rural to urban, 83–84, 170–73; theory, 8–9; transforms plantations, 174–83
milling. *See* central milling, sugar cane milling
Mintz, Sidney W., 54, 175–76, 186, 193
money: Barbados currency, 163; black and

money: (*cont.*)
white control of, 142, 208, 231–32; changes friendly societies, 205–12; circulation, 86, 163–64; controlled by planters, 33, 68–69; creates social change, 72, 183–85; "liquid" nature of, 193; and mutual assistance, 87–93; from Panama, 2–3, 144, 155–69; as "special purpose" medium, 69–70; vital to survival, 55, 63, 69, 197–98; *see also* remittances
Montserrat, 6, 93
Moravians, 51, 90
Morris, Dr. Daniel, 36, 37, 42–43

Netherlands Antilles, 246
Nevis, 101
New Orleans district of Bridgetown, 81
Nietschmann, Bernard, 196

O'Brien, Governor C.R.M., 23, 230–31; plans against violence, 213, 215, 217–20
O'Neale, Charles Duncan, 204–5, 229

Panama: visited by Barbadians prior to Panama Canal, 108, 115–16
Panama Canal, 1–4; Barbadians return from, 139, 143–55; diet of workforce, 197; "gold" and "silver" rolls, 155; injuries in, 152; labor organization, 216, 230; lodges, 227; postal service, 156, 159; *see also* Isthmian Canal Commission
paternalism, 46–47, 94–96, 137–38; disappearance of, 174–76, 186, 242–43
Patterson, W.S., 191
Payne, Clement, 240
peasantry, 53–56, 193–94
pellagra and imported corn, 199–200
Peru, 109–10
physical geography of Barbados, 13–15
Pilgrim, Dr. E.G., 152, 188
plantations, 17–18, 24–26; changes, 173–83; social conditions, 46–50; wages, 68–69, 174
Plantations-in-Aid-Acts, 40
planters, 10, 45–48; react to Panama exodus, 131–39
poems by "Lizzie and Joe," 28, 33, 61, 64, 87; "Janie," 125
police, 70, 215, 241; confront market

police (*cont.*)
  women, 63, 99; monitor political meetings, 230–31
political economy of Barbados in 1900, 18–24
politics, 228–32, 241–42; *see also* Democratic League, Workingmen's Association
poor relief, 26–27, 74–75
Poor Relief Commission of 1878, 83, 89
population of Barbados: Census of 1891, 20; Census of 1911, 171; Census of 1921, 172; changes in, 170–72, 178–79; oversupply of labor, 16–17, 41–42, 84
postal service, 117–18, 161–62; in Panama, 156, 159; *see also* remittances
potato raids, 65–66, 214–15
potatoes, 63, 185, 195
Price, Richard, 193
Probyn, Governor Leslie, 141–42
proletariat, 53–56
Public Health Commission of 1925, 203
Puerto Rico, 176
Putumayo rubber camps, 110, 236

quarantine, 29–31

race relations in Barbados, 10–12, 23–24, 44–52
racism, 10–12, 24, 48; at Panama Canal, 2
railroad, 20–21, 98; construction in Brazil, 109; construction in Ecuador, 108
"Redlegs," 49–50
Reece, H.W., 215, 237
religion, 50–51, 91, 96–97; changes in, 221–23; incorporated into politics, 230–31
remittances, 244–45; from British Guiana, 104; from Panama Canal, 116–17, 155–69; from United States, 235; *see also* money
return migration to Barbados, 139, 143–55
rice imported, 198
rights to emigrate, 136–39
riots, 134–35; in Caribbean, 93, 219; in Bridgetown, 239–45
Robinson, Stanley, 40, 173–74, 213–14; opposes emigration, 142, 236
Royal Commission of 1897. *See* British Royal Commission of 1897
Royal Dutch Line, 30
Royal Mail Company, 29, 113–14, 134

sailing schooners, 100, 130, 234; to Panama, 121–22
St. Andrew parish, 201–2
St. Croix, 130
St. George parish, 178, 195; infant mortality in, 79, 136
St. James parish, 188–89, 202
St. Kitts, 130; riots in, 93, 239
St. Lucia, 114, 130, 236
St. Lucy parish, 117, 185–86; potato raids in, 214, 241; typhoid in, 202
St. Mihael parish, 20, 125–26; land, 189–91, 194; maps, 128–29; pellagra in, 200; population problems in, 82–83, 200–1
St. Peter parish, 202
St. Philip parish, 178; disease in, 76, 181
St. Vincent, 130–31, 187
sanitation problems, 81, 200–5
saving by black Barbadians, 70–72, 164–68
Settoon, S.W., 114
Shanin, Teodor, 54
shopkeepers, 86, 186; return from Panama, 153, 158–59
Skeete, C.C., 193
Skinner, Beresford, 117
Small, Moses, 232
smallpox epidemic of 1902–3, 27–29, 65, 82
social classes of Barbados in 1900, 44–52
Speightstown, 81, 84, 227
Spiller, W.B., 109
steamship travel: to Belgian Congo, 107–8; to Brazil, 109; to Ecuador, 108; to Panama, 106, 113, 120–21
Stevens, John, 2
stoicism, 80, 96
structural view of human migration, 8
subsistence: agriculture in Barbados, 42, 53, 61–63, 69, 181, 201; refuges in Caribbean, 6, 16
sugar beets, 33
sugar cane, 180–82, 197–98, 247; antiquated technology in producing, 17–18, 37–38, 41–42; production hampered by emigration, 119–20
sugar cane milling, 17–18, 174–80
Sugar Commission of 1929, 87–88, 192, 238–39, 243–44
sugar prices, 32, 238; *see also* economic depression
Surinam, 101, 108

Index

suspicion of whites and officials by blacks, 70, 75, 99–100, 158

tenantry settlements, 16, 53; in urban areas, 81–84, 93, 189–91, 200–2
"third-class gangs," xiv, 43–44, 68
Trinidad, 6, 130, 187; disturbances in, 93, 219; as a migration destination, 101–3, 246
typhoid, 31, 74–77, 202

United Kingdom, 22–23, 33–34, 227; as a migration destination, 246
United States, 21, 35, 230; as a migration destination, 5, 234–38, 245–46; *see also* Isthmian Canal Commission
Universal Negro Improvement Association, 229–31

vaccination, 28–30, 75, 118
Vagrancy Act of 1897, 25
Vaughan, H.A., x, 174–75, 245
Vegetable Produce Act, 194, 198–99, 213–14

vestry system, 18–20, 210

wages. *See* plantations
Watson, Athelstan, 191, 235–36
West Indian Agricultural Conference of 1900, 42–43
West Indian Sanitary Convention of 1904, 30–31
West Indies Regiment, 216–20
Wickham, Clennell, 23, 229
wind and sugar milling technology, 178, 182–83
Windward Islands, 6, 16, 48–49, 73, 197
Wolf, Eric, 54, 228
women, 46, 172–73; assume male tasks, 132; migrate to Panama, 122–23, 146–47, 154–55; sell vegetables, xv, 63, 85–86, 99
Workingmen's Association, 204, 228–32
World War I: and world sugar prices, 5, 140–41, 180–81; returnees from, 216–20

Yearwood, H.G., 31
yellow fever, 30, 75, 77, 199

Panama Money in Barbados was set into type on a Mergenthaler Linotron digital phototypesetter in 10½-point Palatino with 1½ point spacing between the lines. Palatino was also selected for display. The book was designed by Ed King at Hillside Studio, composed by Typecraft Company, printed offset by Thomson-Shore, Inc., and bound by John H. Dekker & Sons. The paper on which the book is printed carries acid-free characteristics for an effective life of at least three hundred years.

THE UNIVERSITY OF TENNESSEE PRESS : KNOXVILLE

www.ingramcontent.com/pod-product-compliance
Lightning Source LLC
Chambersburg PA
CBHW030305080526
44584CB00012B/453